PROSPER MÉRIMÉE'S

LETTERS TO AN INCOGNITA

WITH RECOLLECTIONS BY

LAMARTINE AND GEORGE SAND

BRIC-A-BRAC SERIES.

I.

PERSONAL REMINISCENCES BY CHORLEY, PLANCHÉ, AND YOUNG.

II.

ANECDOTE BIOGRAPHIES OF THACKERAY AND DICKENS.

III.

PROSPER MÉRIMÉE'S LETTERS TO AN INCOGNITA; WITH RECOLLECTIONS BY LAMARTINE AND GEORGE SAND.

IV.

PERSONAL REMINISCENCES BY BARHAM, HARNESS, AND HODDER.

V.

PERSONAL REMINISCENCES BY MOORE AND JERDAN.

(Will be published in January.)

Each 1 vol. of 12mo. Per vol. $1.50.

Sent, post-paid, on receipt of price by the publishers.

Bric-a-Brac Series

PROSPER MÉRIMÉE'S

LETTERS TO AN INCOGNITA

WITH RECOLLECTIONS BY

LAMARTINE AND GEORGE SAND

EDITED BY

RICHARD HENRY STODDARD

NEW YORK
SCRIBNER, ARMSTRONG, AND COMPANY
1874

Entered, according to Act of Congress, in the year 1874, by
SCRIBNER, ARMSTRONG, AND COMPANY,
In the Office of the Librarian of Congress, at Washington.

RIVERSIDE, CAMBRIDGE:
STEREOTYPED AND PRINTED BY
H. O. HOUGHTON AND COMPANY.

CONTENTS.

PREFACE.

LAMARTINE, MÉRIMÉE, and GEORGE SAND have added such brilliancy to the French literature of the present century, that their association in this volume is entirely natural and calls for no explanation or justification. Alphonse de Lamartine was born at Mâcon on the Saone, on the 21st of October, 1792, and died in February, 1869; Prosper Mérimée was born in Paris in 1803, and died in Cannes, September 23, 1870; George Sand (Madame Dudevant, whose maiden name was Amantine Lucile Aurore Dupin) was born in Paris on July 1st, 1804; and happily, the date of her death cannot yet be named. The extraordinary brilliancy of the literary reputation of Lamartine, conjoined with the great influence which he at one time exerted in French politics, make him unquestionably the most prominent of the trio. The financial embarrassments in which his extravagant habits plunged him toward the close of his life, placed him in such an unfortunate attitude toward those who had for many years flattered and petted him, that his great popularity suffered a disastrous eclipse; but the matchless eloquence which he repeatedly displayed as an orator, the influence which he now and then possessed as a statesman, and the poetic glow and fervor which breathe through all his writings, have secured for him and his works a reputation and a name which must endure. The wide diversity in the character of the writings of George Sand makes it difficult as yet to assign her a precise place in literature, but some of her works will live as long as the language in which they were written. Both Lamartine and George Sand are nearly as well known to Americans as they are to their own countrymen. For nearly the last half century their names have been widely familiar, and the facts of their respective careers are easily accessible. Until recently, however, Mérimée has been but slightly known, save to his own countrymen. He first appeared before the public in 1825, as the translator from the Spanish of several dramas, under the title "Théâtre de Clara Gazul;" in 1833, he published a moral tale, "The Double Mistake" ("La Double Méprise"), and then there followed at intervals, notes of journeys in the South, and also in the West of France, "Stories in Roman History;" "A History of Don Pedro I., King of Castile;" "An Episode in the History of Russia," etc., etc. "Columba," a novel which was published in 1841, was extremely successful, and upon this, more than upon any other of his works, his popular reputation will probably rest. Whether that reputation can be permanent among his own countrymen is a question which it is hardly worth while to discuss. In the course of his career, however, first as Inspector-General of Historical Monuments, a position to which he was appointed as early as 1834, then as member of the French Academy, with an election to which he was honored in 1844, and afterwards as Senator (1853), he saw French society in all its phases and constantly under circumstances which gave him the most excellent opportunities for observation. Cynical by nature, the lingering disease to which he finally yielded, led him to look at men and things, especially during all the later years of his life, in a morbidly critical way; but that he was capable of loving ardently, these now famous "Letters to an Incognita" abundantly prove. Indeed, they show something even more remarkable than this; that the lover could settle down into the devoted friend, maintaining during a period of over thirty years,—for this singular correspondence extends from 1841 to 1870,—the sincerest admiration for the woman for whom, at one time, Mérimée cherished something more than a Platonic affection. As regards the identity of the "Incognita" and the manner in which the publication of these letters was received in Paris, it is enough to quote the opening paragraphs from a paper suggested by them, which appeared in the "London Quarterly Review" for January, 1874. The writer says: "No literary event since the war, has excited anything like such a sensation in Paris, as the publication of the "Letters a une Inconnue." Even politics became a secondary consideration for the hour, and Academicians or Deputies of opposite parties, might be seen eagerly accosting each other in the chamber or the street, to inquire who this fascinating and perplexing unknown could be. The statement in the "Revue des Deux Mondes" that she was an Englishwoman, moving in brilliant society, was not supported by evidence; and M. Blanchard, the painter from whom the publisher received the manuscripts, died, most provokingly, at the very commencement of the inquiry, and made no sign. Some intimate friends of Mérimée, rendered incredulous by wounded self-love at not having been admitted to his confidence, insisted that there was no secret to tell; their hypothesis being, that the "Incognita" was a myth, and the letters a romance, with which some petty details of actual life had been interwoven (as in "Gulliver's Travels" or "Robinson Crusoe"), to keep up the mystification. But an artist like Mérimée would not have left his work in so unformed a state, so defaced by repetitions, or with such a want of proportion between the parts. With the evidence before us as we write, we incline to the belief that the lady was French by birth, and during the early years of the correspondence in the position of *dame de compagnie* or travelling companion to a Madame M—— de B——, who passes in the letters under the pseudonym of Lady M——. It appears from one of them that she inherited a fortune in 1843; and she has been constantly identified with a respectable single lady residing in Paris with two nieces, and a character for pedantry fastened on her (perhaps unjustly), on the strength of the Greek which she learned from Mérimée."

As regards Mérimée himself, it is only necessary to quote some passages from the "Study," with which the distinguished author Henri Taine prefaces these "Letters to an Incognita." He writes: "I frequently met Mérimée in society — a tall, erect, pale man, who, excepting his smile, had very much the appearance of an Englishman; at least he possessed that cold, distant air that in advance repels all familiarity. One was impressed, merely on seeing him, with his natural or acquired phlegm, his self-control, his habit and determination of holding himself in perfect check. His countenance, especially on ceremonious occasions, was impassible even in intimate circles, and when recounting some drollery his voice remained even and calm, never any outburst nor enthusiasm; while he related the raciest details in fitting words with the tone of a man asking for a cup of tea.

He so strenuously subdued all manifestations of sensibility as to seem destitute of it; but it was not so, indeed quite the reverse; as there are racers so well broken in by their master, that once well in hand they no longer indulge in a caracole. This training began at an early period with Mérimée; for he was but ten years old when, having committed some slight fault, he was severely reprimanded and sent from the room: and weeping, overcome with distress, he had just closed the door, when he heard a burst of laughter, and some one said: 'Poor child, he really thought us angry.' He revolted at the idea of being deceived; he swore to repress thenceforth so humiliating a sensitiveness, and he kept his word. 'Remember to distrust,' was his motto. To guard against impulse, ardor, and enthusiasm, never entirely to allow himself full play, to maintain always a personal reserve, to be the dupe neither of others nor of himself, to act and write as if perpetually in the presence of an indifferent and mocking spectator, — such was the salient feature which, graven more and more deeply into his nature, left its imprint on every phase of his life, his work, and his talent. He lived as an amateur; and indeed, possessed of a critical taste and habit, one can hardly do otherwise; by dint of reversing the tapestry, one ends by looking habitually at the wrong side, seeing instead of handsome personages in fine attitudes, only bits of thread. Early in life, Mérimée possessed a competency, afterwards a congenial and interesting office, that of Inspector-General of Historical Monuments, and subsequently a place in the Senate and a position at court. He was competent, active, and useful in regard to the monuments; in the Senate he had the good taste to be generally absent or silent; while at court he preserved his independence and freedom of speech. To travel, study, observe, to dissect men and events, formed his chief occupation, his official bonds holding him in but slight restraint. A man of such wit as Mérimée possessed, is necessarily held in a certain respect, his irony transpiercing the finest chain-mail of his adversaries. It would be difficult to present a more serious deportment in corporate assemblies, and to entertain less internal respect for them, than Mérimée exhibited. Grave, dignified, studied in attitude, his manners were irreproachable when he visited the Academy or improvised a public discourse; nevertheless, with an occasional sly and comic touch that turned both orator and audience into ridicule. Two distinct personages existed in Mérimée; the one fulfilling with easy propriety the duties, and acquitting himself with grace in the splendors of society; the other holding himself apart and above his second half, whose performance he regarded with a bantering or resigned air; and so also there was a dual self in his ties of affection or sentiment. On the one hand a perfectly natural man, good and even tender, than whom no one was more loyal, unfailing in friendship, and who once having offered his hand, never withdrew it. This characteristic was strikingly shown in his defense of M. Libri against the judges of the court and public opinion; the action of a true knight who singly throws his gage of battle to a whole army. Condemned to fine and imprisonment, he did not assume the air of a martyr, but showed as much grace in submitting to the penalty of his ill-fortune, as bravery in provoking it; and made no mention of it, save with quiet humor, in a preface, saying that he 'had passed fortnight of July in a retreat, where he was in no wise incommoded by the sun, and where he enjoyed profound leisure.' He was obliging and earnest in serving others; and persons who, in begging his good offices, left him disconcerted by his cold manner, would be surprised by his appearance a month afterwards, having in his pocket an affirmative answer to their petition. In his correspondence a striking statement escapes him, which his friends find true, — 'It rarely chances that I sacrifice others to myself, but whenever it happens, I suffer all possible remorse.'

"Towards the close of his life two elderly English ladies were seen at his house, to whom he seldom spoke, and about whom he did not seem to trouble himself greatly; yet a friend saw tears in his eyes because one of them was ill. He never made any allusion to his deepest feelings; and here we have a correspondence, first lover-like, then merely friendly, that continued during thirty years, and yet the name of his correspondent is unknown! By those who read these letters aright, he will be found gracious, affectionate, delicate, earnestly in love, and, almost incredibly, at times a poet, even moved to superstition, like a lyrical German. But by the side of the lover, the critic still appears, and the conflict between these opposing forces in the same nature produces very singular effects; in such a case, however, it is wise not to scan too closely. 'Do you know,' says La Fontaine, 'that however slightly I may love, I no more see the defects of the one exciting the sentiment, than does a mole a hundred feet below the earth. With the sowing of the first grain of love, I never fail to surround it with my entire stock of incense.' In this, perhaps, lay the secret of his charm. In Mérimée's letters harsh words were showered with caresses. Tenderness, altercation, and reconciliation reigned successively: for he seems to have met a character as restive, as unyielding, and independent as his own, — *a lioness though tame.* After a violent quarrel, an affectionate word recalls him to her feet: and these alternations of love and anger finally subside into a calm and enduring friendship. They met at the Louvre, at Versailles, in the neighboring woods, took long clandestine walks together several times a week, even in January; he admired 'a radiant countenance, a subtle charm, a white hand, superb black hair,' an intelligence and attainments worthy of his own, the graces of an original beauty, the attractions of a comprehensive culture, the seductions of delicious toilet and skillful coquetry; he breathed the perfume of an education so choice, and 'a nature so refined, as to epitomize for him a rounded civilization;' in short, he was under the spell. The critic, however, in turn replaced the lover; he unraveled the meaning of a reply, of a gesture; he disengaged himself from sentiment, the better to judge a character; and wrote her rather biting truths and epigrams which were returned to him the following day.

"Such he was in life, and such we find him in his books. He studied and wrote as an amateur, passing from one subject to another, as fancy or occasion prompted, giving himself up to no science, using his talent for the illustration of no theory. This was the want neither of application nor capability; on the contrary, few men possessed more varied attainments. He was master of the Italian, Greek, Latin, Spanish, English, and Russian languages, with their history and literature: and I believe that he also read German. From time to time a phrase, a note shows the point to which he had pursued these studies. He spoke *Calo* in a manner to astonish the Spanish gypsies; he understood the various Spanish dialects, and deciphered ancient Catalonian charters, and scanned English poetry. Only they who have studied an entire literature in print and manuscript, during the four or five successive periods of the language, its style and orthography, can appreciate the facility and the perseverance necessary to enable one to understand Spanish so thoroughly as the author of 'Don Pedre;' and Russian as the writer of the 'Cosaques' and the 'Faux Démétrius.' He possessed a remarkable lingual gift, and acquired languages up to a ripe age, becoming a philologist towards the end of his life, applying himself at Cannes to the minutiæ of study pertaining to comparative grammar. To this knowledge of books he joined extensive learning respecting monuments, his reports proving him to be a specialist as to those of France, comprehending not only the effect but the technicalities of architecture. He studied each church on the spot, aided by the best architects; his memory of locality was excellently trained, and born of a family of painters, he had early handled the brush, being an artist in water-colors; in short, he investigated the subject exhaustively, and having a horror of specious phrases, touched no topic unless with certainty of detail. He travelled frequently; once in the East, twice in Greece, a dozen or fifteen times in England, in Spain, and elsewhere, studying the manners, not only of good company but of bad; consorting familiarly with gypsies and bull-fighters, and relating stories to the peasants beneath the Andalusian stars. Possessed of these varied acquirements, and of such noble faculties, Mérimée might easily have attained an eminent position, both in history and art; but as a historian he occupies only an average rank, while his place, though high, is but limited in art. Nearly always he seems to have written only when occasion prompted, simply to amuse and occupy himself, subjected to no ruling idea, subordinating himself to no task, conceiving no harmonious whole. In this, as in all else, he became disenchanted, and in the end disgusted. Skepticism induced melancholy, and his correspondence in this connection is most sad. His health failed by degrees, and he wintered regularly at Cannes, sensible that his life was fading away; but he carefully watched over it; the one anxiety that accompanies us to the last breath. By order of his physician he practiced archery, sketched for his amusement the lovely scenery of the neighborhood, and could be met every day in the country walking in silence, with his two English lady friends, one carrying his bow, the other his box of water-colors. So he killed time and learned to be patient. He often went to a lonely cabin, half a league distant, to feed a cat; and caught flies for a lizard which he kept by him; and these were his pets. When the railway brought him a friend, he revived, and his conversation was again brilliant and charming; his letters were always so, his mind and wit the most original and exquisite, remaining unimpaired. But happiness failed him; the future looked dark, nearly as gloomy as it does to us of to-day; and before closing his eyes, he sorrowfully witnessed our national disaster, dying September 23, 1870. In summing up his character and talent, it will be found that, born with an excellent heart, endowed with a superior intellect, having lived an honest man, labored much, and produced several works of the first order, yet he neither utilized his gifts to their utmost extent, nor attained the full happiness to which he might have aspired. Through the fear of being deceived, he was mistrustful in life, in love, in science, and in art, and was himself the dupe of this distrust. One is always so to some degree, and perhaps it is better to resign one's self to it in advance."

The mystery which surrounds these "Letters to an Incognita," their freshness, their epigrammatic brilliancy, their keen and flashing wit, the careless boldness with which they dash off the portraits of the leading men and women of the day, in English as well as in French society, combine to draw attention first of all to them, and they are therefore assigned the first place in this volume. In the translation, special care has been taken to avoid the repetitions which were allowed to disfigure the letters as they were originally published. Everything of general interest has been carefully preserved, so that the letters as they stand reflect with sufficient fullness Mérimée's relations to the Incognita, while they give us as well his pointed comments upon the men and events of his day. This translation of the "Lettres a une Inconnue" is, by the way, the only one through which they have thus far been made accessible to the English reader.

In that section of the volume assigned to Lamartine we have his last published work, "Twenty-five Years of My Life," in Lady Herbert's translation, slightly abridged. The passages which have been exscinded, were mainly digressions or rhapsodies, which any reader of the volume itself would be very likely to omit. The integrity of the narrative itself has been carefully preserved, and all those who have ever felt at all attracted toward Lamartine, will turn to it with an eager interest which cannot fail to be satisfied. "In these Memoirs," as M. de Ronchaud who edits them in the original French, remarks, "his whole nature comes out in its living simplicity. Lamartine's books are full of his genius, but nowhere else has he shown us much of his heart." The second volume of these "Memoirs of Lamartine" is occupied by a translation of the diary of Mme. de Lamartine, "Memoirs of my Mother." These traverse to so great an extent the same ground which is covered by "Twenty-five Years of My Life," that only a few pages have been selected from them for this volume. It is enough to say of "Memoirs of My Mother," in general, that they exhibit Mme. de Lamartine as a deeply spiritual and devout woman, a tenderly affectionate mother, keenly anxious for the welfare of her children, and pardonably proud of the brilliant career of her illustrious son. The distressing circumstances of her death were in painful contrast with the peace and serenity which would seem to have been the more appropriate close of so saintly a life. There are few more affecting passages in any of Lamartine's works than the "Epilogue" in which he describes the heart-rending affliction which overwhelmed him in the death of his mother.

Doubtless George Sand might have given us one of the most notable volumes of reminiscences ever published, had she chosen to do so. Possibly she still holds her material for such a book in reserve. Certainly, her "Reminiscences and Impressions" "(Souvenirs et Impressions") is not by any means the work its title would lead the reader to anticipate. It seems to be a *rechauffé* of articles furnished from time to time possibly to reviews, with scattering personal recollections, few of them so pointed as to possess any general interest. If the share of this volume which is assigned to her may seem disproportionate, the only explanation must be found in the fact that we have here all of her "Reminiscences and Impressions" which is likely to interest the American reader.

LETTERS TO AN INCOGNITA.

ARIS, *Thursday.* — Everything about you is mysterious; and the causes inducing in others a certain line of conduct, impel you always to opposite action. I am becoming accustomed to your ways, and nothing any longer surprises me. Spare me, I beg of you; do not put to too harsh a test the unfortunate habit I have contracted of finding good in all that you do. I was perhaps a little too frank in my last letter, in speaking of my character. An old diplomatist, a shrewd man of the world, has often advised me, "Never say any ill of yourself; your dear friends will say quite enough." Do not, however, take literally my self-depreciation; believe, rather, that my chief virtue is modesty, which I carry to excess, and I tremble lest it injure me in your estimation. I may at another time, when inspired, supply you with an exact catalogue of my qualities; for the list will be long, and being today slightly indisposed I dare not project myself into this "progression of the infinite." You cannot guess where I was on Saturday evening, and in what engaged at midnight. I was on the platform of one of the towers of Notre Dame, drinking orangeade and eating ices in the society of four friends and a magnificent moon, with the accompaniment of a great owl flapping his wings. Paris at this hour, and by moonlight, is a superb spectacle, resembling a city of the Thousand and One Nights, the inhabitants of which have been enchanted during their sleep; but Parisians usually go to bed at midnight, and are most stupid in so doing. Our party was a curious

one, four nations being represented, each of us with a different way of thinking; but the bore of it was, that some of us, inspired by the moon and the owl, thought it necessary to assume a poetic tone and indulge in platitudes — in fact, little by little every one began to utter nonsense.

I do not know by what chain of ideas this semi-poetic evening leads me to think of one that was not in the least so; a ball given by some young men, to which all the opera dancers were invited. These women are usually very stupid; but I have observed how superior they are in moral delicacy to the men of their class. Only one vice separates them from other women — that of poverty.

Paris. — Frankness and truth towards women are not desirable — indeed quite the reverse; for see, you regard me as a Sardanapalus because I have been to a ball of *figurantes.* You reproach me as for a crime, and reprove as a still greater crime my praise of these poor girls. Make them rich, I repeat, and only their good qualities will remain; but insurmountable barriers have been raised by the aristocracy between the different classes of society, so that few persons understand how entirely what passes beyond the wall resembles what passes within. I will tell you a story that I heard in this perverse society. In the Rue Saint Honoré lived a poor woman who never left her miserable attic, and who had a little girl twelve years old, neat, reserved, well behaved, who never spoke to any one. Three times a week this child left home in the afternoon, returning alone at midnight, being a supernumerary at the opera. One night she came down to ask for a lighted candle, which being given to her, the porter's wife followed her after a while to the garret, where she found the woman dead on her wretched pallet, and the child occupied in burning a quantity of letters which she drew from a battered trunk. She said, "My mother died to-night, and charged me to burn these papers without reading them." The child knows the name neither of father nor mother, is entirely alone in the world, having no other resource than that of personating monkeys, vultures and devils on the stage. Her mother's last counsel to her was, to remain a *figurante* and to be very good; which she certainly is, even very pious, and does not care to relate her history. Will you be good enough to tell me if there is not infinitely greater merit in this child leading such a life, than belongs to you who enjoy the singular happiness of irreproachable surroundings, and are endowed with a nature so refined as to picture for me, in a measure, the bloom of civilization? I will tell you the truth. I can only endure low society at rare intervals, and through an inexhaustible curiosity respecting all varieties of the human species, seldom entering that of men, there being to me something inexpressibly repulsive in it, especially with us; but in Spain, muleteers and bull-fighters were my friends. I have more than once eaten from the platter of people at whom an Englishman would not look for fear of compromising his self-respect; and I have even drunk from the same leathern bottle with a galley-slave; there was, however, but one bottle, and one must drink when thirsty. Do not believe that I have a predilection for the *canaille.* I simply like to study different manners, different faces, and to hear a different language. Ideas are the same everywhere, and aside from the merely conventional, I do not find good breeding limited to the Faubourg Saint-Germain. All this is Arabic to you, and I know not why I say it. My mother has been very ill, exciting in me great uneasiness, but is now out of danger, and will be in a few days entirely restored to health. I cannot endure anxiety, and during the period of danger I have been in a state of distraction.

As a rule, never select a woman for a confidante; soon or late you would repent of it. Learn also, that there is nothing more common than to do evil for the very pleasure of it. Shake off your ideas of optimism, and be convinced that we are in this world simply to fight against each other. In this connection, I remember that a learned friend who reads hieroglyphics told me that on the Egyptian sarcophagi are often engraved these two words: *life, war;* which proves that I did not originate the maxim just given you. The characters are represented by one of those vases called *canopes*, and a shield with an arm holding a lance.

PARIS. — Your reproaches afford me great pleasure. As to your over-moral relative who says so much evil of me, he recalls Thwackum, who asks: *Can any virtue exist without religion?* Have you read "Tom Jones," a book as immoral as all of mine put together. If it was prohibited, of course you read it. What a droll education you receive in England! And what avails it! Breath is wasted for years in preaching to a young girl, with the certain result that she will desire to know precisely that immoral person for whom it was hoped to inspire her with a holy aversion. What an admirable story is that of the serpent!

All that I know of you pleases me prodigiously. I study you with ardent curiosity. I have certain theories respecting the veriest trifles, — gloves, boots, buckles, to which I attach much importance, having discovered that a certain relation exists between the character of women and the caprice, — or rather, the connection of ideas and the ratiocination, — that dictates the choice of such or such stuffs. I could show, for instance, that a woman who wears blue gowns is a coquette and affects sentiment.

I went the other day on a boating excursion, a number of sailing vessels being on the river, in one of which were several women of a vulgar class. As the vessels reached the shore, from one of them stepped a man about forty years of age who was persistently beating a drum for his own amusement; and while I was admiring the musical organization of this animal a young woman approached him, called him a monster, saying that she had followed him from Paris, and if he declined to admit her to his society he should dearly rue it. The man continued to pound his drum vigorously during this appeal, replying phlegmatically that he would not have her in his boat, whereupon she ran to the vessel moored farthest from the shore and within twenty feet of our own, and sprang into the river, splashing us infamously; but although she had put out my cigar my indignation did not hinder me, aided by my friends, from dragging her out before she had swallowed two glasses of the muddy water. The noble object of such despair had not budged, and grumbled between his teeth: "Why did you pull her out if she wished to drown herself?" Why is it that these cold, indifferent men are the most beloved? I asked myself this question as we sailed home; I ask it still, and I beg you to tell me if you know.

PARIS. — *Mariquita de mi alma* — it is thus I should begin were we at Granada. I believe, notwithstanding my anger, that I love you better in your fits of pouting than I do in any other mood. One sentence of your letter made me laugh like one of the blessed. Without hostile preliminaries for the blow, you tell me *short and sweet:* "My love is promised." You say that you are engaged for life as if it were simply for a quadrille! Very good! My time, it seems, has been profitably employed in discussing love, marriage, and the rest of it! You still say and believe, that when told to "love Monsieur," you at once love. Has your engagement been signed before a notary? When I was a school-boy I received a love-letter with two flaming hearts pierced with a dart, from a seamstress, which precious effusion was captured by the school-master, and I locked up; and, as a denouement of the drama, the object of this budding passion consoled herself with the cruel school-master. Engagements are fatal to the happiness of those who subscribe to them. It is a primal law of nature to hold in aversion whatever savors of the obligatory. All bonds are inherently irksome; and if so trammeled, I seriously believe that you would love *me;* me, to whom you have promised nothing.

To me you appear very devout, superstitious even. This reminds me of a pretty little girl from Granada, who when mounting her mule to cross the Ronda Pass, a route famous for robbers, devoutly kissed her thumb and struck her breast three times, assured by this pious action that the robbers would not dare to show themselves, provided that the *Ingles* — that is myself; with these people all travellers are English — would not swear by the Blessed Virgin and the saints: but only this wicked mode of speech will make these horses move among such roads. See "Tristram Shandy." You are weak and jealous, two qualities not objectionable in a woman, but defects in a man, and I possess them both. Let us cease quarreling and be friends. I kiss the hand that you offer me in pledge of peace.

September. — You allude to special reasons that prevent you from seeking to be with me. I respect secrets, and will not pry into your motives. Some kind busybody may have taken me for the text of a sermon that sways you; nevertheless, in fearing me you would be doing me an infinite wrong. Be reassured I shall never be in love with you; I am now too old and have been too unhappy. I once felt myself falling in love and fled to Spain, one of the finest actions of my life, the cause of the journey never being suspected by the lady. To remain, would have been to commit a great folly — that of offering to a woman in exchange for all that was dear to her, a tenderness that I was conscious of being inadequate to the sacrifice I should have tempted her to make. "Love excuses all, but we must be quite sure that it *is* love;" and this precept, be assured, is more inflexible than those of your Methodistical friends. In me you will acquire a true friend, while I may find a woman with whom I am not in love and in whom I can confide. Should I die this year, you will feel regret at having hardly known me.

The remembrance of your splendid black eyes is no inconsiderable element of my admiration for you. I am old, and nearly insensible to beauty, yet on hearing a fastidious man say that you are very handsome I could not repress a feeling of sadness, and for this reason: that I am horribly jealous (I am not the least in love with you) of my friends, and distressed at the thought that your beauty exposes you to the attentions of men who only appreciate in you that which attracts me the least. The truth is, I am in a frightful humor; nothing makes me so melancholy as a marriage. The Turks who buy a woman after examining her like a fat sheep, are more honest than we who cover our shameful bargain with the transparent varnish of hypocrisy. I have often asked myself what I could say to my wife on my wedding-day, and have found nothing possible unless it be a compliment to her nightcap. The devil would be very cunning to entrap me to such a *fête*. The woman's *rôle* is easier than that of the man. On that day she models herself after the Iphigenia of Racine; but if she observe at all keenly, what droll things she must see! Of course at this *fête* love will be made to you, and you will be regaled with allusions to domestic happiness. When angry, the Andalusians say: "I would stab the sun but for the fear of leaving the world in darkness."

You jest in saying so charmingly that you are afraid of me. You know that I am ugly, capricious in temper, always abstracted, and often tormenting when suffering. Do you not find all this reassuring? You are no pythoness; you will never be in love with me. You are a combination of the angel and the devil, but the latter predominates. You call me a tempter! Dare to say that this word does not apply more strongly to yourself! Have you not thrown a bait to me, poor little fish that I am? And holding me at the end of your line you keep me dancing betwixt heaven and earth, until weary of the sport it may please you to cut me loose, and I shall swim about with the hook in my gills, but never again to find the angler. Adieu, *niña de mi ojos*.

Lady M—— announced to me yesterday that you are going to be married. This being so, burn my letters: I burn yours, and adieu. You know my principle that does not permit me to maintain an intimacy with a married woman whom I have known as demoiselle, with a widow whom I have known as wife. The change in a woman's legal status affects also her various social relations, and always for the worse. In a word, I cannot bear my female friends to marry, therefore, should you marry, let us forget each other. I still love you and commend myself to your prayers.

PARIS. — We are becoming very tender. You say to me, *Amigo de mi alma*, which is very pretty on a woman's lips. It is needless to say that the answer to my question has greatly pleased me. You say, perhaps involuntarily, to my delight, that the husband of a woman who should resemble you would inspire you with true compassion. I believe this readily, and I add that no one would be more unhappy, unless it be the man who should love you. You must be cold and mocking in your fits of ill humor, with an invincible pride that prevents you from saying, "I am in the wrong." Add to this an energy of character causing you to despise complaints and tears. When by the lapse of time and force of events we shall become friends, it will be seen which of the two can more skillfully torment the other. The mere thought of it makes my hair stand on end. Cannot we meet without mystery and as good friends? I am ill and terribly weary. Come to Paris, dear Mariquita, and excite my love anew. I shall never be weary then.

PARIS. — What is your malady? Some heart sorrow? Some mysterious phrases of yours would seem to imply as much. You both suffer and enjoy through the head, but *entre nous*, I do not believe that you are yet in the enjoyment of that viscus (*viscère*) called heart, which is only developed towards twenty-five years of age, in the forty-sixth degree of latitude. Now you are knitting your beautiful black eyebrows and saying: "The insolent fellow, to doubt that I have a heart!" This is, indeed, the great pretension of the day; since the manufacture of such numbers of so-called passionate romances and poems, all women pretend to have a heart. Wait yet a while; when you have a heart in earnest, send me the tidings. You will then regret the happy time in which you only lived by the head, and the ills you now suffer will seem only pin-pricks in comparison with the stabs that will rain upon you with the birth of passion. Your gracious promise to give me your portrait is a double pleasure, as a proof of your increased confidence in me. I am thinking at this moment of the expression of your countenance, which is a little hard: *a lioness, though tame.* I kiss your mysterious feet a thousand times. Adieu.

LONDON, *December.* — Tell me, in the name of God, if you be of God, *querida Mariquita*, why have you not answered my letter? Your last one put me into such a flutter that my reply, on the impulse of the moment, was hardly common sense. Why will you not see me? Your chief motive appears to be the dread of doing something *improper*, as they say here. I do not accept as serious your fear that a more intimate knowledge of me may destroy your illusions. Were this indeed your motive, you would be the first woman, the first human being even, the gratification of whose desires or curiosity had been hindered by a similar consideration. The thing can be *improper* only as regards society. You know in advance that I shall not eat you. Note in passing, that this word *society* makes us unhappy from the moment of donning inconvenient garments at its behests, until the day of our death. A man's discretion, and mine exceptionally, is the greater in proportion that it is trusted. There is, and there will be throughout your life, a conflict between your intuitions and your conventual discipline; thence arises the whole difficulty.

The sea always makes me excessively ill, and *the glad waters of the dark blue sea* are only agreeable to me when seen from the shore; after my first voyage to England it required a fortnight to restore my usual color, that of the pale horse of the Apocalypse. One day at dinner I was seated opposite to Madame V——, who suddenly exclaimed, "Until to-day I thought you were an Indian!"

PARIS, *March*, 1842. — Since you do not refuse my gifts, I send you conserves of rose, bergamot, and jasmine. I offered you Turkish slippers, but have been plundered. Will you have this Turkish mirror in exchange? It may be more acceptable, for you strike me as being even more *coquette* than in the year of grace 1840. It was in December, and you wore ribbed silk stockings.

You are now rich — rich, that is to say free. A capital idea this of your friend, who is another Auld Robin Gray. He must have been in love with you, which you will never confess, for you too dearly love mystery. Why not go to Rome and Naples to see the sun? You are worthy of comprehending Italy, and would return richer in ideas and sensations. I do not advise Greece; your skin is not sufficiently tough to resist all the villainous insects that devour one in that classic land. Speaking of Greece, I send you a blade of grass gathered on the hill of Anthela at Thermopylæ, on the spot where fell the last of the "three hundred." It is not improbable that particles of the dead Leonidas mingle with the constituent atoms of this little flower. It was, I remember, at this very spot, while lying on heaped-up straw and talking to my friend Ampère, that I told him that among the tender memories remaining to me there was only one unmixed with bitterness. I thought of our beautiful youth. *Pray keep my foolish flower.*

I revisited my dear Spain in 1840, passing two months at Madrid where I saw a droll revolution, admirable bull-fights, and the triumphal entry of Espartero, the most comical show possible. I stayed at the country-house of a friend, who in her devotion to me is a sister, and went every morning to Madrid, returning to dine with six charming women, of whom the eldest was thirty-six years old. Owing to the revolution I was the only man permitted to go and come freely, so these six unfortunates had no other *cortejo*. They spoiled me prodigiously. I was not in love with any of them, in which perhaps I was wrong; and though not deceived by these privileges conferred by the revolution, I found it very sweet to be Sultan, even *ad honores*. On my return I indulged in the innocent pleasure of having a book printed, not published, magnificent in binding and engravings. I would offer you this rarity, but it is historic and pedantic, and so bristling with Greek, Latin, and even Osque (do you know in the least what Osque is?), as to be beyond your mark. Last summer, finding myself with money in my pocket, I roved between Malta, Athens, and Constantinople for five months, during which there were not five tedious minutes. I saw the Sultan in varnished boots and a black frock coat, afterwards, covered with diamonds, in the procession of Baïram; on which occasion a very handsome dame, on whose slipper I trod inadvertently, gave me a tremendous blow with her fist, calling me a *giaour*, and this was my sole association with Turkish beauties. At Athens and in Asia I saw the finest monuments in the world, and the loveliest landscapes. The drawback consisted in fleas, and gnats the size of larks. With all this I have grown very old. My firman gives me turtle-dove hair, which is a pretty Oriental metaphor for expressing an ugly truth. Imagine your friend quite gray! Your claim to rival Ionic and Corinthian capitals in my heart, made me laugh. In the first place, I like only the Doric, and there are no capitals, not even those of the Parthenon, which are worth to me the memory of a friendship.

PARIS, *May*, 1842. — If I must be frank, and you know that I cannot correct myself of this defect, I will confess that you struck me as much improved physically, not at all so morally; that you have a very fine complexion, and beautiful hair which I looked at more than your cap, which probably was worthy of admiration, as you seem to be provoked that I did not appreciate it; but I have never been able to distinguish lace from calico. You have still the figure of a sylph, and though rather *blasé* as to black eyes, I never saw finer ones at Constantinople nor at Smyrna.

Now for the reverse of the medal. You have continued a child in many things, and have acquired into the bargain a nice little dash of selfishness and hypocrisy, which may be serviceable, only it is nothing of which one need boast. You do not know how to conceal your first impulses, but think to make amends by a host of puerile evasions. What do you gain by it? Remember Jonathan Swift's fine maxim: *A lie is too good a thing to be wasted.* This magnanimous idea of being hard to yourself, will, assuredly, lead you very far, and a few years hence you will find yourself as happy as the Trappist, who, after having perseveringly scourged himself should one day discover that there is no Paradise. It is your Satanic pride that has hindered you from seeing me. You believe, at least, that you have pride, but it is only a petty vanity well worthy of a devotee. The fashion of the day tends to sermons — do you frequent them? This alone is lacking in you! As respects myself, I am not more of a hypocrite, in which perhaps I am wrong: certain it is that I am not therefore the better liked. Ah! great news! The first Academician out of the forty who shall die will be the cause of my paying thirty-nine visits. I shall pay them as awkwardly as possible, and shall gain thirty-nine enemies. It would be tedious to explain to you this fit of ambition. Suffice it that the Academy is now my blue cachemire. Be happy, but remember this maxim: Never to commit other follies than those agreeable to you. Perhaps you prefer M. de Talleyrand's apothegm, that one must guard against good impulses, because they are nearly always honest.

PARIS, *June*, 1842. — I have received your purse, which exhales a charmingly aristocratic perfume, and if embroidered by yourself does you honor; in it also I recognize your recent taste for the positive. It would have been poetical to value it at one or two stars; and I should prize it even more had you deigned to add to it some lines from your white hands. No, I will not accept your pheasants which you offer in a detestable way, saying, moreover, disagreeable things about my Turkish sweetmeats. It is you who have the palate of a *giaour* in not appreciating the food of houris. Your conscience, I am sure, is often less lenient than I, whom you accuse of hardness and indifference. The hypocrisy that you now cleverly practice, merely as a game, will, in the end, play you a trick — that of becoming a reality. As to coquetry, the inseparable companion of the deplorable vice that you affect, you have long been duly convicted of it, and it became you when tempered by frankness, by heart and imagination. Is it your friendship that you designate as an *essence?* a word I like. Since all that you wish for comes to pass, I humbly pray you to intercede with destiny that I may be an Academician; but the plague must supervene among these gentlemen to favor my chances, to improve which I must also borrow a little of your talent for hypocrisy. I am too old to reform, and in making the effort I should perhaps become even worse than I am. Formerly I had no high opinion of my precious self, but my self-esteem has increased, simply because the world has degenerated. I pass my evenings in re-reading my books which are being republished, and find myself very immoral and sometimes stupid. The question now is to diminish the immorality and stupidity with the least trouble; but at the cost of *blue devils* to myself.

CHALON-SUR-SAONE, *June*, 1842. — Thanks for your prayers, if they are not a mere rhetorical figure. I am aware of your devoutness, which is now the fashion, like blue cachemires. Our French devotion displeases me, being a species of shallow philosophy proceeding from the head and not the heart. When you have seen the Italians you will agree with me that their devotion is alone genuine: only one cannot have it at will, and one must be born beyond the Alps or Pyrenees to possess such faith. You cannot imagine the disgust with which our present society inspires me, and one would say that it had sought by every possible combination to augment the mass of *ennui* apparently necessary in the order of the world; while in Italy everything tends to render existence easy and endurable.

AVIGNON, *July*, 1842. — Since you assume this tone *ma foi*, I yield. Give me brown bread, which is better than none at all, only permit me to say that it *is* brown, and write to me again. You see that I am humble and submissive. The figure of rhetoric of which you believe yourself to be the inventor has been long in use, and might be clothed with an uncouth Greek name, but in French it is known under the less lofty term of lying. Make use of it with me as little as possible, and do not lavish it on others: it must be kept for great occasions. Do not seek to find the world foolish and ridiculous; it is only too much so in reality. It is better to cherish illusions, and I hold several which are perhaps rather transparent, but I exert myself to retain them. I am sorry that you read Homer in Pope, and recommend as preferable Dugas-Montbel's translation, which is the only readable one. If you had the courage to brave ridicule and the time to spare, you would read Planché's Greek Grammar a month to make you sleep, which would not fail of this effect; at the end of two months you would amuse yourself by comparing M. Montbel's translation with the Greek; and two months afterwards you would easily perceive from the ambiguity of phrase, that the Greek has a meaning other than that given by the translator. At the end of a year you would read Homer as you do a melody and the accompaniment; the melody being the Greek, the accompaniment the translation. It is possible that this would incite the wish to study Greek in earnest; but such assiduity is also to presuppose you with neither dresses to occupy you, nor people to whom they may be displayed. Everything in Homer is remarkable. His epithets, so seemingly strange in French, are singularly appropriate. I remember that he calls the sea "purple," and I never understood its application until last year. I was in a little caïque on the Gulf of Lepanto, going to Delphi. The sun was setting, and as it disappeared the sea wore for ten minutes a magnificent tint of dark violet — but this requires the air, the sea, the sun of Greece. I hope that you will never become sufficiently an artist to discover that Homer was a great painter. I hope that you find me this time passably resigned and decorous, *Signora Fornarina!*

PARIS, *August*, 1842. — I congratulate you on your Greek studies, and to begin with something that may interest you, will tell you the word by which in Greek persons possessing like yourself hair of which they are justly proud are described: *efplokamos. Ef*, much; *plokamos*, curl. Homer, somewhere says: —

"Nimfi efplokamouça Calypso."
(Curly-tressed nymph Calypso.)

I am sorry that you should set out so late in the season for Italy, which you will see only through atrocious rains that obscure half the charm of the loveliest mountains in the world, and you will be obliged to accept on faith my eulogies on the exquisite skies of Naples. Moreover, you will have no good fruit, but in compensation, *becaficos*, so called because they live on grapes.

While packing my trunk at Avignon, two venerable figures entered, announcing themselves as members of the Municipal Council. I supposed them emissaries from some church, when they informed me with much pomposity and prolixity that they wished to commend to my loyalty and virtue a lady about to travel with me. I replied very crossly that I should be very loyal and virtuous but that I detested travelling with women, whose presence precluded smoking. The mail coach arrived, within which I found a large, handsome woman, simply and coquettishly attired, who declared herself to be always very ill in a carriage, and despaired of reaching Paris alive. Our *tête-à-tête* began, and I was as polite and amiable as I find it possible to be while remaining in a cramped position. My companion talked well, without any Marseillaise accent, was an ardent Bonapartist, very enthusiastic, believed in the immortality of the soul, not too much in the Catechism, and saw things generally *en beau;* nevertheless, I was conscious that she felt a certain fear of me. We were some fifty odd hours alone; but though we chatted immensely I found it impossible to come to any conclusion respecting my neighbor except that she was married, and a person of good society. On arriving at Paris she precipitated herself into the arms of an excessively ugly man, no doubt her father, and raising my hat I was about entering a cab, when my unknown, leaving the gentleman, said in an agitated voice: "Monsieur, I am much moved by the respectful consideration shown me by you, for which I cannot sufficiently express my gratitude; and I shall never forget my good fortune in travelling with so *illustrious* a man."

And this word explains the Municipal Councilors, and the terror of the lady. They had evidently seen my name on the register, and the lady, having read my books, expected to be swallowed alive, which opinion no doubt is shared by many of my feminine readers. This incident put me into a bad humor for two days. It is a singular thing, that having at one period of my life become a very worthless fellow, I lived during two years on my former good reputation ; and since resuming my very moral life, I now am considered a scamp. . . . . If you are surprised that the goddesses are blondes, you will be still more astonished at Naples at seeing statues whose hair is painted red. It seems that beautiful women formerly used red, even gold powder ; but on the other hand you will see in the pictures of the *Studij*, a number of goddesses with black hair, descriptive of which there is in Greek a terrible word : *mélankhètis :* the χα being a diabolical aspirate.

It distresses me to perceive your rapid progress in Satanism, that you are becoming ironical, sarcastic, and even diabolical, all which words are drawn from the Greek, the meaning of the last being calumniator. You jest at my finest qualities, and even your praise is impaired by a reticence and cautiousness that deprive the commendation of all merit. As for good company, I have often found it mortally tedious. I am vain enough to believe myself not out of place with unpretending persons whom I have long known, and at a Spanish inn with muleteers and Andalusian peasant women. Write that in my funeral oration and you will have told the truth. And if I speak of this, it is that I believe the time approaches for you to prepare it ; for I suffer excessively from confused sight, spasms, and frightful headaches, which would indicate some serious affection of the brain, and I may soon become, as Homer says, a guest of gloomy Proserpine. I should be delighted were it to sadden you for a fortnight.

I believe the ancients to have been more amusing than ourselves : they had not such paltry aims, were not preoccupied by such inanities. Julius Cæsar at fifty-three was guilty of follies for Cleopatra, and forgot all for her, nearly to the point of drowning himself actually and figuratively. What statesman of our generation is not callous, completely insensible at the age at which he can aspire to be a Deputy?

The little that I have seen of Greece has enlarged my comprehension of Homer. Throughout the Odyssey one sees the incredible love of the Greeks for their own country. To dwell in a foreign land is to them the greatest of misfortunes; but to die in exile is to them beyond all imagination frightful. You jest at my gastronomy; do you appreciate the entrails so greedily devoured by ancient heroes? They are still eaten, and are truly delicious, being composed of spiced and appetizing little crusts skewered by perfumed mastic wood, which at once explains why the priests reserved for themselves this tempting morsel of the victims.

You ask if there are any Greek novels — there are many, but very tedious in my opinion. "Daphnis and Chloe," translated by Courier is pretentiously *naïf* and not over exemplary. An admirable novel, but very immoral, is "L'Ane de Lucius;" one does not boast, however, of reading it, though a masterpiece. The worst of the Greeks is, that their ideas of morality and decency differ so essentially from our own. If you have the courage to attempt history you will be charmed with Herodotus, who enchants me. Begin with "Anabasis or the Retreat of the Ten Thousand;" take a map of Asia and follow these ten thousand rascals in their journey; it is Froissard *gigantesque.* Lucien is the Greek with the most wit, or rather *our* wit: but he is a libertine and I dare not commend him.

I gratefully appreciate your condescension at the opera in permitting me to look at your face during two hours, and I owe it to truth to say that I admired it greatly, as also your hair, which I had never seen so near. As to your assertion of having refused nothing that I have asked of you, several millions of years in purgatory will be your penance for this fine falsehood. I do not remember comparing you to Cerberus, but you certainly bear him a resemblance, not only in your love for cakes, but in possessing three heads, or rather brains — one of a frightful coquette, the other of an old diplomatist; the third I will not name, as to-day I wish to tell you nothing agreeable. I have returned from seeing "Frédégonde," which was excessively tedious, notwithstanding Mademoiselle Rachel, who has very handsome black eyes without white, as it is said has the devil. You tell me amiably that you do not wish to see me for fear of becoming wearied of me. If I am not mistaken, we have met six or seven times in six years, and adding up the minutes, we may have passed three or four hours together, the half of which was in silence. Admit that it is little flattering to my self-love to be treated thus after an intimacy of six years, and in face of the proofs of regard that you have vouchsafed me ; moreover, pardon the word, I think it somewhat silly. If you believe yourself to be doing wrong in meeting me, do you commit no fault in writing to me ? As I am not well versed in your catechism, this remains a perplexing question. I speak harshly perhaps, but you wound me, and I cannot imitate you in ridding myself of a weight on the heart by eating cakes. But I will ask nothing more of you, — for you become every day more imperious, and develop a scandalous refinement in coquetry. You are careful to recall your eyes to me, which I have not forgotten though so seldom seen. You should see me were it only to escape from the atmosphere of flattery surrounding you. When I met you at the house of our friend, your extreme elegance greatly surprised me, and the quantity of cakes necessary to restore you after the fatigue of the opera astonished me still more ; not that I do not place coquetry and *gourmandise* in the first rank of your faults, but I thought the form of these defects a moral one ; believing that you bestowed little thought on your toilette, that you were a woman who eat merely through abstraction, and preferred to make an impression on men by your eyes and clever sayings rather than by your dresses. See how deceived I have been.

December, 1842. — Formerly the absurdities of others amused me, but now I prefer to conceal them from the world. I have also become more humane, and when witnessing lately the bull-fights at Madrid, the pleasurable sensations of ten years previous were not renewed. I have a horror of all suffering, and for some time past have believed in moral suffering. In short, I strive as much as possible to forget my *me;* and this in few words is a list of my perfections. No, I have no *Vanagloria.* I see things too practically, perhaps, having been *escarmentado* through regarding them too poetically. I have passed my life in being praised for qualities that I do not possess, and calumniated for defects that are not mine.

Your letter does not surprise me in the least: for I now know you well enough to be certain that when a good thought strikes you it is at once repented of, and you strive to have it speedily forgotten—but this justice I will do you: that you understand admirably how to gild the most bitter pill. You compare me to the devil. I was quite conscious on Tuesday of not thinking enough about my old books and too much of your gloves and *bottines.* But in spite of all that you say with such diabolical coquetry, I cannot believe that you have the slightest fear of renewing at the Museum our former follies. It pleases you to have some vague mark for your coquetry, and you find it in me; but you do not wish it to be too near, for should you miss the target your vanity would suffer, and perhaps in approaching it closely you would discover it to be not worth your shaft. Have I read you aright?

I suffer terribly and cough incessantly, nevertheless I shall go to hear Rachel declaim tirades from "Phèdre" before several great men, and she will believe my cough to be a cabal against her. This evening I heard Madame Persiani sing, and she has reconciled me to human nature; were I King Saul I should choose her in place of David.

I am told that M. de Pongerville, the Academician, is about to die, which throws me into despair, for I shall not be chosen to replace him, and I wish he could wait until my time shall arrive. He has translated into verse a Latin named Lucretius, who died at the age of forty-three from having taken a philtre to make himself beloved, previous to which he wrote a great poem, atheistic, impious, abominable, on "The Nature of Things." You appear to me to grow more handsome, which I had thought impossible; but one always improves in beauty when in good health; and that comes with a hard heart and good digestion.

December, 1842. — I have been exceedingly ill with my throat, and all the fires of hell in my breast, and have passed several days in bed meditating on the strangeness of this world. I find myself on the declivity of a mountain whose summit, with much fatigue and little pleasure, I have hardly attained, the descent being so steep and tedious that perhaps it would be rather an advantage to fall into a crevice before reaching the bottom; while the only ray of consolation along the whole route has been a little distant sunshine, a few months passed in Italy, Spain, or in Greece while forgetting the whole world, the present, and especially the future. All this is far from gay: but some one brings me four volumes by Doctor Strauss, "The Life of Jesus," which in Germany is called *exegesis*, a pure Greek word they have found by which to express discussion on the point of a needle, but it is very amusing. I have remarked that the more closely a thing is shorn of any useful conclusion, the more amusing it becomes.

There are people who buy furniture of a color to suit their taste, but for fear of spoiling it shroud it in linen covers that are only removed when the furniture is worn out. In all that you do and say, you substitute a factitious for a true sentiment — this perhaps is *decorum*. You say in your letter, "I believe that I have never loved you so well as yesterday" — you should have added, "I love you less to-day." I often repent of being too loyal in my *rôle* of statue. You gave me your soul yesterday: I would have given you mine in return but you did not wish it. Always the linen cover!

Yesterday on returning from a dinner I discovered that I knew by heart the speech of Tecmessa that you admired, and being in a somewhat pensive mood I translated it into English verse, as I abhor French verse.

PARIS, *January*, 1843. — I heartily forgive your jest about the Academy, of which I think less than you believe. Should I ever be an Academician, I shall not be hard as a rock, though perchance a little case-hardened and mummified ; but rather a good fellow at heart.

I am reminded of an incident that occurred a fortnight ago at a dinner given by an Academician for the purpose of presenting Bèranger to Mademoiselle Rachel. A number of celebrities were assembled. Rachel came late and her manner of entering displeased me ; while the men said so many silly things to her, and the women did so many on seeing her, that I remained in my corner ; besides, it is a year since I have spoken to her. After dinner, Bèranger with his candor and usual good sense told her that she was wrong to fritter away her talent in *salons*, there being for her only one true public, that of the Théâtre Français. Rachel appeared to appreciate the advice, and to prove that she benefited by it, at once declaimed the first act of "Esther." Some one was needed to give her the cue, and by her direction a Racine was formally brought to me by an Academician who was officiating as *cicisbeo ;* but I replied rudely that I knew nothing about verses and that there were persons present who being in that line would scan them much better. Hugo excused himself on account of his eyes ; another for some other reason, the master of the house being finally victimized. Picture to yourself Rachel costumed in black, standing between the piano and tea-table, with a door behind her, assuming a theatrical pose and expression, the transformation being very fine and vastly amusing. This lasted about two minutes, then she began : —

"Est-ce toi, chère Elise?"

The confidante in the middle of his reply lets fall both book and spectacles, ten minutes passing before he can recover his page and his eyes. The audience perceive that Esther is getting into a rage. She resumes. The door behind opens, a servant enters, who is signed to withdraw. He hurriedly retreats but does not succeed in shutting the door, which remaining ajar swings to and fro, accompanying Rachel with a melodious and most comical creak. This not ceasing, Rachel puts her hand to her heart and grows faint, but, like a person accustomed to die on the stage, giving one time to come to her assistance. During this interlude Hugo and M. Thiers fall to quarreling on the subject of Racine, Hugo asserting that Racine had a narrow mind (*un petit esprit*) and Corneille a master intellect (*un grand*). "You say that," replied Thiers "because you are *un grand esprit;* you are the Corneille" — here Hugo's head assumed an air of great modesty — "of an epoch of which Casimir Delavigne is the Racine." Meanwhile the swoon passes off and the act is finished, but *fiascheggiando.* One of the guests who knows Rachel well, remarked: "How she must have sworn this evening on going away." This is my story; do not compromise me with the Academicians.

I deeply regret having exposed you through my persistency to such a frightful drenching. It rarely happens to me to sacrifice others to myself, and when it occurs I am filled with all possible remorse. Happiness only gives me strength, while it diminishes yours. *Wer besser liebt?* You laughed at me and received as a jest what I said as to the wish to sleep, or rather the torpor that sometimes steals over one when in a state of happiness so great as to preclude its utterance in words. I observed yesterday that you were under the influence of this sleep, which is worth many vigils, and I was too content to wish to disturb my happiness. It is in exaggerating facts by brooding on them that you have succeeded in making a star-chamber matter of what you have yourself termed *frivolities;* and allow me to say, that the very obstinacy and rabid ferocity with which you thwart me as to these frivolities render them more dear to me, and endue them with a fresh importance. If I must see you only to resist the most innocent temptations, it is the *rôle* of a saint surpassing my strength, and the condition exacted by you that I transform myself into a statue, like the king in the "Arabian Nights," is simply insupportable. The only hypocrisy of which I am capable is that of concealing from those whom I love all the ill they do me; I might sustain the effort for a season; but forever, no. As to our walk, I am like a cat that continues to lick his moustache after lapping milk. Acknowledge that repose, even the *kef*, which is superior to all that is best of this nature, is nothing in comparison with the happiness "that is almost a pain." You claim to have spoiled me, but you do not understand the art; your triumph is to put me in a fury. Adieu, *dearest!*

PARIS, *February*, 1843.—Since seeing you I have been much in society, committing a multitude of academic meannesses which cost me a painful effort, having lost the habit, but doubtless I shall quickly pick it up again. To-day I saw five illustrious poets and writers of prose, and had night not overtaken me the thirty-six visits might possibly have been achieved at a dash. The drollery of it is the meeting one's rivals, several of whom glared as if they wished to eat me alive. Truth to say, I am worn out with this odious drudgery and should be glad to forget it all in an hour with you.

I have been this evening to the Italiens, where, thanks to the *claquers*, my enemy Madame Viardot had a success. I find that I have omitted to attend the Opera House Ball—where, alas! is the happy time in which I so enjoyed it? now it bores me horribly. Do I not seem to you very old? Theodore Hook is dead. Have you read Bulwer's "Ernest Maltravers," and "Alice," which contain charming pictures of old love and young love. You may reflect with pride on the strange influence you have exercised over my ideas and resolutions; you have read my thought as quickly as it was conceived—and yet yesterday, on the strength of a Greek verse, I went to Saint-Germain-l'Auxerrois, full of hope but fruitlessly. Do you remember when we always divined each other's wishes? The other evening at the opera your rainbow costume inspired me with various fancies, but you have no need of coquetry with me. I do not love you better as a rainbow than in black. I have long suspected something diabolical in you, but am somewhat reassured in thinking that I have seen your feet, neither of which is cloven; nevertheless it may be that beneath these *bottines* you have a little claw concealed. I have passed a wretched night of suffering, and as a diversion shall think of your feet and hands.

I have received the sad news of the death by paralysis of poor Sharp,[1] one of my most intimate friends whom I was about to visit in London. I cannot yet accustom myself to the thought of seeing him no more.

My fate will be decided at the Academy on the fourteenth, which corresponds with the ides of March, the day of the death of my hero, Cæsar. Ominous, is it not? Reason encourages me to hope, but a depressing intuition whispers of failure. Meanwhile I conscientiously pay my visits. I find people very polite, quite accustomed to their parts and enacting them very much in earnest, while I strive to play mine with equal gravity, though I find it difficult. Does it not strike you as comical to say to a man, "Monsieur, I believe myself to be one of the forty cleverest men of France; I am worthy of you," and similar facetiæ. This must, moreover, be translated into civil and fitting phrase to suit the various persons; an occupation to weary me beyond endurance if prolonged. I envy the fate of women who have no employment but to make themselves beautiful, and to rehearse the effect to be produced on others. I return your *cravate*, which was found in the anteroom of His Royal Highness the Duke de Nemours, but no one has asked any explanation of its presence in my pocket.

I am full of remorse for my fury, my only excuse being that the transition from our delicious halt in a strange species of oasis, to our walk, was too abrupt — it was falling from heaven to hell. You reproach me with being indifferent to every one; I suppose you simply mean that I am undemonstrative — when untrue to my nature I suffer. Admit also that it is sad, after becoming all that we are to each other, to find you still distrustful of me. Two personalities exist in you: the one all heart and soul; the other a beautiful statue polished by society, draped in silk and cachemire, a charming automaton with most skillfully adjusted springs. We speak to the first, and find only the statue; but why need it be sc

[1] Mr. Sutton Sharp, a very distinguished English barrister.

lovely! You ask if I believe in the soul — not over much; nevertheless, on reflection I find an argument in favor of the hypothesis, namely: how could two inanimate substances give and receive a sensation by a union that would be simply insipid but for the idea that we associate with it? This is rather a pedantic mode of saying that when two persons who love, embrace each other, they experience a sensation quite different from that communicated by kissing the softest satin. But the argument has its value, and we will discuss metaphysics at our next meeting — a subject of which I am fond, for it is inexhaustible.

You shall have your portrait *en Turquesse*, and I have placed a *narghilé* in your hand to add a local coloring; but I must have my pay, or prepare for a terrible vengeance. I have been asked to-day to contribute a sketch for an album to be sold for the benefit of sufferers by an earthquake, and I shall give them your portrait!

PARIS, *April*, 1843. — You do well not to speak of Catullus. He is not an author to be read during Holy Week, and there are passages in his writings quite impossible to translate into French. We clearly see what love was at Rome towards the year 50 before J. C.; it was, however, a little better than love at Athens in the time of Pericles. Women were already a recognized force: they made men commit follies. Their power arose, not, as is commonly said, through Christianity, but I think through the influence that the barbarians of the North exercised over Roman society. The Germans were capable of exaltation. They loved the soul; the Romans loved little save the body. It is true that for a long period women were without souls: they have none as yet in the East, and it is a pity. You comprehend how two souls speak to one another, but yours seldom responds to mine. I am glad that you value the verses of Musset, and you are right in comparing him with Catullus, who, however, wrote his native tongue better, while Musset has the defect of not believing more in the soul than Catullus, whom his time excused. Would you believe that a

Roman could say pretty things, and could be tender? I will show you some verses that will fit in like wax *à propos* of our usual disputes. You will see that the ancients are worth more than your Wilhelm Meister.

Our walks have become a part of my life, and I hardly understand how I previously existed. In what mood shall I find you? Each time that we meet you are mailed in a fresh panoply of ice that only melts at the end of a quarter of an hour. By the time of my return you will have accumulated a veritable iceberg.

AVALLON, *August*, 1843. — I came here to visit an old uncle whom I have seldom seen. I dislike relations; one is obliged to be familiar with persons whom one has rarely met because they happen to be the son of the same father as one's mother. My uncle, however, is a good fellow, not too provincial, and whom I should find agreeable if we possessed two ideas in common. The women here are as ugly as those of Paris, having, moreover, ankles as thick as posts. In addition to our moral perfections we have the advantage of being the ugliest and most stunted people in Europe. At Vezelay I found myself in a horrible little town perched on a high mountain, bored to death by the country people, and preoccupied by a speech I was to deliver. I am a Representative, and you know me well enough to judge how odious to me is the *rôle* of a public man. While I sketched, a crowd gathered about me, emulating each other in conjectures as to the nature of my occupation. To console me there was an admirable church which owes to me its escape from demolition, and which I first saw soon after meeting you; and I asked myself to-day if we were more mad then than now. There was also a natural terrace that a poet might well call a precipice, where I philosophized on the *me*, on Providence, in the hypothesis that it exists; and finished with the despairing thought that you are far away. I send you an owl's feather that I found in the abbatical church, having read in some book of magic that when a woman places it beneath her pillow she dreams of her friend.

SAINT-LUPICIN, *August*, 1843, 600 *metres above the level of the sea — in the midst of an ocean of very active and famished fleas.* — This village is in the Jura Mountains, is ugly to the last degree, filthy, and populous with fleas. I shall pass a night like those at Ephesus, but at my awaking, unfortunately, I shall find neither laurels nor Greek ruins. There are immense quantities of colossal flowers, a singularly keen and pure air, and the human voice can be heard at a league's distance. I have had leaden skies, a broken wheel, and a poulticed eye, all tolerably remedied: but I cannot become habituated to solitude — solitude in motion, than which there is nothing more sad; and were I in prison, I should be more at my ease than thus roving alone about the country.

AVIGNON, 1843. — The district that I am now traversing is very fine, but the natives are stupid beyond measure. No one opens his mouth but to praise the country, and this from the priest to the porter. There is no appearance of that tact constituting the gentleman, which I found among the common people of Spain; but with that exception it is impossible to find a country more nearly resembling Spain. There is the same aspect of town and landscape; the workmen lie in the shade and drop their cloaks with a tragic air that is Andalusian; the odor of garlic and oil is mingled with that of oranges and jasmine; the streets are shaded with linen during the day, and the women have small, well-shod feet; there is nothing, even to the *patois*, that has not a flavor of Spain. A still closer relation exists in its abundance of gnats, fleas, and other insects, and I have yet two months of this life to pass before seeing human beings!

I have sent my sketches to Paris; besides, a Roman capital would not interest you, — devils, dragons, and saints forming the decoration. The devils of the first centuries of Christianity are not very seductive, and I am sure that you would not value dragons and saints. I have sketched a Maçon costume for you, the only graceful one I have seen, though the sash is so drolly placed as to afford no advantage in a slender over a thick waist, — the dress would seem to require a special physical organization. The cheapness of cotton stuffs and the facility of communication with Paris have wrought the disappearance of our national costumes. Avignon is filled with churches and palaces, all provided with battlemented and machicolated towers. The palace of the Pope is a model of a fortification for the Middle Ages, which proves what amiable security reigned toward the fourteenth century. There are subterranean chambers used by the Inquisition, with the remains of an infernal complicated machine, and furnaces for heating the irons with which heretics were tortured. The natives are as proud of their Inquisition as the English of their Magna Charta. "We also," say they, "have had *auto-da-fé*, and the Spaniards had none until after us!"

TOULON, *October*. — It is impossible to find a place dirtier or prettier than Marseilles; and these words are especially appropriate to its women. They have expressive countenances, fine black eyes, beautiful teeth, very small feet, and imperceptible ankles; but the pretty feet are shod in thick, cinnamon-colored stockings the color of Marseilles mud, and darned with cotton of twenty different tints. Their dresses are badly made, untidy and covered with stains, while their fine hair owes its lustre mainly to candle-grease. Add to this an atmosphere redolent of garlic mixed with fumes of rancid oil, and you have a picture of the Marseilles beauty. What a pity that nothing can be perfect in this world! Yet, in spite of all, they are ravishing — a positive triumph.

Your letter is admirably diplomatic; you practice the axiom that language has been given to man to conceal his thought; and yet I see between the lines the tenderest things in the world. I think unceasingly of my return to Paris, and my imagination paints I know not how many delicious moments passed at your side.

PARIS, 1843. — *I weary for you*, to make use of an ellipsis that you affect. I did not clearly realize that we were about to part for so long a time. Shall we really see each other no more? We separated without a word, almost without a look. I was sensible of a calm happiness not usual with me, and for a few moments I seemed to wish for nothing more. How ingenious you are in depriving others and yourself of an enchantment that comes so near! Doubtless I am wrong to use the word enchantment, as marmots probably never experience the sensation, and you were one of those pretty animals before Brahma transferred your soul to the body of a woman. But nowithstanding my ill-humor I love better to see you with your grand air of indifference than not at all. The affection you bear me is merely an emanation of the intellect. You are all mind, one of those chilly women of the North who live only through the head. Our characters are as opposite as our *stamina*, and though you may divine my thoughts, you can never comprehend them. Yet, with all these conflicting characteristics a great affinity exists between us; it is Goethe's *Walverwandschaft.* Throw away your faded flowers and come with me to seek fresh ones. You say that sunshine exercises a cheering influence over you, — and for myself, though I love you at all seasons, in all weather, the happiness of seeing you in sunshine is a more exquisite happiness still. Is it possible that you cannot *say* to me all that you write? What is this *bizarre* timidity that hinders frankness, prompts you to wrap your thoughts in words more perplexing than the Apocalypse, and to assert the most extraordinary falsehood rather than allow a word of truth to escape which would give me such pleasure? Do you believe in the devil? In my opinion the pith of the matter lies there. If he terrifies you, contrive that he do not carry you off. I do not guaranty my catechism, which, however, I believe to be the best. I have never sought to make converts, but, up to the present time, neither has my conversion been accomplished by others.

Yesterday evening I went to the opera, where they proposed to close the doors, Ronconi being drunk or in prison for debt; but yielding to our clamor they gave us "L'Elisir d'Amore;" after which I corrected proofs until three o'clock in the morning. I do not concern myself so much about the Academy as you suppose. I have hardly a chance of success. Do you know any magic that will conjure my name from the deal-box called Urn?

PARIS, *March*, 1844.[1] — Many thanks for your congratulations, but I wish for something better; to see and walk with you. I think you take the matter too tragically. Why do you weep? The "forty chairs" were not worth one little tear. I am very heartily gratified, the more that I expected defeat; and my mother who was suffering from acute rheumatism was suddenly cured. I am worn out, demoralized, and completely "out of my wits." Then my novel, "Arsène Guillot," makes a signal *fiasco* and rouses the indignation of all the self-styled virtuous people, especially the women of fashion who dance the polka and throng to the sermons of Père Ravignan, and who go so far as to liken me to a monkey who climbs to the top of the tree and makes grimaces at the world below. I believe that some votes have been lost by this scandal; on the other hand, some have been gained. Now, to show my greatness of soul, I must rush about thanking friends and enemies. I had the good fortune to be blackballed seven times by persons whom I detest, yet who tell me that they were my warmest partisans; but it is a happiness not to be burdened with gratitude towards those whom we hold in slight esteem. My Homer deceived me, or rather it was M. Vatout to whom the threatening vaticination was addressed.

March, 1844. — I fear that the address may have seemed too long. I am still shivering from the cold, and you may have perceived my terrible cough, which might have been mistaken for a cabal. Did you prefer the full dress to the frock coat? I had some difficulty in discovering you hidden beneath your neighbor's bonnet — another bit of childishness. Did you see what I sent you, in full view of the Academy? But of course you never wish to see anything. Why will you dispute on

[1] His election to the French Academy.

this text: "Which loves the best?" A desirable preliminary would be to come to an agreement as to the meaning of the verb, and this we shall never do; we are both too ignorant, and above all too ignorant of each other. More than once I have fancied you to be clearly revealed, but you always escape me. I was right in calling you Cerberus, "three gentlemen in one." Our mutual concessions only result in making us more unhappy; and, more clear-sighted than you, I greatly blame myself, for I have made you suffer in prolonging an illusion that I should never have conceived. For you I have no reproaches. You wished to reconcile two incompatible things, but in vain. Should I not be grateful that you essayed the impossible for my sake? On the whole, perhaps you will one day come to regard our folly only in its fairest light, will remember only the happy moments we have passed together.

Consider if it be not sad for me to find myself always in conflict with your pride, my great enemy, or rather rival in your heart, and which triumphs over your tenderness, in comparison with which it is a Colossus to a pigmy. This premeditated pleasure, or, I prefer to believe, instinct that leads you to excite in me a desire for what you obstinately refuse, is in reality a species of selfishness. All that wounds your pride stirs you to rebellion; and unconsciously this colors the most trivial details. You are happy, you tell me, when I kiss your hand, and you yield yourself to the feeling because your pride is satisfied by this demonstration of humility. You wish me to be a statue that you may be my life, my soul-awakener; but you wish for no reciprocity in the happiness to which I aspire, as that would imply an equality that displeases you. I shall never place my pride and happiness in the same scale, therefore if you will kindly suggest new formulas of humility, I will adopt them without hesitation. Is not the friendship which so strangely unites us, a sweeter, more living force than all the victories gained by your demon pride?

PARIS, 1844. — It is decided that I go to Algeria next month; and while you are learning Greek I am studying

4

Arabic, a diabolical language of which I shall never acquire two words. I passed a day at Strasbourg, exhorting the authorities with sublime eloquence to restore an ancient church ; their reply being that they were in greater need of tobacco than monuments, and that they should convert the church into a storehouse. The cathedral that formerly I liked so much appears absolutely ugly, and even the wise and foolish virgins of Steinbach hardly found grace in my eyes. You are right in liking Paris so well ; it is, after all, the only city in which one can truly live.

I dined yesterday with General Narvaez — an entertainment in honor of his wife's birthday. Few ladies except Spanish were present. One was pointed out to me who is starving herself to death through love, and is gently fading away. This species of suicide must seem very cruel to you. There was another demoiselle, whom General Serrano has deserted for her fat Catholic Majesty ; but she is not dying of it, and seems even to be in excellent health. There was also Madame Gonzalez Bravo, sister of the actor Romea, and sister-in-law of the same Majesty, who, it is said, gives herself a large number of sisters-in-law. This one is very pretty and very clever.

Paris, 1844. — We separated yesterday mutually discontented, and both were in the wrong. It is evident that we can no longer meet without quarreling horribly. We both desire the impossible. You — that I should be a statue ; I — that you should cease to be one. Every fresh proof of this impossibility, which at heart we have never doubted, is cruel for both. For my part I regret all the pain I have caused you. I too often give way to impulses of absurd anger ; it would be as reasonable to feel angry against ice for being cold. I hope that you will forgive me ; no resentment remains, only a heavy sadness. Adieu, since only at a distance can we be friends. When both shall be old, we may perhaps meet again with pleasure ; meanwhile, in misfortune or in happiness, remember me. Once more, while I have the courage, adieu.

PARIS, 1844. — My occupation at this moment is tedious and low beyond measure; I am soliciting votes for the Academy of Inscriptions. The most absurd scenes occur, and I am often seized with a wish to laugh, which must be repressed for fear of shocking the gravity of the Academicians. I embarked somewhat blindly in the affair, but my chances are not bad. You are wrong to be jealous of Inscriptions. I have a little *amour propre* in the matter; just as in a game of chess with a skillful adversary, but neither loss nor gain will affect me a quarter so much as one of our quarrels. But what a vile calling is this of solicitor! Did you ever see dogs enter the hole of a badger? When experienced in the game they have an appalled look on entering, and often come out more quickly than they go in, for it is an ugly brute to visit, is the badger. I always think of the badger when about to ring the bell of an Academician, and "in the mind's eye" I see myself an exact likeness of that dog. However, I have not yet been bitten.

POITIERS, 1844. — No doubt you have amused yourself exceedingly, which I cannot but believe to be synonymous with an indulgence in coquetry. Since leaving Paris my life has been unspeakably disagreeable. Like Ulysses, I have seen much of manners, men, and cities, and find them all very ugly. I have had several attacks of fever that astonished and grieved me as proving that I am growing old. I find the country the flattest and most insignificant in France, but fine forests, great trees, and vast solitudes abound, wherein I should like to meet you. I pass my time in meditating on our walks. I applaud Scribe for having made a virtuous and neo-catholic public laugh with the prizes for virtue; and I am equally surprised as to what you say of his elocution, as formerly he read abominably. It must be the academic robe that bestows this self-command; and this restored a little hope to me.

PERPIGNAN, 1844. — I have been tormented by an absurd idea which I hardly dare to tell you. While visiting the arena of Nîmes with the architect of the department, who was explaining some repairs under his direction, I observed ten paces from me a charming bird a little larger than a titmouse, gray body, with white, red, and black wings, which, perching itself on a cornice, looked fixedly at me. The architect, a great sportsman, had never seen one resembling it. As I approached it flew off, poising itself again a few steps distant, still regarding me closely; and wherever I went, in every story of the amphitheatre, it followed me, its flight being noiseless, like that of a night bird. The next day the scene was repeated. I brought bread, it would not touch it; I then threw it a grasshopper, which it equally disregarded, still watching me. The most learned ornithologist of the town tells me that no bird of this species exists in this region. Finally, at my last visit to the amphitheatre, my bird still followed my steps so far as to enter a dark and narrow corridor where a day bird would seldom venture. I then remembered that the Duchess of Buckingham saw her husband under the form of a bird the day of his assassination, and the idea flashed upon me that you were dead and had assumed this shape to visit me. In spite of myself this nonsense distressed me, and I was enchanted to find your letter dated the day on which I first saw my marvelous bird.

A fair is in progress here, and the town additionally thronged with Spaniards flying from the epidemic, so that I was unable to obtain lodging at an inn, and should have been reduced to a bed in the street but for the commiseration of a hatter. I write in a cold little room with a smoking chimney, cursing the rain that dashes against my window; the woman who serves me speaks Catalan, and only understands me when I speak Spanish; while, worst of all, the flood threatens to carry away the bridge and detain me here, a wretched prisoner. An admirable situation for the expression of ideas.

I have been to the Fountain of Vaucluse, where I wished to inscribe your name, but there were so many atrocious verses, so many Sophies and Carolines, that I would not profane it by such bad company. Parthenay I found a horrible town of *chouans*, with an abominable tavern where they made an infernal noise, and mixed so much stable with my dinner as to make it impossible for me to eat. At Saint-Maixent I saw women with headgear of the fourteenth century, and the waist of the dress of nearly the same period, allowing the chemise to be seen, which is of coarse house-cloth, buttoned under the chin, and open like men's shirts ; and in spite of the gingerbread beneath I thought it very pretty.

PARIS, *February*, 1845. — Everything passed off better than I had hoped.[1] I was perfectly self-possessed, and am well content with the public, though I know not if it be so with me. All is well since you did not find me ridiculous. I should have lost my confidence had I known you to be present, in view especially of my tarragon-colored coat, and my face *idem*.

TOULOUSE. — Fortunately I find here your letter, for I was furious at your silence. You are never so near forgetting me as when persuading me that I am in your thought. You ask me to pet you, but I am in too bad a humor, having been in a continuous rage this past fortnight against you, against myself, the weather, and the architects. I passed four-and-twenty hours at the house of a Deputy and if I were ambitious of being a politician this visit would have completely quenched my aspirations. What a calling ! what people one must see, conciliate, flatter ! I say with Hotspur : "I had rather be a kitten and cry mew." Slavery for slavery, I prefer the court of a despot ; at least the greater part of despots wash their hands. In England, no doubt, Lady M—— will beset you again with her fine theories "about the baseness of being in love." God knows if you will not return three quarters English. While you are luxuriating in melting peaches, I am eating yellow, acid ones of a singular but not unpleasant flavor, and figs of every color. I am immeasurably bored in the evening, and begin to wish for the society of bipeds of my own species. I count the provincials as naught, being fatiguing to my eyes and entirely foreign to my circle of thought.

[1] His reception at the French Academy.

BARCELONA, 1845. — I have reached the goal of my long journey, and have been admirably received by my archivist, who had already prepared my tables and the ancient books in which I shall lose what remains of my sight. To find his *despacho*, a gothic hall of the fourteenth century must be traversed, and a marble court planted with orange-trees as tall as our lime-trees, and covered with ripe fruit. This is very poetical, and as regards comfort and luxury recalls, as does my chamber, the Asiatic caravanserai. However, it is better than Andalusia, though the natives are inferior and have a fatal defect in my eyes, or rather ears, in that I understand nothing of their gibberish. At Perpignan, I met two gypsies who were cropping mules, and I spoke *caló* to them to the great horror of my companion, a colonel of artillery; while they, finding me even more skilled than themselves in the *patois*, offered a striking testimony to my attainments of which I was not a little proud. In summing up the results of my journey, my conviction is, that it was unnecessary to come so far, and that my history could have been satisfactorily accomplished without disturbing the venerable dust of Aragonese archives.

MADRID, *November*, 1845. — I have been installed here a week in the midst of intense cold, rain, and a climate quite similar to that of Paris; only, I look on snow-capped mountains and live familiarly with very fine Velasquez. Thanks to the ineffable slowness of these people, I have only to-day begun to ferret among the manuscripts, as an academic council was necessary to permit me to examine them, and I know not how many intrigues to enable me to obtain information as to their existence.

I find this country much changed, and less agreeable since my last visit. Persons whom I left friends are now mortal enemies; many of my former acquaintances have become grandees, and very insolent. Every one thinks aloud, with but slight consideration for others, and a frankness prevails that amazes us Frenchmen, and me the more, inasmuch as you have lately accustomed me to something very different. You should make a tour beyond the Pyrenées to take a lesson in frankness. You can form no conception of the expression of the swain's face when the beloved object does not arrive at the appointed hour, nor of the noise of the escaping sighs; but such scenes are so common as to create no scandal nor tittle-tattle. I see happy lovers, and find that they take advantage of the confidence and intimacy accorded by their *innamoratas.* The most romantic do not comprehend in the least what we term gallantry: the lovers here, truth to say, are merely husbands non-authorized by the church. They are the *souffre douleur* of the legal husband, execute commissions and nurse Madame when she takes medicine. Notwithstanding your infernal coquetry, and your aversion for the truth, I love you far more than all these over-frank people. Do not take advantage of this avowal. It is so cold that we shall have no bull-fight; but a number of balls are announced, the tedium of which is inexpressible.

August, 1846, *on board a steamboat.* — I have been among the mountains seeking some spot remote from electors and candidates, but I found such quantities of flies and fleas that I am not sure if the elections be not preferable. Yesterday evening I spent with peasant men and women, making their hair stand on end with ghost stories. There was a magnificent moon that lighted up their regular features and showed the fine black eyes of these damsels, while idealizing the condition of their hands and stockings. I went to bed very proud of my success with this, to me, novel audience; but in the morning on seeing my *Ardéchoises* by sunlight, *con villanos manos y pies,* I almost regretted my eloquence.

PARIS, 1846. — I find the provinces more stupid and unendurable each year. I could not well describe the tedium and various annoyances of this little tour. It recalls Clarence's dream: —

> "I would not spend another such a night,
> Though 't were to buy a world of happy days."

Paris is absolutely empty of intelligent inhabitants, only cap-makers and Deputies remaining, which is nearly the same thing. I am even more isolated here than usual, depressed by something of the feeling of an *emigré* who on returning to his country finds a new generation. It will strike you that I have grown horribly old — all of which simply means that I am sad, very cross, and that it is you, our walks, which I need. Perhaps when the sea air shall have tarnished your dresses, or fresh ones arrive from Paris, you will send me a thought. There is nothing on earth half so charming to a woman, it is said, as to display pretty toilettes. I can offer you no equivalent for these joys ; but I should suffer too much in believing you to be so constituted. I learn, with pleasure, that you are so heartily wearied at ——, which I predicted. After living in Paris, the provinces are insupportable ; one says and does numberless enormities that are overlooked in Paris, but which in a village are magnified to the size of a house.

BONN, 1846. — When once launched on a journey I have the utmost difficulty in coming to a halt ; and very seductive promises will be needed to prevent me from pushing on to Lapland. I have been six days in this admirable country, I mean Rhenish Prussia, where civilization is very advanced, with the exception of the beds, which are still four feet long, the sheets three. I lead an altogether German life. I rise at five o'clock and go to bed at nine, after partaking of four meals, which routine suits me quite well ; and I am not yet ill with doing nothing save opening my mouth and eyes. Only, the German women have become horribly ugly since my last visit.

With respect to monuments, I am by no means satisfied with those I have seen, the German architects appearing to me even worse than our own. They have denuded the Minster at Bonn, and painted the Abbey at Lahr in a way to make one grind one's teeth. The scenery of the Moselle is very much overpraised, and I have seen nothing really striking since passing the Tmolus. My admiration is exclusively reserved for the umbrageous foliage and for their fine conception of the *cuisine;* here the most important occupation is *zu speisen.* All honest people after dining at one o'clock take tea and cakes at four, go to a garden at six to eat a roll and stuffed tongue, which enables them to sustain nature until eight, when they go to a hotel to have their supper. What becomes of the women during this period I do not know, but it is certain that from eight to ten o'clock not a man remains in the house, each one being at his favorite hotel, eating, drinking, and smoking; and the reason of this may, I think, be found in the large feet of these ladies and the excellence of Rhenish wine.

PARIS, *March*, 1848. — I have never been more sadly shocked by the stupidity of the Northern people, and also by their inferiority to those of the South, than during my recent tour, the average native of Picardy striking me as much below the lowest class of Provence; in addition to which I nearly perished with cold in all the inns to which my evil destiny led me.

I am tormented by the failure of the —— firm, in which I fear your interests also are at stake; and each day will bring us fresh disturbance. We must sustain each other and share the little courage remaining to us. You are too much alarmed; but it is difficult to give advice and to see clearly through the fog that stretches over our future. Many persons believe Paris, all things considered, to be safer than the country, and I am also of this opinion. I have no fear of a street battle, first, because no sufficient motive exists; then that strength and audacity are on the one side, while I see only dullness and cowardice on the other. If civil war should break out, it will be first declared in the country, as great irritation has been aroused against the dictatorship of the capital, and perhaps measures, now impossible to foresee, may lead to this result in the West. As to the consequence of the riots, contrast those of the first revolution in Paris with the one two years ago at Buzançais, — more deplorable than all those of '93. Everything passed off quietly yesterday, and we shall have numerous similar processions before any shot will be fired, if indeed that should ever happen in this timid country.

Paris, *May*, 1848. — All has passed off well, for the reason that they are such fools that the Chamber, notwithstanding all its faults, has proved to be stronger than they. There are neither killed nor wounded, everything is quiet, and an excellent feeling prevails between the people and the National Guard. The leading insurgents have been arrested, and so many troops are under arms that for some time to come there will be nothing to fear. I have witnessed some highly dramatic scenes. I am worn out with a night's service with the Guards, but, after all, fatigue has its advantage at this time. The happiness of seeing you is as great under the Republic as under the Monarchy, and you must not be avaricious in its bestowal. But the most important, pressing thing to tell you is, that each day I love you more and more, and I should be glad could you summon courage to say the same to me.

June, 1848. — I returned this morning from a little campaign of four days, during which I ran no danger and was enabled to see the horrors of the day and of this country. In the midst of my distress I grieve above all for the folly of France: it is unequaled. I cannot see that it will ever be possible to turn her aside from the savage barbarism in which she shows so strong an inclination to wallow. I hope that your brother is safe: I do not think that his legion was seriously in action. I will hastily relate a curious incident or two before going to bed. The La Force prison was protected for several hours by the National Guard and surrounded by the insurgents, who said to the soldiers: "Do not fire on us and we will not fire on you — take care of the prisoners." To watch the battle I entered a house that had just been rescued from the rebels, and asked the occupants, "Did they take much from you?" "They stole nothing." Add to this, that I led a woman to the abbey who had employed herself in cutting off the heads of the Guards with her kitchen knife; and that I saw a man whose two arms were red with the blood of a dying soldier whose belly he had ripped up, laving his hands in the gaping wound. Do you begin to understand somewhat of this great nation? What is quite certain is, that we are going headlong to the devil.

July, 1848.—Paris is, and will be quiet for some time to come. I do not think that the civil, or rather the social war is at an end, but another battle so frightful as the recent one seems impossible, the recurrence of the infinity of circumstances necessary to bring it about not being probable. Of its hideous results which your imagination doubtless paints, you will find but few traces, the glazier and house-painter having already effected their removal; but you will see many long faces. What can one do? the *régime* is *de facto*, and we must accustom ourselves to it. By and by we shall cease to think of the morrow, and on awaking in the morning shall be happy in the certainty of an undisturbed evening. The days are long and warm, and as tranquil as could be wished, or rather hoped for under the Republic. All the signs foretell a prolonged truce. The disarming is effected with vigor, and produces good results. One curious symptom is remarked; namely, that in the insurgent faubourgs any number of informers can be found to point out the hiding-places and even the leaders of the barricades. It is a good sign, you know, when wolves fall to fighting among themselves. The 14th of July passed by very quietly, notwithstanding the sinister predictions with which we were favored. The truth—if it can be discovered under the government under which we have the good fortune to live—the truth is, that our chances for tranquillity have been singularly increased. To bring about the events of June, several years of organization and four months of arming were requisite. A second representation of this bloody tragedy appears to me impossible; nevertheless, some little plot, several assassinations, and a few riots are still probable. We shall have perhaps a half century in which to perfect ourselves, the one party in the construction of barricades, the other in their destruction. Paris is now being filled with mortars and howitzers, both transportable and efficacious—a novel argument, and said to be excellent.

I went yesterday to Saint-Germain to order a dinner for the Society of Bibliophiles, where I found a cook not only capable, but eloquent, who comprehended at once the most fantastic dishes that I proposed. This great man resides in the portion of the palace in which Henry IV. was born, which commands one of the loveliest views in the world, while a few steps bring one to a wood with great trees and magnificent undergrowth. And not a soul to enjoy all this !

You resemble Anteus, who renewed his strength in touching the earth. *You* no sooner touch your native soil than you relapse into your old defects. Your letter does not tell me how long I am to suffer the purgatory of your absence. It was redolent of a perfume so much the more delicious from being familiar to me, and which brings to me so many charming associations. I think of you unceasingly; even while looking at the fighting at the Bastille my thoughts were of you.

August, 1848. — This evening while my friend M. Mignet was strolling with Mademoiselle Dosne in the little garden fronting the residence of M. Thiers, a ball came down without the least noise, struck the house very near Madame Thiers's window and glancing thence wounded a little girl seated beyond the garden railing. The ball was quickly extracted, and no ill will ensue save a slight scar: but for whom was it intended? Mignet? that is impossible. Mademoiselle Dosne? still more so. Neither Madame nor M. Thiers was at home. No one heard the explosion, the ball was of regulation size, and air-guns are of a much smaller calibre. I believe it to have been a republican attempt at intimidation, as foolish as all else that is done in this our day. Cavaignac says: "They will kill me, Lamoricière will succeed me, then Bedeau; after whom will come the Duc d'Isly, who will sweep everything clean." Does this not strike you as prophetic? No one believes in an intervention in Italy. The Republic will be even rather more cowardly than the Monarchy; they may, however, make a pretence of allowing it to be supposed that intervention is probable, hoping by this ruse to obtain a congress, protocols, and a compromise. One of my friends, just returned from Italy, was plundered by the Roman volunteers, who find that travellers are made of better stuff than the Croats. He asserts that it is impossible to make the Italians fight, with the exception of the Piedmontese. Throw aside your Romaic; it will be love's labor lost. In vainly trying to learn it I forgot my Greek, and it will play you the same trick. I am surprised at your facile comprehension of this gibberish, which as a language, moreover, will soon disappear, for Greek is already spoken at Athens, and Romaic will only be used by the lower orders. Since 1841, not a single Turkish word, formerly so frequent, has been heard in the Greece of King Otho.

Yesterday, at the general competition for prizes, one was awarded to an urchin named *Leroy*, whereupon his comrades exclaimed "*Vivė le roi!*"

General Cavaignac who assisted at the ceremony laughed with a very good grace: but the same boy receiving yet another prize, the applause became so uproarious that the general lost countenance and twisted his beard as if he would pluck it out by the roots.

August, 1848. — We hear rumors of fresh riots; and now the cholera is coming to complicate matters. M. Ledru is thought to be inciting a disturbance by way of protest against the administrative inquiry. The situation closely resembles that of Rome during Catiline's conspiracy, only there is no Cicero. A most grievous symptom is, that Citizen Proudhon has a great number of adherents, his little sheets being sold in the faubourgs by thousands — all of which is sad, but to me the *ennui* of the approaching rain and cold is more serious and much more certain than the riot. I suffer much, and should be excessively vexed to die before our breakfast at Saint-Germain.

LONDON, *June*, 1850. — The most decided impression received from this journey is that the English are individually stupid (*bêtes*), but an admirable people *en masse*. Everything that can be done by the aid of money, good sense, and patience, they do; but of the arts they have no more notion than my cat.

The Nepaulese princes are here, with whom you would fall in love. They wear flat turbans bordered with enormous pear-shaped emeralds, and are a mass of satin, cachemire, and gold. They are of a deep milk and coffee color, have a good air, and appear to be intelligent.

We are going to Hampton Court to avoid the chances fc suicide that the *Lord's Day* in this city would not fail to offeı I dined yesterday with a bishop and a dean, who have madc me even still more a socialist. The bishop belongs to what the Germans call the rationalist school; he does not even believe what he preaches, and on the strength of his black silk apron enjoys five or six thousand pounds a year and passes his time in reading Greek. The women all look as if made of wax; and wear such expansive bustles that the pavement of Regent Street is only wide enough to hold one woman at a time. I passed yesterday morning in the new House of Commons, which is a frightful monstrosity; I had previously no conception of what could be accomplished with an utter want of taste and two millions sterling. I have strong fears of becoming a thorough socialist by dint of eating admirable dinners from silver gilt plates, and seeing persons who win forty thousand pounds sterling at the Epsom races. There is as yet no probability of a revolutionary outbreak here. The servility of the lower orders, of which we see each day some fresh example, conflicts with our democratic ideas: it is a question of moment to know if they are more happy.

SALISBURY, *June*, 1850. — I begin to have enough of this region. I am worn out with the perpendicular architecture, and the manners, equally perpendicular, of the natives. I have passed two days at Cambridge and Oxford with the reverends, and, all things considered, I prefer the Capuchins. I am especially furious against Oxford. A Fellow had the insolence to invite me to dinner. There was a fish four inches long, in a great silver dish, and a lamb cutlet in another: all this served in magnificent style, with potatoes in a dish of carved wood. But never was I so hungry. This is the result of the hypocrisy of these people. They like to show their abstinence to foreigners, and, eating luncheon, they do not dine. Were it not broad day at eight o'clock in the evening, one might believe it to be December, which does not hinder the women from going out with open parasol. It is impossible to see anything more ridiculous than an Englishwoman in the hoop that is worn here.

I have just committed a blunder. I gave half a crown to a man in black who showed me over the cathedral, and then I asked him for the address of a gentleman for whom I had a letter from the dean. He proved to be the very person to whom the letter was addressed. He looked very foolish, and so did I: but he kept the money.

Who is a Miss Jewsbury, rather red-haired, who writes novels? I met her recently and she told me that she had dreamed all her life of a pleasure that she believed impossible, that of seeing me — *verbatim*. She has written a novel entitled "Zoe." Will you, who read so much, tell me who is this person for whom I am a romance.

PARIS, *June*, 1851. — Yesterday I accepted an invitation from the Princess Mathilde to see the Spanish dancers, who are very *médiocre*. The dance at the Mabille has killed the *bolero*, and these dames wore such a quantity of crinoline as to prove clearly the encroachment of civilization. A girl and her old duenna amused me by their intense surprise at finding themselves beyond the *tierra* of Jesus; they were as perfect barbarians as could be desired.

PARIS, *December*, 1851. — The last battle, I believe, is now being fought; but who will win? Should the President lose, it seems to me that the heroic Deputies should give way to Ledru-Rollin. I have returned home horribly fatigued, and have met none but madmen. The look of Paris recalls that of February, except that now the soldiers are very fierce and terrify the citizens. The military are sure of success, but we understand their almanac. However this may be, we have just escaped a reef and are sailing towards the unknown.

PARIS, 1852. — I am threatened with a lawsuit for contempt of court and attack upon the final judgment; while the School of Charts is also sharpening its claws to tear me to pieces. I shall be compelled to undergo an examination and to engage in desperate polemics. In case I fail, try to keep well and come to see me in prison. I do not know whether they will hang me, but I am very *fidgetty* at the thought of a public ceremony in presence of the very cream of the rabble, and three imbeciles in black gowns as stiff as pickets and convinced of their own importance, to whom one cannot dream of expressing one's contempt for their gowns, their person, and their mind.

May, 1852. — Four days in prison and a thousand francs fine! My lawyer argued well, the judges were civil, and I not at all nervous. I shall not appeal. I pass my time in reading Beyle's correspondence. It has rejuvenated me twenty years. It is as if I were making the autopsy of the thoughts of a man whom I have known intimately and whose ideas respecting men and things had grown singularly colorless by the side of my experience. This renders me sad and gay twenty times within the hour, and makes me regret having burned Beyle's letters to me.

CARABANCHEL, 1853. — On arriving here I found preparations for a *fête* at which a comedy was to be played and a *loa* (a dithyrambic dialogue) recited in honor of the lady of the house and her daughter. My services were called into requisition to paint skies, repair decorations, and design costumes, not to enumerate the rehearsals of five mythological goddesses, who on the fatal day looked exceedingly pretty but were overcome with terror. The audience applauded warmly, without understanding in the least the nonsensical rigmarole of the poet author of the *loa*. The comedy was better, and I admire the facility with which the young girls of society transform themselves into passable actresses. During supper a *protégé* of the Countess improvised some pretty verses that moved the heroine to tears and disposed every one else to drink rather too generously. As there are nine ladies here without a gentleman, I am called at Madrid, "Apollo." Of the nine Muses five unfortunately are mothers, but the remaining four are true born Andalusians with little ferocious airs that are ravishing, especially when in their Olympian costume with peplum, which through love of euphony they persist in calling *peplo*.

MADRID, *October*, 1853. — I went yesterday to see Cucharès, the best matador since Montès. The bulls were so indifferent that it was necessary to excite them by little fiery darts. Two men were thrown into the air, and for a moment we thought them dead, which imparted some slight interest to the spectacle; otherwise everything was detestable. The bulls no longer have any spirit, and the men are not much better than the bulls. The ugly convent of the Escurial is as sad as when I saw it twenty years ago, but civilization has penetrated its walls and one finds iron bedsteads and cutlets, but no longer fleas and monks. The absence of the latter distinctive element renders Herrera's heavy architecture still more ridiculous.

I will bring you the garters, which I had dfficulty in finding. Civilization makes such rapid progress that on nearly every leg the *elastic* has replaced the classic *ligas* of former days; and when I asked the chamber-maids to show me a shop where they were sold they indignantly crossed themselves, saying that they no longer wore such obsolete fashions, which were only in use by the common people. Mantillas are nearly as rare; they are superseded by bonnets; and such bonnets!

Last week the *fête* of *Saint Eugénie* was celebrated at the French embassy by a ball, at which Madame ——, wife of the United States Minister, appeared in a costume so designed as to make one split with laughter — black velvet bordered with gold lace and tinsel, and a tawdry diadem. Her son, who looks like a boor, made inquiries respecting the position of the persons present, and having obtained satisfactory information sent a challenge to a very noble, very rich duke, a great simpleton, and desirous of living yet a long time. The parley still continues, but no one will be killed.

I am re-reading "Wilhelm Meister," a strange book, in which the finest possible things alternate with the most absurd childishness. In all that Goethe wrote there is a singular mingling of genius and German silliness (*niaiserie*): was he laughing at others or at himself? On my return remind me to give you "The Elective Affinities," the oddest, most anti-French of all his works. No one reads at Madrid. I have asked myself how the women pass their time when not making love, and I find no plausible reply. They are all thinking of being empresses. A demoiselle of Granada was at the play when it was announced in her box that the Countess de Teba was to marry the Emperor. She rose with impetuosity, exclaiming: "*En ese pueblo no hay parvenir.*" [1]

The absorbing question here is, whether the Ministry will remain in, or whether there will be a *coup d'état*. The house in which I reside is neutral ground, where the Ministers and leaders of the Opposition meet, which is agreeable for lovers of news. What is called here society is composed of so small a number of persons, that to break up into factions would be fatal. In all public places one is sure of meeting the same three hundred faces, from which results a more amusing and infinitely less hypocritical society than elsewhere.

It is the custom here to offer in return everything that is praised. At a recent dinner I sat next the Prime Minister's fair friend, who is as stupid as a cabbage and excessively stout. She displayed somewhat handsome shoulders, on which rested a garland with glass or metal acorns, and not knowing what to say to her, I praised both beads and shoulders, to which she replied: "*Todo ese a la disposicion de V.*"

PARIS, 1854. — You will find the Sydenham Crystal Palace a vast Noah's Ark, marvelous as to its collection of curious objects, but regarded from an artistic stand-point, perfectly ridiculous; yet there is something at once so grand and so

[1] In this country there is no chance of rising.

simple in its construction that one must go to England to form a conception of it. It is a toy costing twenty-five millions; a cage in which several churches might waltz; and to you who are *gourmande*, I recommend its dinners.

The last days I passed in London interested me. I met socially all the eminent politicians, and was present at the debates on the Supplies in the Houses of Lords and Commons, in which the most renowned orators spoke, but in my opinion very abominably. I have brought a pair of garters from London. I do not know with what Englishwomen keep up their stockings, nor how they procure this indispensable article, but I believe it to be a very difficult matter and very trying to their virtue. The shopman who gave me these garters blushed up to the eyes. All the charming things you say to me would be a delight if experience had not taught me to distrust you. I dare not hope for what I desire so ardently. There is something very painful in conforming to your protocols, which, in point of contempt of logic and probability, are worthy of Nesselrode. I returned this morning from Caen. On my arrival there I proceeded to the hall of the Law School, where I found about two hundred men and a dozen ladies. I delivered my little discourse without the slightest emotion, being very civilly applauded. The ceremonies terminated with the reading of some rather good verses by a humpbacked dwarf, immediately after which I was conducted by the authorities to the *hôtel de ville*, where a banquet was given in my honor, at which excellent fish and delicious lobsters were enjoyed. At last the hoped-for moment of release came, when to my dismay the President of the Antiquaries arose, every one standing, and proposing my health, referred to me as remarkable in the three qualities of senator, a man of letters, and a scientist. Only the table separated us, and I was much inclined to throw a dish of rum jelly at his head. While he spoke I was meditating my reply, with no apparent possibility of finding a word. I returned thanks, however, in a speech of five minutes, with but a slight idea of what I was saying, which, however, I was assured was very eloquent. But my sufferings were not over.

I was seized by the mayor and led to a concert of the Philharmonic Society, where I was exhibited to a large number of well dressed people, the women very fair and very pretty, attired much like Parisians except in a less lavish display of shoulders, and in wearing maroon colored half boots with their ball dress.

INNSPRUCK, *August*, 1854. — I am intoxicated with magnificent landscapes and panoramas. From Basle to Schaffhausen, on the right hand and left, are enchanting mountains, far finer than those of the lower Rhine so much admired by Englishwomen. At Constance we had capital trout and heard Tyroleans play on the *zitther.* Thence to this place we have traversed a region of forests, lakes, and mountains of increasing beauty and grandeur, but are overcome with fatigue such as one experiences after examining a fine picture gallery. I am recruiting here with delicious woodcock and extraordinary soups. The drawback of the journey lies in an ignorance of the manners and ideas of the people, far more interesting to me than all the landscapes. In the Tyrol the women seem to be treated according to their merit. They are harnessed to wagons and easily draw heavy loads, are excessively ugly, with enormous feet; and the ladies whom I met on the railway and boats are not much better. They wear indecent bonnets, sky-blue boots with apple-green gloves. It is in great part the above peculiarities that constitute what the natives call *gemüth*, and of which they are exceedingly vain. It strikes me that the radical deficiency in the works of art of this country is that of imagination, upon which, nevertheless, they pique themselves, falling consequently into the most pretentious extravagances.

PRAGUE, *September*, 1854. — This city is exceedingly picturesque and there is admirable music. Yesterday I strolled through several gardens and public concerts, and saw the national dances performed decently and soberly; while nothing can be more captivating than a Bohemian orchestra. The physique here differs much from that of Germany ; very large heads, broad shoulders, very small hips, and no legs whatever — that is a picture of Bohemian beauty. We have exhausted our knowledge of anatomy in striving to understand how these women walk. They have, however, fine black eyes, very long and fine black hair, but feet of a length, thickness, and breadth to surprise travellers accustomed to the most extraordinary sights. Crinoline is unknown. At the public gardens in the evening they drink a bottle of beer, after which they take a cup of coffee, which disposes them to partake of three veal cutlets with ham, the interstices being filled up with some light pastry cakes resembling our buns. The blanket of my bed of various pretty colors, is one metre long, to which is buttoned a napkin that serves me for sheet, and when I have arranged that in equilibrium, my servant places over the whole an eider down coverlet which I pass the night in throwing down and replacing.

VIENNA, *October*, 1854. — Really, this good city is an agreeable place of sojourn, and it requires a certain degree of courage to leave it, now that I have learned to enjoy sauntering about its pleasant places, and have made many friends. We are agitated by news from the Crimea. Is Sebastopol taken ? It is believed so here ; and the Austrians, with the exception of a few ancient families who are Russian at heart, congratulate us. God grant that the news may not be an invention such as the telegraph delights in when at leisure. However it may be, I think it a fine thing that our troops, six days after landing, should have pommeled the Russians so vigorously. We enjoy the looks of the Russians now here. Prince Gortschakoff says that it is an "incident" that will effect no change as to principles. The Belgian Minister, the wit of Vienna, says that Gortschakoff is right to intrench himself behind principles, because they are never taken with the bayonet. *À propos* of wit, willing or unwilling, I have been made a *lion*. Society here being so *gemüthlich*, everything that a Frenchman says is accepted as wit. I am thought very amiable. I write sublime thoughts in albums, I make drawings, in a word I have been perfectly ridiculous. I passed three days at Pesth, where my modesty suffered in being shown a public bath, in which Hungarian men and women were together in the hot mineral water. I saw one beautiful Hungarian who hid her face with her hands; in this unlike the Turkish women, who wear the chemise for that purpose. I have heard Bohemian musicians play very original Hungarian airs that intoxicate the natives. The music begins lugubriously and ends with a mad gayety that quickly spreads to the audience, who stamp, break the glasses, and dance on the table; but foreigners are not affected by these phenomena. Magnificent furs are obtained here for a trifle — the only bargains in the country. I am ruined by hack hire and dinner parties. The custom is to pay the domestics who serve the dinner, and the hall porter; in fact one pays at every turn.

LONDON, *July*, 1856. — I am about to visit a real Scotch chieftain, who has never worn any breeches, has no staircase in his house, but maintains a bard and a seer. I find the people here so amiable, so pressing, so monopolizing, that my arrival is evidently a relief to their *ennui.* Yesterday I saw two of my former beauties; the one has become asthmatic, the other a Methodist. I have also made the acquaintance of eight or ten poets, who struck me as rather more ridiculous even than our own.

EDINBURGH. — I have passed three days at the Duke of Hamilton's, in an immense castle, and a very fine country. At no great distance is a herd of wild oxen, said to be the only ones now remaining in Europe, but which appeared to me as tame as the deer at Paris. Throughout this castle are pictures by the great masters, magnificent Greek and Chinese vases, and richly bound books from the greatest collections of the last century. All this is arranged without taste, and one sees that it affords the proprietor but small enjoyment. I now understand why the French are so much in request in foreign countries ; they take pains to be amused, and in so doing amuse others. I found myself the most entertaining person of the very numerous society assembled, and was at the same time conscious of being rather the reverse. I find Edinburgh altogether to my taste with the exception of the execrable architecture of the monuments, the claim of which to be Greek is about as well founded as an Englishwoman's pretension to be a Parisian because her toilettes are prepared by Madame Vignon. The accent of the natives is odious to me. The women, as a rule, are very ugly. The country necessitates short skirts, and they conform to the fashion and to the exigencies of the climate, by holding up their gown with both hands, a foot above the petticoat, displaying sinewy legs and half-boots of rhinoceros leather, with feet to match. I am shocked at the proportion of red-haired women whom I meet.

August, 1856, *at a country house near Glasgow.* — I lead a pleasant life, going from château to château, and everywhere entertained with a hospitality for which I despair of finding adequate expression, and which is only practicable in this aristocratic country. I am contracting bad habits. The guest here of poor people who have little more than thirty thousand pounds a year, I have thought myself not sufficiently honored because of dining without wind instruments and a piper in grand costume.

At the Marquis of Breadalbane's I passed three days in driving about the park. There are about two thousand deer, besides eight or ten thousand in his forests not adjacent to the castle. There are also, for the sake of singularity, at which every one aims here, a herd of American buffaloes, very fierce, inclosed in a peninsula, and which one goes to look at through the palings. Every one there, Marquis and buffalo, had the air of being bored. I believe that their pleasure consists in making people envious, and I doubt whether this compensates for the pother of playing innkeeper to all sorts of people. Amidst all this luxury, I observe, from time to time, bits of stinginess which amuse me.

KINLOCH-LINCHARD, *August*, 1856. — I begin to be satiated with grouse and venison. The truly remarkable scenery has still a charm for me, but my curiosity is satisfied. What I am not weary of admiring is, the bristling attitude the people here maintain: being chained together at the galleys even would not make them more sociable. This arises from their fear of being "caught in the act of being stupid," as Beyle says, or rather an organization that inclines them to prefer selfish pleasures. We arrived here at the same time with two gentlemen and a middle-aged woman accustomed to high society, and who had travelled. At dinner the thick ice necessarily thawed; but in the evening the husband took up a newspaper, the wife a book, the other gentleman began to write letters, while I was left to play a single-handed game against my hosts. I am told that the Celtic race (who live in frightful holes near the palace in which I am a guest) know how to talk. The fact is, I fancy, that on market day a continual noise of animated voices, laughter and shouts, is heard. Gælic is very soft. In England and the Lowlands, complete silence.

CARABACEL, *December*, 1856. — I have been besieged by Russian and English cards, and have been offered a presentation to the Grand Duchess Helen, an honor that I pointedly declined. To furnish us with gossip we have a Countess Apraxine, who smokes, wears round hats, and keeps a goat in her *salon*, which she has strewn with grass. But the most amusing person is Lady Shelley, who commits some fresh drollery every day. Yesterday she wrote to the French Consul: "Lady S—— informs M. P—— that she has a charming dinner party of English people to-day, and she will be delighted to see him afterwards, at five minutes past nine o'clock." She wrote to Madame Vigier, ex-Mademoiselle Cruvelli: "Lady Shelley would be charmed to see Madame Vigier if she would be good enough to bring her music with her." To which the ex-Cruvelli immediately replied: "Madame Vigier would be charmed to see Lady Shelley, if she would be good enough to come to her house and behave as a lady."

LONDON, *British Museum*, 1858. — You can form no conception of the beauty of the Museum on Sunday when there is no one present except M. Panizzi and myself; it seems to be permeated by a marvelous atmosphere of thought. Last Wednesday I fell into rather a droll scrape. I was invited to the Literary Fund dinner presided over by Lord Palmerston, and at the moment of setting out was notified that I should be expected to make a speech, as my name would be associated with a toast to the literature of Continental Europe. I was victimized with a satisfaction that you may imagine, and during fifteen minutes uttered nonsense in bad English before an assemblage of three hundred literary men, and a hundred women admitted to the honor of seeing us eat stringy chickens and tough tongue. I have never been so saturated with foolishness, as Pourceaugnac says.

Yesterday I received a visit from a gentleman and wife who brought me a number of autograph letters from Napoleon to Josephine, which they wished to sell. They are exceedingly curious in the fact of touching on nothing but love, and are doubtless authentic; but it is difficult to understand why Josephine did not burn them as soon as read.

PALACE OF FONTAINEBLEAU, *May*, 1858. — I am excessively annoyed and half poisoned from having taken too much laudanum; in addition to which, I have written verses for His Majesty of the Netherlands, played charades, and "made a fool of myself" generally. Shall I describe the life we lead here? Yesterday we took a stag and dined on the grass; the other day we were all drenched with rain; every day we eat too much, and I am completely exhausted. Destiny did not fashion me for a courtier. I shall try to snatch a little sleep while awaiting the fatal hour of getting under arms, which is to say, donning tights. How much I should prefer to stroll through this fine forest with you, chatting of fairy-land. I am exceedingly vexed with your ridiculous prudery. The book in question has the misfortune to be badly written, that is to say, in an enthusiastic tone that Sainte-Beuve extols as poetic, so much do tastes differ. One does not, when possessed of your taste, exclaim that it is frightful, immoral, but finds all that is good in the volume very good. You allow your prejudices to sway your judgment, and each day you grow more prudish, more in consonance with the affectation of the age. Your crinoline I overlook, but not your prudery.

VENICE, *August*, 1858. — Venice filled me with sadness. I have been moved to indignation by all the commonplaces uttered of the architecture of the palaces, which is effective, but destitute of taste and imagination. The canals resemble the Bièvre, and the gondola an inconvenient hearse. The pictures of the second-rate masters at the Academy pleased me; but there is not a Paul Veronese worth "The Marriage of Cana," not a Titian to be compared with "Christ with the Tribute Money" at Dresden, or even "The Crown of Thorns" at Paris. On the other hand, I am pleased with the physiognomy of the people. The streets swarm with charming girls with bare feet and head, who, if bathed and scrubbed, would serve as models for the Venus Anadyomene. I was present at an amusing *funzione* in honor of the Archduke. A serenade was given, six hundred gondolas following the colossal boat that carried the music, all bearing lanterns and burning red and blue Bengal lights, which touched the palaces on the grand canal with a magical tint. In passing the Rialto no gondola would draw back, nor give way, so that the mass formed a solid bridge, and at every moment was heard the crash of collision and breaking oars; but an observable feature was, that amid all the excitement of the throng, which in France would have led to a general battle, no abusive language was heard, not even a cross word. These people are made of milk and maize. To-day I saw a monk, in the middle of St. Mark's Square, fall on his knees before an Austrian corporal about to arrest him. There was never any thing more pitiable, and in front of the lion of St. Mark!

In a pretty villa on the banks of Lake Como I saw Madame Pasta, whom I had not met since her palmy days at the Italian

Opera. She has singularly increased in size, cultivates cabbages, and says that she is as happy as when crowns and sonnets showered on her. We discussed the theatre, music, and she remarked, justly, that since Rossini, no opera had been composed in which there was unity of thought and treatment.

CHÂTEAU DE COMPIÈGNE, *November*, 1858. — This morning I saw my friend Sandeau in the frame of mind natural to one who has appeared in knee-breeches the first time. He asked me a hundred questions with a *naiveté* that alarmed me. We have had great men from over the Channel, Russians and the Ministers, but the greater part of the guests took their departure yesterday, and we are left *en petit comité*, that is to say, we are but thirty or forty at table. One cannot sleep in this place. The time is passed in being frozen or roasting, and this has given me an irritation of the chest that exhausts me. But it is impossible to imagine a more amiable host or a more gracious hostess. When I think that I could have seen you to-day in Paris, I am tempted to fly from here ; and also to hang myself at your resignation : a virtue that I do not possess, and which enrages me in others. Nothing is easier here than to absent one's self from breakfast, or the morning walk, but dinner is the momentous ceremony ; and when I spoke to the old courtiers of my intention to dine in town, they frowned in such evident consternation that I saw it must not be thought of.

CANNES, *January*, 1859. — There are great numbers of English here. I dined yesterday with Lord Brougham and I know not how many Misses freshly arrived from Scotland, whom the sight of the sun appeared greatly to surprise. Had I the talent to describe costumes, I could amuse you with those of these ladies ; you have never seen anything to parallel it since the invention of crinoline.

I have just read the Memoirs of Catherine II., which present a strange picture of the people and courts of that period.

Catherine on her marriage with the Grand Duke, afterwards Peter III., had a quantity of diamonds and superb brocaded robes, and for her lodgings a chamber that served as a passageway for her women, who, to the number of seventeen, slept in a single room next that of the queen. There is not to-day a grocer's wife who does not live more comfortably than the empresses of a hundred years ago. Catherine gives us sufficient strong reasons for believing Paul I. to be the son of Prince Soltikoff; and the curious thing is, that the manuscript in which she narrates these fine histories was addressed to her son, this same Paul, an animal for whom strangling was the best mode of suppression. I am glad that my critique on Mr. Prescott has pleased you. I am not altogether satisfied with it as I only expressed half of what I should like to say, acting on the aphorism of Philip II.: that one must say only good of the dead. In fact, the work is only of slight interest, and not above mediocrity. It strikes me that had the author been less Yankee, he could have done something better. We have marvelous moonlight, the sea like glass, and the heat of June. I am more and more convinced that heat is my great restorative. When it rains I have horrible spasms: as soon as the sun returns Richard is himself again. Cannes is becoming too civilized: one of the loveliest walks is to be destroyed for the railway; we shall become the prey of Marseilles, and the picturesque will be lost.

PARIS, *April*, 1859. — The war in Italy will be sharp, but not long; the financial state of the world could not allow it; and after the first shock I hope that England will intervene. Austria has no money, and many persons believe her motive to be simply a pretext for declaring her bankruptcy. Our people are warlike and confident, the soldiers gay and sanguine. There is an enthusiasm, a buoyancy in our army, in which the Austrians are totally deficient. Little of an optimist as I may be, I have full faith in our success. Our reputation is so well established that those who fight against us enter into it with little heart. A Russian alliance is still spoken of, in which I have no faith, for Russia has nothing to lose in the quarrel, and however it may terminate she will find it to be to her advantage : meanwhile she amuses herself with panslavist intrigues among the Austrian subjects, who regard the Emperor Alexander as their Pope. The Austrians are said to wear a modest, somewhat shamefaced air. The mass of our people are intensely interested and offer vows for success. The *salons*, especially those of the Orleanists, are perfectly anti-French and arch fools, who imagine that they will float back with the tide, and that their burgraves will resume the thread of their discourse that was snapped in 1848. Poor people ! who do not understand that after this will come division, a republic, and anarchy. Germany is bawling against us ; a mere jet of underlying red liberalism which just now assumes the Teutonic form. Russia is a terrible ally who would devour Germany, but who would gain for us England's ill-will, and perhaps hostility. We have so long led a sybaritic life as to ignore the emotions of our fathers ; but we must now return to their philosophy. Our troops, rest assured, will be well taken care of, and will eat *macaroni stupendi* while the Austrians will sometimes find verdigris in their soup. Were I a young man, an Italian campaign would be to me the most attractive way of seeing a spectacle always noble — the awaking of an oppressed people.

PARIS, *May*, 1859. — Germany is still fermenting, which will result, apparently, rather in beer drinking than in blood shedding. Prussia resists to her utmost the pressure of the *Franzosenfresser*, and proclaims her intention to retake not only Alsace, but also the German provinces of Russia. This last jest would indicate that this Teutonic enthusiasm is neither serious nor well-considered. M. Yvan Tourguenieff, who comes direct from Moscow, says that all Russia is offering prayers for us, and that the army would be delighted to have a brush with the Austrians, whom, the priests are preaching, God will punish for their persecution of the orthodox Greeks of the Sclavonic race ; and subscriptions are open to send

Sclavonic Bibles and tracts to the Croats to preserve them from papal heresy. This looks very like a political propaganda of panslavism.

A strong attack is now being organized against the Derby Ministry. Lord Palmerston and Lord John would be reconciled — rather an improbable event — or still more unlikely would unite for the destruction of the present Cabinet. The radicals will support them. Whatever may be the issue, we shall gain little by the change. Lord Palmerston, though the main promoter of the Italian agitation, would no more uphold it than would Lord Derby, only he would treat Austria with less consideration and would not seek to embarrass us. The wiseacres announce that all Europe will intervene : not improbable ; but after the famous phrase *Sin all' Adriatico*, how can we leave Italy only half-delivered ? How hope that a young emperor, suckled and governed by the Jesuits, beaten and in a bad humor, should confess his folly and ask pardon ! Would not the Italians, who until now have been circumspect, be goaded into every imaginable imprudence pending the negotiations ?

PARIS, *July*, 1859. — You alone reconcile me to the Peace. Perhaps it was necessary ; but on the whole what matters to us the liberty of a parcel of smokers and musicians ? We heard this evening the Emperor's speech, which was well delivered, with a grand air, an air of frankness and good faith : there is sense and truth in it. The returning officers say that the Italians are brawlers and cowards ; that only the Piedmontese can fight, who, however, pretend that we were in their way, and that without us they could have done better. The Empress asked me in Spanish what I thought of the speech ; to which I replied, combining candor with courtesy : "*Muy necesario.*"

PARIS, 1859. — I am reading the "Letters of Madame du Deffand." They are very amusing, giving an excellent picture of the society of her day, which was very amiable and somewhat frivolous. A striking contrast to the present era is manifest in their general and earnest endeavor to please ; as also in the sincerity and fidelity of their affections. They were more obliging people than ourselves, and especially than you, whom I no longer love.

PARIS, *September*, 1859. — The other day I met Edmond About, who is always charming. He resides at Saverne and passes his life in the woods, where a month ago he encountered a singular animal walking on all fours, wearing a black coat and varnished boots without soles. It proved to be a professor from Angoulême, who had been driven to the Baden gambling table by conjugal unhappiness, where he lost everything. Returning to France through the forests he missed his way and had eaten nothing for eight days. About carried and dragged him to a village where he was supplied with linen and food, but he survived only a short time. When the man-animal lives in solitude for a certain period, and reaches a certain state of physical dilapidation, it appears that he walks on all fours. About assures me that this *chef-d'œuvre* makes a very ugly animal.

You are growing stout and brown with the sun : but however you may be, fat or thin, I shall love you always tenderly. I have frightful spasms, am still ill, and suspect that I am on the great railway leading beyond the tomb. At some moments this thought is painful, at others I find the consolation that one experiences on the railway — the absence of responsibility in the presence of a superior and irresistible power.

PARIS, *September*, 15, 1859. — I was summoned from Tarbes by letter to Saint-Sauveur to pass the day, my visit being returned by their majesties ; which occasioned a great disturbance in M. Fould's household, Madame Fould improvising a dinner and breakfast, taxing to the utmost the resources of the little village. Their majesties were in excellent health and capital spirits at Saint-Sauveur, and I admired the natives, who had the good taste to leave them entirely to themselves. The

Emperor has bought a dog rather larger than a donkey, of the ancient Pyrenean breed: a magnificent brute which climbs rocks like a chamois.

MADRID, *October*, 1859. — Everything here is changed. The ladies whom I left as thin as spindles have become elephants, the climate of Madrid having a very fattening quality. Not only the manners, but the picturesque aspect of old Spain are notably altered by politics and a parliamentary government. At this moment nothing is discussed but war, the question of avenging the national honor exciting a general enthusiasm that recalls the Crusades. It is imagined that the English view the African expedition with displeasure and even wish to prevent it, which redoubles the warlike ardor. The army wish to lay siege to Gibraltar, after taking Tangiers!

CANNES, 1860. — Baron Bunsen is here with his two daughters, both mounted on crane's feet, with ankles resembling the club of Hercules; one of the young ladies, however, sings very well. Bunsen is clever enough and knows the news, of which you keep me but ill-informed. I have read the pamphlet by Abbé ——, which strikes me as even more clumsy than violent. He must be thought an *enfant terrible* at Rome, where neither good sense nor finesse is lacking, and where the priests are skillful intriguers. Ours have the national blustering instinct, and are devoid of tact.

Here is a nice little incident characteristic of this region. A farmer in the neighborhood of Grasse is found dead in a ravine where he had fallen or been thrown during the night. Another farmer comes to see a friend and tells him that he has killed the man. "How? and why?" "Because he cast a spell over my sheep; then I asked the advice of my shepherd, who gave me three needles to boil in a pot, over which I pronounced the words he taught me. The same night that I put the pot on the fire the man died." Do not be surprised should my books be burned in the church square at Grasse.

The recent brochure by my colleague Villemain, is singularly vapid. When one has attempted to write a book against the Jesuits, and has boasted of being the defender of liberty of conscience against the omnipotence of the Church, it is droll to hurl forth a recantation and to support it by such feeble argument. I believe that every one has gone mad, except the Emperor, who reminds one of the shepherds of the Middle Ages whose magic flute inspired the wolves to dance. I am seriously told that the French Academy, which has been markedly Voltairian these few years past, wishes to nominate Abbé Lacordaire as a protest against the violence to which the Pope is subjected. The matter is really one of perfect indifference to me. So long as I shall not be compelled to listen to their sermons, all the members of the Sacred College may be nominated to the Academy.

I have been on a little excursion in the region of eternal snow, where I saw fine rocks, cascades, and precipices, and a great subterranean cavern of unknown extent, supposed to be inhabited by all the gnomes and devils of the Alps. In fact, I passed a week in the enjoyment of pure nature and lumbago. We have here a Siberian wind, and this morning some snowflakes fell before my window; an unheard-of scandal in the memory of the oldest inhabitant of Cannes. I am ill, melancholy, wearied. My sight is failing and I can no longer sketch. What a sad thing is this growing old! Bulwer's novel, "What will he do with it?" appears to me senile to the last degree; nevertheless it contains some pretty scenes and has a very good moral. As to the hero and heroine, they transcend in silliness the limits of romance. A book that has amused me is a work by M. de Bunsen on the origin of Christianity and on *everything*, to speak more exactly; but it styles itself: "Christianity and Mankind." M. de Bunsen, though calling himself a Christian, has little respect for the Old and New Testaments.

Paris, *May*, 1860. — The ball at the Hôtel d'Albe was superb; the costumes were very fine, many of the women very pretty, and typifying the audacity of the age being *décolletées* in the most outrageous fashion both as to skirt and waist.

During the waltz I saw a number of charming feet and many garters. Crinoline is declining. Be assured that within two years dresses will be worn very short, and the natural advantages of those so fortunate as to possess them will be distinguished from artificial charms. Some of the Englishwomen passed belief. The captivating daughter of Lord —— represented a Dryad, or some mythological personage, in a dress that would have left the entire bust exposed but for the semi-veil of a sort of swaddling band. It was nearly as conspicuous as the scanty drapery of the Mamma. The *ballet* of the Elements was danced by sixteen quite pretty women in short petticoats and covered with diamonds. The Naiads were powdered with silver, which, falling on their shoulders, resembled drops of water. The Salamanders were powdered with gold; one among them, Mademoiselle Errazu, being wondrously beautiful. The Princess Mathilde, painted a deep *bistre*, personated a Nubian, and was much too exact in costume. In the midst of the ball, a domino embraced Madame S——, who uttered loud screams. The dining-room with its surrounding gallery, the servants in their dresses as pages of the sixteenth century, and the electric light, recalled Martin's picture of Belshazzar's Feast. The Emperor changed his domino in vain; he would have been recognized at a league distant. The Empress wore a white bournous and black velvet mask, which did not disguise her in the least. There were many foolish dominos; the Duc de —— walking about as a tree, — an excellent imitation. At the ball given by M. Aligre, a wife was pinched black and blue by her ferocious husband. The wife screamed and fainted; general tableau! The jealous idiot was not thrown out of the window, which would have been the only sensible thing to do. At a recent masked ball a lady had the temerity to appear in a costume of 1806, without crinoline, which produced a great sensation. These are fine commentaries on the times and women.

An amusing incident occurred lately. M. Boitelle, Prefect of Police, who should certainly be the best informed man in Paris, learned through the reports of faithful agents that M.

Fould, the Minister of State, had gone to sleep in his newly built house in the Faubourg Saint-Honoré. Very early in the morning the Prefect appeared, pressed the Minister's hand very demonstratively, explaining the important part he had taken in what had just occurred. M. Fould thought that he referred to his son, who is committing follies in England. This *quid pro quo* lasted until the Prefect asked permission to know the name of his successor in the Cabinet, to which M. Fould replied, that he had come to his new residence merely as a house-warming, and had found it more convenient to sleep there than at the Ministerial palace.

It appears that Lamoricière is already somewhat weary of the imbroglio that greets him in the papal territory. Cardinal Antonelli remarked a short time ago to a foreign minister, that he had never met a man of more comprehensive mind than Lamoricière. "I have discussed the intricate situation of affairs with him, for which he immediately suggested five or six remedies; and he talks so well, that within the hour he gave me four different opinions on the same question, all so strongly fortified that I am perplexed as to a choice." Every one here is preoccupied by Garibaldi's expedition, which will, it is feared, result in a general complication. Should he break his back in Sicily, I think that perhaps M. de Cavour would not be too much distressed, but if he succeed, he will become ten times more dangerous.

Read Granier de Cassagnac's book on the Girondins. Portions of it are exceedingly curious, and it presents a horrible picture of the massacres and revolutionary atrocities; all written with much fire and vigor. Three days ago I received a visit from M. Feydeau, who is a very fine fellow, but artlessly betrays an extreme vanity. He is going to Spain to complement what Cervantes and Lesage have merely outlined! He has still thirty romances to write, the scene of which will be laid in thirty different countries; this is why he travels. I think of you incessantly in spite of your faults.

Paris, *July*, 1860. — The funeral of Prince Jerome was a terrible ceremony. I do not know how many vacancies it has created in our ranks, but fear that only the undertakers have profited by it. More than thirty thousand persons came to sprinkle holy water, which shows the flunkyism of this high-minded nation! It is even more senseless than is supposed, and that is saying much. You lost a fine spectacle, that of seeing me *in fiocchi* and black gloves, pass through the Rue de Rivoli amid the admiring populace. We were one hour and three quarters in defiling between the Palais Royal and the Invalides, then came the mass, then the funeral oration by Abbé Cœur, who praised the principles of '89, while declaring our soldiers to be ready to die in defense of the Pope. He also said that the first Napoleon had no love for war, but was always forced to the defensive. The finest part of the ceremony was a *De profundis* chanted in the vault, and which we heard through black crape that separated us from the grave. Were I a musician I would profit in opera by the admirable effect of this crape in modifying sound.

The Orleanists pretend that M. Brénier has been knocked in the head by an uncivil husband; but the more credible rumor is that the lazzaroni have thus sought to avenge the violence offered to their king. The liberals, in retaliation, have assassinated the police, which has been of much benefit to M. Brénier. The northern Italians have not the quick sensibility of the Neapolitans. They have logic and common sense, as Stendhal said, while the Neapolitans are merely badly trained children.

In the evening every one goes to the Champs-Elysées to hear Musard's music; fine ladies and *lorettes* mingled pell-mell, and are difficult to distinguish one from the other. And people go to the circus to see the learned dogs roll a ball up an inclined plane by leaping on it! This generation is losing all taste for intellectual pleasures.

South Parade, Bath, *August*, 1860. — Such a life as mine here would make a thorough-bred horse broken-winded:

in the morning, walks, shopping, and visiting; in the evening, dinners with the aristocrats, where I always find the same dishes and nearly the same faces. I could hardly remember the names of my hosts, for in their white cravats and black coats, all Englishmen look very much alike. We are extremely detested here, and still more dreaded. Nothing is more droll than the fear they have of us, which they are at no pains to disguise. The volunteers are even more stupid than the National Guard was with us in 1830; for in this country everything is invested with an air of gravity not to be seen elsewhere. I know a very honest fellow sixty years of age, who drills every day in Zouave breeches. The Ministry is very weak and does not know its own mind, and the Opposition is not more wise. But great and small agree in believing that we covet general annexation. At the same time, there is no one who supposes a war to be possible, unless the question of annexing the three kingdoms should be agitated. I am not very well pleased with the Emperor's letter to M. de Persigny. It would have been much better in my opinion, to say nothing at all, or simply to tell them what I repeat every evening: that they are great fools.

LONDON, 18 *Arlington Street,* 1860. — Only after some time in London do I accustom myself to its singular light, which seems to pass through brown gauze, the effect being that of an eclipse. This atmospheric peculiarity and the curtainless windows will annoy me for some days to come; but on the other hand I am regaling on all manner of good things, breakfasting and dining like an ogre.

It is evident that the affairs of the East are becoming more complicated every moment. The disembarking of the French in Syria would be followed by a general explosion of massacre and pillage throughout the East; very probably, also, the Turkish provinces of Greece — that is to say, Thessaly, Macedonia, and Christian Albania — would be excited to retaliation. Everything will be on fire this winter in the East, and to visit Algeria at such a moment seems to me perfect madness. The "Times" to-day announces four feet of snow at Inverness. Shall I find enough charcoal and plaids in Scotland to remedy this evil?

GLENQUOICH, *August*, 1860. — The weather here is always detestable, but it does not hinder people from going out. They are so accustomed to rain, that unless it be of extraordinary violence they are not deterred from walking. The paths are sometimes torrents, and the mountains are invisible within a hundred paces; but these people return, saying "Beautiful walk." One of the greatest annoyances of this region is a little fly called midge, which is exceedingly venomous; and though there are two young ladies here, the one blonde, the other red-haired, and both with skin of satin, these horrible insects prefer to attack me. Our chief amusement is fishing, and fortunately the insects do not venture on the lake. There are fourteen persons here. During the day each one goes his own way; in the evening, after dinner, each one takes a book or writes letters. To chat and seek to amuse each other is a thing unknown to the English. The Highland air has benefited me, and I breathe more easily. Our hunters kill deer and grouse; and every day we have excellent birds; but I cannot eat, the main pleasure amid this rain and fog; and I sigh for a *soupe maigre*, or for a solitary dinner at home, or with you at Saint-Cheron: this last wish will never be realized, I fear.

PARIS, *September*, 1860. — Panizzi has been with me for ten days, and I am acting cicerone, showing him everything, from cedar to hyssop. I understand nothing of the disorders that have begun. My guest thinks that the Pope and the Austrians will be driven out. For the first, appearances are unfavorable; as to the others, I believe that if Garibaldi meddles with them he will burn his fingers. From Naples comes a royal philosophical witticism. Previous to embarking, His Majesty received, every five minutes, the resignation of a General or an Admiral: "Now they are too thoroughly Italians to fight against

Garibaldi ; a month hence they will be too much of royalists to fight against the Austrians." It would be impossible for you to imagine the fury of the Orleanists and Carlists. A rather sensible Italian tells me that M. de Cavour caused the Sardinian army to enter the States of the Church, because Mazzini was about to incite a revolution there.

I hear that the *fêtes* at Marseilles in the Imperial honor were very fine : that the enthusiasm was at once deliberate and clamorous, and that perfect order was maintained notwithstanding the immense, overexcited Southern multitude. The spectacle of the Marseillaise, in their ordinary state, is always sufficiently amusing, but, when under excitement, they must be still more absurd. But they not only lost their heads on the occasion of the Emperor's visit, but also two barrels of Spanish wine that I have been expecting. The merchant who should have received them writes to me very naïvely, that he was too much occupied with the *fêtes* to think of my wine, and could only attend to it after taking a little rest.

I lately passed a few days at Saintonge, where I found every one discomfited, weeping their eyes away for the misfortunes of the Holy Father and General Lamoricière. It is said that General Changarnier is writing a narrative of his colleague's campaign, in which, after bestowing the highest eulogies, he proves that Lamoricière committed the most enormous follies. In my opinion, the only one of the martyr heroes at whom one cannot laugh, is Pimodan, who died like a brave soldier. Those who exclaim against the martyrs because they have been taken, move me to no pity. Moreover, the present time is perfectly comic ; and it is comfortable to learn every morning, through one's paper, of a catastrophe, to read Cavour's notes and the encyclicals. I see that they have shot Walker, in America, which surprises me, for his case is precisely that of Garibaldi whom we all admire.

Two evenings ago, wishing for some music, I went to the Italiens, where they gave the "Barber of Seville." This music, the gayest ever written, was executed by people with the air of having just returned from a funeral. Alboni, who played

Rosina, sang admirably, with the expression of a bird organ. Gardoni sang like a gentleman who fears to be mistaken for an actor. Had I been Rossini I should have beaten them every one. Only Basilio, whose name I do not recall, sang as if he understood the words.

I am told that the Empress, whom I have not yet seen, is still terribly afflicted. She sent me a fine photograph of the Duchesse d'Albe, taken twenty-four hours after death, which was very calm ; she looks as if in a quiet sleep. Five minutes before her death she laughed at her waiting-maid's Valencian *patois*. I have no direct news of Madame de Montijo since her departure, but I fear that the poor lady will not bear up under this dreadful blow.

I am in the midst of academical intrigues ; the question not one touching the French Academy, but that of the fine arts. An intimate friend of mine is the favored candidate, but he has received an intimation from His Majesty to give place to M. Haussmann, the Prefect. The Academy is annoyed, and wishes to nominate my friend in spite of himself, which I encourage to the utmost ; and I should like to tell the Emperor the wrong he does himself in mingling with matters that do not concern him. I hope for success, and that the Colossus will be finely blackballed.

Italian affairs are very amusing, and what is said of them by the few honest people here is still more droll. The martyrs of Castelfidardo are beginning to arrive, among them a young man of eighteen years who allowed himself to be taken, and whose aunt I saw a few days ago. She said : "The Piedmontese behaved in an atrocious manner to my nephew." I awaited some appalling revelation. "Only imagine, Monsieur, five minutes after being made prisoner the poor fellow's watch was gone. A gold hunting watch that I had given him !"

October, 1860. — I quite understand that the first view of Oriental life should dazzle you. One sees things both droll and to be admired at every step ; in fact, there is always something droll in Orientals as in certain strange, pompous beasts that we formerly saw at the Jardin des Plantes. Decamps has caught this ludicrous phase, but not the very fine, noble side of their character.

Thanks to your sex you are privileged to enter the harems and chat with the women. Do they in Algeria, as in Turkey, make a display of their charms? Tell me how they dress, what they say, and what they think of you. What is the character of the dances that you saw? Were they modest, and did you comprehend their sentiment? I imagine that they are more interesting than those of Parisian balls; and they probably resemble the dances of the gypsy women of Granada. I do not doubt that an Arab, from Sahara, in witnessing a waltz in Paris, would conclude, and naturally, that the Frenchwomen were enacting pantomime. In going to the root of things we always find the same primal ideas. Have you seen the women at the Moorish baths? I am inclined to believe that the habit of living with crossed legs must give them horrible knees. I suppose you will adopt kohl for your eyes, which is very pretty, being also, it is said, an excellent preservative against ophthalmia, an affection common and dangerous for European eyes in hot climates. I grant you my permission to try the effect. You give me sketches; I wish for details. There is nothing that you cannot say to me, and besides, you are renowned for your euphuisms. You have the art of academical expression. I congratulate you on your courage in learning Arabic. I once glanced through M. de Sacy's grammar and recoiled in terror, but I remember that there are lunar and solar letters, and I know not how many conjugations. My cousin, one of the most learned Arabists, who had passed twenty-five years at Djeddah, told me that he never opened a book without learning some new word, of which there were, for instance, five hundred for the one word lion.

PARIS, *October*, 1860. — I went to Saint-Cloud yesterday, where I breakfasted almost *tête-à-tête* with the Emperor, the Empress, and "Monsieur fils," as they say at Lyons. I talked a long while with the Emperor, principally of ancient history and Cæsar. He surprises me by the ease with which he comprehends erudite subjects, for which he has only recently acquired the taste. The Empress related some curious anecdotes of her journey to Corsica. The Bishop spoke to her of a bandit named Bosio, a thoroughly honest youth, whom the counsels of a woman had driven to commit several little murders. He is pursued for some months, but uselessly; women and children suspected of carrying him food are thrown into prison, but to lay hands on him is impossible. Her Majesty, who has read a certain romance,[1] became interested in this man, and said she should be very glad if he could be enabled to leave the island and go to Africa or elsewhere, where he might become a good soldier and an honest man. "Ah! Madame," said the Bishop, "will you allow me to have this told to him?" "How, Monseigneur, you know where he is?" General rule: the most worthless fellow in Corsica is always related to the most honest man. It greatly surprised the Imperial party that they should have been asked for a prodigious number of favors (*grâces*), but not for a sou; so the Empress returns full of enthusiasm.

The meeting at Warsaw is a failure. The Emperor of Austria invited himself, and was received with the politeness that is accorded to the indiscreet. Nothing of importance was accomplished. The Emperor of Austria essayed to prove that if Hungary was a source of danger to Austria, Russia had Poland; to which Gortschakoff replies: "You have eleven millions of Hungarians, and you are three millions of Germans. We are forty millions of Russians, and have no need of assistance in bringing six thousand Poles to their senses. Consequently, there is no necessity for mutual guaranties." England is calming down, and it is possible that she may make us overtures to adopt a joint policy with regard to Italy. In that event war would be impossible unless Garibaldi should attak Venice. They write me from Naples that the muddle is at its height, and the Piedmontese are expected there with

[1] Merimée's novel of *Colomba*.

the same impatience with which we in Paris in 1848 looked for the arrival of the troops of the line. They sigh for order and rest their hopes for its restoration on Victor Emmanuel alone. Moreover, Garibaldi and Alexandre Dumas have prepared their minds for peace, much in the same way as a a freezing rain disposes one to a hot dinner.

PARIS, *November*, 1860. — Affairs are still complicated by the condition of the East, which is such that our Ambassador at Constantinople expects the old machine to crack from top to bottom at any moment. The Sultan is selling his cachemires, and does not know if he will be able to buy a dinner next month. Do you know the Emperor Francis Joseph's greeting to the Emperor Alexander? "I bring you my guilty head!" The serf's formula on approaching his master in the fear of being beaten. This he said in good Russian, for he knows all languages. His servile meanness did not profit him much; Alexander preserved a most discouraging coldness, and the Prince Regent of Prussia, following his example, put on airs. After the departure of the Emperor Alexander, the Austrian emperor remained four hours alone at Warsaw, where there was no great Russian or Polish noblemen so poor to do him reverence. All this has been a great triumph to the old Russians, who detest the Austrians still more than the English or ourselves.

You have heard of our victory over these poor Chinese. What an absurdity to go so far for the purpose of killing people who have done us no harm. True, being a species of ourang-outang, the Grammont law alone can be invoked in their favor. I am preparing for our Chinese conquests by reading a new romance just translated by Stanislas Julien. It is the story of Mademoiselle Cân and Mademoiselle Ling, who are very witty, making verses and crambo on every occasion. They meet with two students possessing the same poetic facility, and a never-ending combat of quatrains ensues, the prominent idea of which is the blue lotus and white doves. It is impossible to conceive of any imaginative effort more uncouth and more barren of passion. The people who can be amused by this style of literature are evidently abominable pedants, who well deserve to be beaten and conquered by us, who are disciples of the noble Greek literature.

I dined to-day with Prince Napoleon. The Princess Clotilde admired my wrist buttons, and asked the address of my jeweler.

MARSEILLES, *November*, 1860. — My friend Mr. Ellice, of Glenquoich, will be my neighbor this winter. He has just purchased a Scotch estate next his own; or rather lakes, rocks, and heaths several leagues in extent. I cannot conceive what it will produce, unless it be grouse and deer.

I have brought with me a new edition of Pouschkine's works, and have promised to write a notice of him. I find magnificent things in his lyric poems, entirely after my own heart; that is to say, Greek in their truth and simplicity. I should like to translate several that are marked by great sprightliness, in which, as in precision and clearness, he strikes me as preëminent. One in the style of Sappho's ode reminds me that I am writing in the chamber of an inn, dreaming of happy moments in the past. I am ill and suffering; but of all petty miseries the worst for me is sleeplessness, when thoughts are gloomy, and one takes a dislike to one's self. The journey of the Empress to Scotland creates much gossip, and every one is mystified.

CANNES, *December*, 1860. — The political disturbance has somewhat agitated me, however unprejudiced in the premises I may be. You know how intimate I have been with the chief victim, M. Fould. As yet I know nothing positive respecting the reasons for his disgrace. It is evident, however, that a beautiful woman is somewhat implicated, who is anxious to dislodge him, and who has long sought to accomplish this end. M. Fould is less philosophical than I had thought, or than I should have been in his place; but he has been wounded by certain proceedings. As to the liberal measures, we must wait to see the result. As a principle, it is better to take the initiative in giving than to grant what has been long and impatiently demanded. On the other hand, the Emperor may be seeking support in the Chambers to enable him to withdraw from our false position in Italy, — protecting a Pope who excommunicated us *in petto*, while we risk a quarrel with our friends out of tenderness for the vanity of a puppet (the Emperor of Austria) who has never wished us well. Here, throughout France, the people who wear black coats and claim to be powerful are in favor of the Pope and the King of Naples, as if they had incited no revolution in France, but their love for the papacy and legitimacy does not stretch to the point of expending a crown for them. What will be the effect of the recrudescent eloquence with which the new concessions threaten us? The old Parliamentarians begin to prick up their ears. M. Thiers, it is said, will enter the lists as a candidate for the Deputies, and this example will be followed by many others. I can hardly imagine what will become of the Ministers without portfolio commissioned to represent the eloquence of the Legislative Body and the Senate; but it will be diverting to see orators like Messieurs Magne and Billault, with the Jules Favres and *tutti quanti.*

My friend Mr. Ellice is at Nice, whence he occasionally comes to visit me; he complains of finding no intellectual associates. I see that you have had a visit from Mr. Cobden, a man of talent and very interesting, the opposite of an Englishman, in that he never utters commonplaces and has few prejudices. I can give you no political news, for my correspondents tell me nothing, except that nothing is done. It is a characteristic of our generation to set out with a great hubbub that ends in loitering and amusing ourselves on the road.

CANNES, *February*, 1861. — I have been to Nice on a visit to my friend Mr. Ellice who is cruelly tortured by the gout. I confess to an involuntary sentiment of satisfaction in passing the bridge of the Var free from custom-house officers, gensdarmes, and passports. It is a fine annexation and makes one feel several millimetres taller.

M. Fould has been on a visit to me, and related many curious stories touching both men and women who intermeddled in his affairs. I doubt if he will have the courage to persevere in sulking. It appears that when one has carried a red portfolio under the arm for some time, the loss of it reduces him to the state of an Englishman without his umbrella.

If you find some pretty silk stuff that washes, and not too much like a woman's gown, order me a *robe de chambre* the longest possible, and buttoned down the left side, and in the Oriental fashion. Bring it with you, for I have no wish to wear silk gowns when the ice of the Seine is two feet thick. The cold reported at Paris makes my hair stand on end; nevertheless I am summoned there by the President. Do not be alarmed to see my illness announced. A dignity has been conferred on me which I could very well have dispensed with, but which compels me to be punctual; and they also write me that our Senate is papistical and legitimist, and that my vote will not be one too many for the ballot.

The poor Duchess of Malakof is an excellent person, not very bright, especially as to French. She appears to be entirely domineered over by her frightful monster of a husband, who is rough by habit and perhaps through policy. It is said, however, that she accommodates herself to the inevitable. Should you see her, speak of me and of our theatrical performances in Spain. I am told that her brother is an amiable fellow, very handsome, and a poet into the bargain. Thanks for the tobacco pouch, the gold and colored embroidery of which is exquisite. Only barbarians can do these things, our workmen having too much acquired art and not enough sentiment to equal them. Thanks also for the bananas, to my taste the most delicious fruit in the world.

PARIS, *March*, 1861. — Since my return to Paris I have been in a condition of utter stultification; first, as regards our exhibition at the Senate, where, I may say with M. Jourdain, I have been surfeited with nonsense. Every one had a speech prepared, that it was necessary to display, and so contagious was the example of dullness that I delivered my own like an idiot. I was cruelly frightened, but overcame it by reminding myself that I was in the presence of two hundred imbeciles, and with no reason for agitation. The joke of it was that M. Walewski, for whom I wished to obtain a satisfactory budget, was offended by my praise of his predecessor, and honestly declared that he would vote against my resolution. M. Troplong, near whom in virtue of my office as Secretary I was seated, condoled with me in a low tone; to which I replied that it was impossible to make a Minister drink who was not thirsty. This was repeated piping hot to M. Walewski, who took it for an epigram, and has frowned at me ever since.

The second *ennui* of the day is the official and private dinners, where one sees the same turbot, fillet, and lobster, and the same tiresome persons as on the preceding occasion. But the most irksome of all is Catholicism. You can hardly imagine the degree of exasperation to which Catholics are moved, flying in one's face for a mere nothing; for example, if one does not show the whites of one's eyes in hearing them discourse of the sainted martyr; and still more if one innocently inquires, as I have done, who has been martyrized. I have also got into a scrape in expressing astonishment that the Queen of Naples should be photographed in boots! — an exaggeration of my words and a surpassing stupidity. The other evening a lady asked me if I had seen the Empress of Austria. I said that I thought her very pretty. "Ah! she is ideal!" — No, it is an irregular face, more agreeable perhaps than if perfectly classical. — "Ah! Monsieur, she is beauty itself! Tears of admiration come to one's eyes!" And this is the society of to-day! I fly from it as from the plague. What has become of the French society of former years!

The latest, but a colossal bore, has been "Tannhauser." Some persons say that its representation at Paris was one of the secret clauses of the treaty of Villafranca; others, that Wagner has been given to us to compel our admiration of Berlioz. The fact is, it is prodigious. I am convinced that I could write something similar if inspired by the scampering of my cat over the piano keys. The Princess de Metternich bestirred herself enormously in feigning to understand it and to lead the applause, which, however, never came. Every one yawned; but at first the audience assumed the air of comprehending this keyless enigma. Beneath Madame de Metternich's box, it was said by the wits that the Austrians were taking their revenge for Solferino. It was also said that one wearies of the recitatives, and tires of the airs (*se tanne aux airs*). Try to catch the pun. Your Arabic music, I fancy, would be a capital preparation for this infernal uproar. The failure is stupendous! Auber says that it is Berlioz without melody.

I am satisfied that within two months the Pope will either be off, or that we shall leave him to his own devices, or that he will come to some arrangement with Piedmont; but matters cannot remain in their present status. The bigots are raising a horrible outcry, but the Gallic *bourgeois* and the people are anti-papists.

You tell me nothing of your health, which appears to be good, nor of your complexion, which must be, I fear, somewhat browned.

PARIS, *May*, 1861. — You must have been sadly impressed with the aspect of winter in Central France, coming as you do from Africa. Whenever I return from Cannes I am horrified at the sight of the leafless trees and damp, dead earth.

The Catholics have rendered our *salons* insupportable. Not only have the former devotees become acid as verjuice, but all of the ex-Voltairians of the political opposition have turned papists. What consoles me, is, that some among them believe themselves obliged to attend mass, which must bore them sufficiently. My old Professor, M. Cousin, who formerly never spoke of the Pope but as the Bishop of Rome, is converted and never misses a mass. It is even said that M. Thiers is becoming devout, but I find some difficulty in believing it, for I have always had a weakness for him.

I am, at this very moment, a prey to the herrings that the sea-calves of Boulogne have raised up to torment us, and I await the Maronites as a finishing stroke — that is to say, we are disputing in the Senate, and very sharply, *à propos* to herrings, and we are menaced with daily sittings. Is it true that all the Boulogne herring fishers are thieves who buy the herrings taken by the English, and which they pretend to have caught themselves? Is it also true that the herrings have been seduced by the English, and pass no more along our coasts?

CHÂTEAU DE FONTAINEBLEAU, *June*, 1861. — I am resting under the trees with great happiness after my tribulations. Never have I seen men so enraged, so out of their senses as the magistrates. I console myself in thinking that if twenty years hence some antiquary shall burrow in the "Moniteur" of this week, he will say that one philosopher of moderation and calmness was found among an assembly of lunatics. This philosopher, without vanity, is myself. In this country magistrates are selected from men too stupid to gain their living as lawyers; they are badly paid, and are allowed to be crabbed and insolent. I have done my duty, and all is at an end. I was well received here, with no raillery on my defeat. I very clearly gave my opinion of the matter, and they do not appear to think me in the wrong. It is magnificent weather and the air of the forest is delicious. There are rocks and heather which would have their charms could I walk with you among them, chatting of all manner of things; but we go in a long file of *chars à bancs*, where one is not always well matched in point of capacity for amusing. There is not a republic, however, where one can have more freedom or find a host and hostess more amiable and kind to their guests. There are few people here. We have the Princess de Metternich, who is very animated after the German fashion, that is to say, she affects a species of originality composed of two parts *lorette*, one part great lady. I suspect that in reality there is not too much wit to sustain the *rôle* that she has adopted. One accomplishes nothing here. Sometimes I am summoned for a stroll in the woods; sometimes to make verses; but time is especially wasted in waiting. The great philosophy of the day is to know how to wait, and I have some difficulty in educating myself in the art. Thanks to Cæsar, doubtless, I shall be here until the end of the month. I am working for the *bourgeois* (the Emperor), with whom I am more pleased every day. I went last week to Alise with the Emperor, who is becoming an accomplished archæologist. He passed three hours and a half on the mountain, under the most terrific sun, examining the vestiges of Cæsar's siege, and reading the "Commentaries." We returned with the skin peeled from our ears, and the color of chimney-sweeps.

CHÂTEAU DE FONTAINEBLEAU, *June*, 1861. — We have had a capital ceremony here, reminding me of that in the "Bourgeois Gentilhomme." It was the most diverting spectacle possible, that of twenty black men exceedingly like monkeys, dressed in gold brocade with white stockings and varnished shoes, and swords at their side, all flat on their face and crawling on hands and knees the whole length of the Henri II. gallery, each one with his nose level with the back of the crawler preceding him. The hardest task fell to the first ambassador, who wore a felt hat embroidered in gold that danced on his head with each motion, and who held a bowl of gold filagree work within which were two boxes containing each a letter from their Siamese Majesties. The letters were inclosed in purses of gold-woven silk, the whole being very pretty. After delivering the letters to the Emperor, it became necessary to retire backward, and confusion fell upon the embassy. A succession of blows on the face of those behind them by the first rank, whose swords pierced the eyes of the second rank, who in turn made blind of one eye the third rank, was the result of this masterly retreat. They presented the appearance of a swarm of black beetles on the carpet. The Minister of Foreign Affairs had arranged the ceremony and exacted that the ambassadors should crawl, the effect of which moreover failed, for the Emperor at length lost all patience, rose, made the beetles rise, and spoke in English with one of them. The Empress kissed a little monkey whom they had brought, said to be the son of one of the ambassadors, who ran about on all fours like a little rat, but had an intelligent expression. The temporal king of Siam sent his portrait to the Emperor, and that of his wife, who is hideously ugly. You would be charmed by the beauty and variety of the stuffs they brought; gold and silver tissues so light and transparent as to resemble the clouds of a fine sunset. They gave the Emperor trowsers embroidered with ornaments in enamel and gold, and a vest of gold brocade as flexible as foulard, the designs, gold on gold, being really exquisite; while the buttons are of filagree gold, diamonds, and emeralds. They have a red gold and a white gold which produce an admirable effect when blended. In short, I have never seen anything at once so bewitching and splendid. The tastes of these savages is singular, in that their fabrics are not glaring although they use only brilliant silks, gold, and silver. All this is marvelously combined, producing on the whole a quiet and harmonious effect.

LONDON, *British Museum*, *July*, 1861. — You know, or you do not know, that there is a new Lord Chancellor, Lord B——, who is old, but his morals by no means so. A lawyer named Stevens sends his clerk with a card for the Chancellor; the clerk makes inquiries, and is told that my lord has no house in London, but that he often comes from the country to Oxford Terrace, where he has a temporary lodging. Thither the clerk proceeds and asks for my lord. "He is not here." "Do you think he will return for dinner?" "No, but to sleep certainly; he sleeps here every Monday." The clerk leaves the letter, and Mr. Stevens is greatly astonished that the Chancellor should look frightfully black at him. The gist of the story is, that my lord maintains a clandestine *ménage*.

I have not had a moment's rest since my arrival; dinner parties, balls, and concerts without cessation. Yesterday I attended a concert at the Marquis of Lansdowne's, where there was not a single pretty woman, a remarkable circumstance here; but, on the other hand, they were all dressed as if the first *modiste* of Brionde had composed their toilette. I have never seen anything to parallel their headdresses; one ancient dame, who wore a diamond crown composed of small stars with a huge sun in the centre, being an absolute counterpart of the wax figures that one sees at fairs!

Yesterday I dined at Greenwich with some great personages who exerted themselves to be lively, not like the Germans by throwing themselves from the windows, but by making an excessive noise. The dinner was abominably long, but the white bait excellent. We have unpacked two cases of antiquities just arrived from Cyrene. There are two statues and several remarkable busts, one of a good period and quite Greek; a Bacchus, that is especially captivating though with rather a mincing expression, the head being in an extraordinary state of preservation.

M. de Vidil is committed and will be tried at the next assizes. He is not admitted to bail, and the worst that can happen to him will be a sentence of imprisonment for two years; for where death does not supervene the English law does not recognize murder.

Lord Lyndhurst said to me that one must be extremely *maladroit* to be hung in England. I went the other evening to the House of Commons and heard the debate on Sardinia. Anything more verbose, more pointless (*gobe-mouche*), and fuller of bragadocio than the majority of the speakers it is impossible to imagine, and notably so Lord John Russell, now Lord Russell.

I have been interrupted by a visit to the Bank. They placed in my hand four small packages amounting to four million pounds sterling, but I was not allowed to bring them away. They showed me a very pretty machine that counts and weighs three thousand sovereigns per day. It hesitates a moment, and after a short deliberation throws the good sovereign to the right and the bad to the left. There is another that takes a bank bill, stoops and gives it, as it were, two little kisses, impressing on it marks that forgers have not as yet been able to imitate. Finally, I was conducted to the vaults, where I might have imagined myself in a grotto of the Arabian Nights; all filled with sacks of gold and ingots sparkling in the gaslight.

PARIS, *August*, 1861. — I do not know whether in consequence of too much turtle soup, or exposure to the sun, but I have again suffered from my former agonizing pains, which must resemble those of hanging, and which create in me no desire to be suspended. After six weeks of dinner parties I find it very comfortable not to don a white cravat. I passed a week in Suffolk County in a fine château, almost in solitude. It is a flat country, but covered with magnificent timber, with much water; it is very near the fens whence Cromwell came. The quantity of game is astonishing, and at every step one runs the risk of crushing partridges or pheasants.

Should Madame de Montijo go to Biarritz I shall join her and pass some days with her. She is inconsolable, and I find her even more sad than last year when her daughter died.

I see by your letter that you are as much occupied as a general-in-chief on the eve of battle. I remember reading in "Tristram Shandy," that in the house with a newly born babe all the women believe themselves entitled to tyrannize over the men; and I feared to be treated with the disdain inseparable from your present height of grandeur. For myself, I am but slightly inclined to love children; nevertheless, I can imagine that one may be attached to a little girl as to a kitten, an animal to which your sex bear a strong resemblance. There is perfect solitude here, by which I profit in preparing something promised to my master, and which I wish to take to Biarritz. I read little except Roman history; nevertheless, I have read M. Thiers's nineteenth volume with great pleasure. It strikes me as being written with greater negligence than its predecessors, but full of curious matter. In spite of his desire to speak ill of his hero, he is continually carried away by his involuntary love. He gives exceedingly amusing stories of Montrond, to whom I only regret not having related them while he was living. M. Thiers paints him correctly as an adventurer in love with his trade, and honest towards his employers during the period of his service, much the same as Dalgetty in the "Legend of Montrose."

BIARRITZ, *September*, 1861. — I am still here, dear friend, like a bird on a branch. It is not the custom here to make plans in advance, indeed they are resolved on only at the last moment. It is excessively cold after dinner, it being impossible to keep warm with the system of doors and windows that has been contrived here. The sea air is of service, and I breathe more easily, but sleep badly, as I am immediately on the shore, for the slightest wind rouses the waves to a terrific uproar. Time passes here as in all imperial residences — in doing nothing and in waiting that something may be done. I work a little, sketch from my window, and walk a great deal. There are but few persons at the Villa Eugénie, and all agreeable. Yesterday we took a charming walk along the Pyrénées, sufficiently near the mountains to see them in all their beauty and escaping the discomfort of constant ascents and descents. We lost our way and found only people who were ignorant of our fine French tongue : and this happens as soon as one quits the suburbs of Bayonne.

Yesterday the Prince Imperial gave a dinner party to a troupe of his young friends. The Emperor himself mixed the champagne with seltzer-water, but the effect was the same as if they had drunk the pure wine. They were all tipsy a quarter of an hour afterwards, and my ears still ache with the noise they made. I boldly undertook to translate a Spanish memoir respecting the site of Munda for His Majesty, which I begin to perceive is terribly difficult reading. I am working like a negro for my master, whom I shall go to see in a few days.

COMPIEGNE, *November*, 1861. — Our anticipated *fêtes* have been postponed by the death of His Majesty of Portugal. As lions we have four Highlanders in kilts, the Duke of Athol, Lord James Murray, with the son and nephew of the Duke.

It is droll enough to see these eight bare knees in a drawing-room where all the men are in knee breeches or pantaloons. Yesterday his Grace's piper was introduced, and they all four danced in a way to alarm the company when they whirled about. But there are some ladies here whose crinoline is still more alarming as they enter a carriage. As lady guests are not obliged to wear mourning, legs of every color are seen, the red stockings having a very good effect. In spite of walks through damp, icy woods, and red-hot drawing rooms, I have escaped a cold ; but I am oppressed and do not sleep.

I was present at the great ministerial comedy, where we were in expectation of several additional victims. The faces were a study, the speeches still more so ; inasmuch as M. Walewski, the tottering Excellency, paraded his griefs indiscriminately to friends and enemies. An inveterate prejudice is the strongest provocation to the utterance of nonsense, especially when one is in the habit of it. Oh human platitude ! His wife, on the contrary, was wonderfully cool and self-possessed. What is said of the Emperor's letter? He has a way peculiar to himself of saying things, and where he speaks as a Sovereign contrives to convey the impression that he is of a finer porcelain. I believe it to be precisely what is needed by our high-toned nation which has no love for common clay.

Yesterday the Princess of ——, when taking tea, asked a footman, in her German accent, "*De lui aborder ti sel bour le bain.*" After a quarter of an hour the man returned with thirty pounds of bay salt, supposing that she wished to take a salt bath.

A picture by Müller, representing Queen Marie Antoinette in prison, was lately brought to the Empress. The Prince Imperial asked who this lady was and why she was not in a palace. They explained to him that it was a Queen of France, and told him the meaning of a prison. He immediately ran off to ask the Emperor to be pleased to pardon this Queen whom he kept in prison. He is an odd child, and sometimes *terrible.* He says that he always bows to the people because they drove away Louis Philippe who was not on good terms with them. He is a charming child.

CANNES, *January*, 1862. — I have here as neighbor and companion M. Cousin, who has come to be cured of laryngitis, and who talks like a one-eyed magpie, eats like an ogre, and is surprised that he does not get well under this beautiful sky, which he sees for the first time. He is, moreover, very amusing, for he has the tact to draw out every one around him. I believe that when he is alone with his servant he talks with him as with the most coquettish Orleanist or Legitimist Duchess. The Cannites, *pur sang*, cannot get over their astonishment, and you may fancy, their look on being told that this man, who talks on every subject, and talks well, has translated Plato and is the lover of Madame de Longueville. The inconvenient part of it is that he does not know when to stop talking. For an eclectic philosopher it is a misfortune not to have adopted the conspicuous virtue of the sect of peripatetics.

How do you govern the little children who absorb you so much? It appears to be an interesting occupation. The worst thing about children is their tardy development which leaves us so long uncertain if they have mind or power of reasoning; it is vexatious that their struggling intelligence cannot be demonstrated by themselves. The main question is to know whether we shall talk sense or nonsense to them; each system has its pros and cons. I have made the acquaintance of a poor cat that lives in a cabin deep in the woods; I carry it bread and meat every day, and it runs a quarter of a league to meet me. I regret not being able to carry it off, for it has marvelous instincts.

LONDON, *British Museum*, *May*, 1862. — Frankly, the Exhibition is something of a failure. True, everything is not yet unpacked, but the building is horrible; although very large it does not impress one with its size, and one must walk and be lost in it to appreciate its extent. The English have made great progress in taste and the art of arrangement; we make furniture and painted paper assuredly better than than they, but we are in a deplorable path, and if this continue we shall be distanced. Our jury is presided over by a German who speaks English that is nearly incomprehensible, and nothing can be more absurd than our conferences ; no one even understands what subject is under discussion. Nevertheless, we vote. The worst of it is, that in our division there are some English manufacturers, and medals must necessarily be given to these gentlemen, who do not merit them. I am bombarded by speeches and routs. Two days ago I dined with Lord Granville. There were three small tables in a long gallery, which arrangement was expected to promote general conversation, but as the guests were but slightly known to each other nearly a general silence prevailed. In the evening I went to Lord Palmerston's, where the Japanese Embassy wore great swords which kept getting caught in all the women's dresses. I saw some women who were very beautiful and others who were very ugly; both making a complete exhibition of their personal charms; some attractive, others quite the reverse; but each one displaying the same assurance.

LONDON, *June*, 1862. — I read my report yesterday to the International Jury, in the purest Anglo-Saxon, not a word drawn from the French. In vain do the Commissioners appeal and beat the drum, they cannot attract a crowd. Since the price has been reduced to a shilling fashionable people no longer go, and the lower class seem to find little pleasure in it. The restaurants are detestable, the American restaurant being the amusing feature, where may be found more or less diabolical beverages that one drinks through a straw: mint julep or "*raise the dead.*" All of these drinks are disguised gin. I am tired out with British hospitality and dinners which give the idea of all being prepared by the same inexpert cook. You cannot imagine how I long for a plate of soup from my own *pot-au-feu.*

I do not know which of two recent important events has produced the greatest effect, — one, the defeat of the two Derby favorites by an unknown horse ; the other, the defeat of the Tories in the House of Commons. The number of mournful faces in London was really ludicrous. A young married lady at the races fainted on learning that Marquis was beaten a head's length by a rustic without pedigree. Mr. Disraeli puts a better face on the matter and shows himself at every ball.

PARIS, *July*, 1862. — Madame de Montijo arrived last week, so changed that it is distressing to see her. Nothing consoles her for the death of her daughter, and I find her less resigned even than on the day of her death. I dined last week at Saint-Cloud with a small circle quite agreeably, and where the feeling struck me as being less papistic than is generally supposed. I was permitted to scandalize matters without being called to order. The little Prince is charming. He has grown two inches and is the prettiest child I have seen.

BAGNÈRES-DE-BIGORRE, *The Upper Pyrénées*, 1862. — I have arrived here with M. Panizzi after a little tour beneath a terrible sun, and find weather worthy of London: fogs and an imperceptible rain that penetrates to one's bones. The physician of this watering-place is an old comrade of mine who has auscultated me and punched my chest and back, discovering two mortal ailments of which he undertakes to cure me, provided that I drink daily two glasses from the hot mineral spring, which is not ill-tasting; and that I bathe in a warm spring that is very agreeable to the skin. Already I am better. There are not many persons here, the English and the grapes having failed this season. In point of beauty we have Mademoiselle A. D——, who formerly captivated Prince ——. I have only seen her back, and she wears the vastest crinoline to be found in all the country. Balls are given twice a week, which I shall not attend, and amateur concerts, which I shall religiously avoid. Yesterday I was compelled to undergo a musical mass, to which I was conducted by gensdarmes; but the *soirée* given by the Sub-Prefect I declined, not to accumulate too many catastrophes in a single day. I should like to show you the incomparable verdure of this region, to talk with you beneath the shade of the great beech-trees, and make you drink the bright water for which crystal would be no fitting comparison. The petty quarrels and occupations of which you complain are lamentably incidental to a provincial place, and one can only deplore the fate of persons condemned to live there. Nevertheless it is certain that in the course of a few months one sinks to the level of the natives, and becomes interested in provincial inanities. The confession is sad, but human intelligence accepts the aliment offered and with satisfaction.

Last week I made a mountain excursion to see a farm belonging to M. Fould. It is on the shore of a small lake, facing one of the finest panoramas imaginable, surrounded by great trees, a rare thing in France ; and one breakfasts there most capitally. He has many magnificent horses and oxen, the whole managed with English order.

Have you read " Les Misérables," and heard what is said of it ? This is another of the subjects in respect to which I find the human species below that of the gorilla. The world becomes more stupid every day.

BIARRITZ, *Villa Eugénie, September*, 1862. — Dear friend, I am here on the sea-shore, breathing more easily than for a long time. The waters of Bagnères made me ill, a proof, it was said, of their beneficial action ; but on leaving them I began to revive, and now the sea-air and perhaps also the superb *cuisine* have perfected my cure. There are but few guests at the Villa, and only amiable persons whom I have long known. There is no crowd in the town, not many French, the Spaniards and Americans predominating. At the Thursday receptions at the Villa the Northern and Southern Americans have to be placed on different sides of the *salon,* lest they should eat each other.

On these occasions there is full dress, but usually there is not the least toilette ; the ladies dine in high dresses, and we of the ugly sex in morning coats. There is not a château in France or England where one is so free and without etiquette, nor where the chatelaine is so good and so gracious to her guests. We take beautiful walks in the valleys skirting the

Pyrénées, returning with prodigious appetites. The lady bathers are, as usual, very odd in the matter of costume. There is a Madame ——, the color of a turnip, who arrays herself in blue and powders her hair, — the powder, however, is said to be ashes, with which she sprinkles her head because of her country's misfortunes.

Have you seen Victor Hugo's speech at a dinner of Belgian booksellers and other swindlers at Brussels? What a pity that this good fellow, who has such fine imagery at his command, should not possess an iota of common sense, nor the discretion to refrain from uttering platitudes unworthy of so clever a man! I find more poetry in his comparison of the tunnel and railway than I have met with in any book these five years. But they are, after all, merely metaphors, containing nothing of depth, solidity, or judgment. He is a man who intoxicates himself with his own words and does not take the trouble to think. The twentieth volume by Thiers pleases me, as it does you. I have read it a second time with renewed pleasure, and shall do so again. It was immensely difficult, in my opinion, to extract anything from the confused rubbish of the St. Helena conversations as reported by Las Cases, and Thiers has come out of it wonderfully well. I am also pleased with his comparison of Napoleon with other great men, although he is somewhat severe upon Alexander and Cæsar; nevertheless, there is much truth in what he says as to the absence of virtue on the part of Cæsar. It attracts great interest here, and I fear that there is not overmuch love for the hero; for instance, they will not concede the anecdote of Nicomedes, nor you either, I fancy. Adieu — keep well, and do not sacrifice yourself too much for others; they will come to accept it as a habit, and what is now a pleasure to you, will perhaps some day become an irksome duty.

Paris, *October*, 1862. — I returned from Biarritz with my Sovereigns. We were all quite doleful, having been poisoned, as I believe, by verdigris. The cooks swear that they scoured their saucepans, but I do not credit their oaths. The fact is, fourteen persons at the Villa were seized with vomiting and cramps, and having formerly been poisoned with verdigris, I know the symptoms and hold to my opinion. What with the poisoning and the political stir, I have led an agitated life. I have been divided between the desire that M. Fould should remain in the Ministry, in the interest of our master, and the wish that he should resign for the sake of his own dignity and personal advantage. It has ended by concessions which have benefited no one, while, in my opinion, they have lowered the *dramatis personæ.* The joke of the matter is that Persigny, whom the non-papist Ministers cannot endure, has become their standard-bearer, and that he shall continue in office they have made the condition on which they retain their portfolios. So, Thouvenel, an intelligent, very good fellow, has been dismissed, while Persigny, who is crazy and understands nothing of business, remains. Here we are then, in the clutches of the clergy, and you know where they lead their friends.

I am now reading a book that may entertain you: the history of the "Revolt of the Netherlands," by Motley. There are not less than five thick volumes; but although not over and above well written, it is smooth in style and interesting. He yields too much to anti-Catholic and anti-Monarchical prejudice, but he has made immense researches, and though an American, is a man of talent.

I am suffering with my lungs. You will learn some day that I have ceased to breathe for want of this organ, which should induce you to be very amiable to me before this misfortune shall occur.

CANNES, *January*, 1863. — I have received the last novel by M. Gustave Flaubert, the author of "Madame Bovary," which I believe you have read, though you will not confess it. The new romance is "Salammbo," a crazy production; but the writer has talent which he fritters away under the pretext of realism. One obtains an amusing idea of the author, and a still more ludicrous one of his admirers, the ***bourgeois***, who discuss such things with decent people. I recommend you to read a romance by M. de Tourguenieff, the proofs of which I am expecting for the "Revue des Deux Mondes," and which I have read in Russian. It is called "Les Pères et les Enfants." It offers a contrast between the passing and coming generation. The hero, the representative of the new generation, is a socialist, materialist, and realist, nevertheless a sensible and interesting man. This novel has produced a great sensation in Russia, and a great outcry against the writer, who is accused of immorality and impiety. When a work excites such public exasperation, it is, in my opinion, a signal proof of success.

Before leaving Paris I consulted an eminent physician, wishing to ascertain how long a time would be allowed to prepare for my funeral ceremonies. I was satisfied with the consultation, first, because the ceremony would not take place so soon as apprehended; secondly, because he explained clearly and anatomically the seat of my malady — not the heart, but the lungs. True, I can never be cured, but there are alleviations for my suffering. I have been in bed a week from an attack of spasms and suffocation, having contracted a painful lumbago, the effect of this fine climate, where, so long as the sun remains above the horizon one may fancy it to be summer; but as soon as it disappears we have a quarter of an hour of damp cold that penetrates to one's very marrow.

It appears that they are becoming more and more religious in Paris. I receive sermons from people from whom I should have expected something quite different. I am told that M. de Persigny has shown himself ultra papist on the Senate's committee of address. I do not believe that there was ever a period when the world was more senseless (*bête*) than now. Last as long as it may, the end is ominous.

Paris, *April*, 1863. — Of all the Italian cities, Florence appears to me to have best preserved her characteristics of the Middle Ages. As to Rome let me give you two bits of advice: first, never to be a moment in the air at night-fall, for fear of the Roman fever; but a quarter of an hour before the Angelus go to St. Peter's and wait until the strange, damp precipitate in the air shall pass by. There is nothing finer for meditation than this great church at that hour, the indistinctness of its vast proportions makes it truly sublime. Think of me when there. My second recommendation is to employ a rainy day in seeing the Catacombs. When there, turn into one of the narrow corridors debouching from the subterranean streets, extinguish your taper and remain alone for a few moments. You will tell me your sensations. I should have great pleasure in the experience with you, but perhaps our sensations would not be the same. I never succeeded in Rome in carrying out my programme of sight-seeing, for at each street corner one is drawn off by something unforeseen, and the great charm is to yield to impulse. As regards objects of art, study the frescoes, and the views as to nature and art combined. At the Capitol make them show you the wolf of the Republic, which bears trace of the thunderbolt that struck it in the time of Cicero. It is not a thing of yesterday. Try to understand that you cannot see the hundredth part of all that is interesting, and do not regret it; there will remain one great, harmonious memory worth more than a crowd of souvenirs in detail. Do not forget to see Pompey's statue, at the foot of which Cæsar was assassinated. Rome is pervaded with a gentle, agreeable melancholy which one recalls with pleasure; for a vivid comparison with which it would be well to pass a week at Naples. Of all transitions it is the most abrupt and amusing; it is comedy succeeding tragedy; and sends one to bed the mind filled with ludicrous images.

I do not know whether the *cuisine* has made any progress in the States of the Holy Father, but in my time it was the "abomination of desolation," while in Naples it was possible to subsist.

Society here is astir with the actual or reputed eccentricities of Madame de ———. Certain it is that she is crazy enough to be placed under restraint. She beats her servants, cuffs, boxes the ears, and makes love to her favorites in the same breath. She carries her Anglo-mania so far as to drink brandy and water, that is to say, much of the former with little of the latter. The other evening she presented one of her friends to M. Troplong, saying: "*Monsieur le President*, I bring you my *darling*." To which M. Troplong politely replies, that he is happy to make the acquaintance of M. Darling. If all that is told me of the manners of the *lionnes* be true, it is to be feared that the end of the world is near. I dare not tell you all that takes place in Paris among the young representatives of the generation that is to bury us.

CHÂTEAU DE FONTAINEBLEAU, *July*, 1863. — No one has time here for anything, and the days pass one knows not how. The chief occupation is eating, drinking, sleeping: I succeed in the first two, in the last very badly, after passing several hours in knee-breeches, in rowing on the lake and getting a frightful cough. There are many well assorted guests here, fewer officials than usual, which does not, however, detract from the prevailing *entente cordiale*. Sometimes we walk in the woods, after having picnicked on the grass like tradesmen from the Rue St. Denis.

Two days ago some very large chests arrived from his Majesty Tu-Duc, Emperor of Cochin China. They were opened in one of the court-yards. Within the large cases were smaller ones painted in red and gold, containing two very yellow elephant's teeth, two rhinoceros' horns, and a package of mouldy cinnamon, the whole exhaling inconceivable odors. There was also a large quantity of narrow gauze-like stuffs, of every ugly color, more or less soiled, and all musty. Medals, that were among the expected gifts, were absent, and probably remained in Cochin China; from which it appears that the great Tu-Duc is a swindler. Yesterday we attended the manœuvres of two regiments of cavalry, and were all cooked by the heat; all the ladies had a sun-stroke. To-day we are to have a Spanish dinner in the Forest, and I am intrusted with the *gaspacho*, that is to say, imposing raw onions on the ladies, who would swoon at the mere mention of the vegetable. I have forbidden that they be warned, and after they have eaten it, I shall make my confession to them in the style of Atreus.

LONDON, *August*, 1863.—I expected to find London empty, and in fact such was my first impression; but at the end of two days I discovered the great ant-hill to be still swarming, and, alas! that they dined quite as often and as interminably as last year. Is not the slowness of the dinners inhuman in this country! It really deprives me of appetite. We are never less than two hours and a half at table, and if the half hour during which the men leave the women to speak ill of them be added, it is always eleven o'clock when we return to the drawing-room. This would be but a demi-evil could one eat all the time; but, with the exception of the roast mutton, I find nothing to my taste.

The great men seem to me to have grown somewhat old since my last visit. Lord Palmerston has given up his false teeth, which changes him very much; but has preserved his whiskers, and has the air of a gay gorilla. Lord Russell looks less good-humored. The great beauties of the season have left town, but they are not very enthusiastically lauded. The toilettes, as usual, struck me as very inferior and crumpled; but nothing can resist this climate, of which my throat is also a proof. I am hoarse as a wolf, and suffer from suffocation. On my return to Paris, Panizzi will join me, and we are to be carried off to Biarritz by my gracious Sovereign Lady, who will lodge us for some time on the sea-shore.

Have you read Renan's "Life of Jesus?" It is the stroke of an axe to the edifice of Catholicism. The Bishop of Tulle has issued an order that all the nuns of his diocese shall recite *Aves* in M. Renan's honor, or rather to hinder the devil from flying off with everybody because of this same Renan's book. The author is so frightened at his own audacity in denying the Divinity, that he loses himself in hymns of admiration and adoration, to the disparagement of the philosophical intelligence by which alone the doctrine is to be judged.

CHÂTEAU DE COMPIÈGNE, *November*, 1863. — Since my arrival here I have led the perturbed life of a manager, having been author, actor, and director. We have played with success a rather immoral piece, of which I will tell you the story on my return. We have had very fine fireworks, though a woman who examined the fusees too closely was killed outright. You do not tell me what has become of the charming child in whom you are interested. Train her, I beg of you, so that she be not a fool like the majority of women of the present day. If those in the Provinces are worse than in Paris, I do not know in what desert we shall seek refuge. We have here a fine slip of a girl, five feet four inches tall, with the pretty ways of a grisette, and a mixture of ease and honest timidity sometimes very amusing. Some fear was entertained lest the second part of a charade should not correspond with the beginning — (a beginning of which I was the author): "It will go off very well," said she: "We shall show our legs in the ballet, and that will make up for all." — N. B. Her legs are like flageolets and her feet are far from aristocratic.

CANNES, *January*, 1864. — I am charmed that Aristophanes is so fortunate as to please you. There are doubtless many things that shock your prudery, but which will interest you now that you have learned from Cicero something of ancient morals. You ask if the Athenian ladies attended the theatre. Learned men are divided in opinion on this point. It is probable that tolerance and intolerance prevailed at different periods in the same country, but it is certain that women never appeared on the stage, their *rôles* being enacted by men, which was the more easy from the custom of wearing masks during the performance. In Algeria you would have found, doubtless, women at the play. In the East, they have not now, and never had in ancient times, the prudery that prevails with women at the present day. An extraordinary point about Aristophanes is the unrestrained way in which he speaks of the gods, even on the occasion of their festival, for it was at the Dionysia that "The Frogs" was represented, in which

Bacchus plays so singular a part. The same thing took place in the first ages of Christianity. Comedies were played in church. There was the mass "des sots," and the mass "de l'Ane," the text of which still remains in a very curious manuscript. Apart from the nonsense that Aristophanes threw into his comedies as a seasoning of coarse salt, there are choruses of the finest poetry. My venerated master, M. Boissonade, was of opinion that no Greek had surpassed them. I recommend you to read "The Clouds," the masterpiece of Aristophanes. There is in it a dialogue between the Just and the Unjust, of the most elevated style. I think there is truth in his reproaches against Socrates ; even after listening to him in Plato, one is tempted to forgive the hemlock. A man is a pest who, like Socrates, proves every one to be only a fool.

PARIS, *April*, 1864. — I rarely go into society, but I wished to pay my respects to my masters, whom I found in excellent health ; which gave me also an opportunity of seeing the new fashions, which I admire but indifferently. It is a sign of old age. I cannot become accustomed to the mode of dressing the hair. Not a woman adopts the style suited to her own face ; but all model themselves after the barber's blocks. One of my friends presented me to his wife, a young and pretty person, who was whitened, daubed with rouge, and her eyelashes painted. I was horrified.

Have you read About's book, "Le Progrès ?" I do not know if it is successful, but it is very witty. Perhaps the clericals have had the good sense to withhold the excommunication that never fails to insure wide circulation to a work. It was their fulmination that secured Renan great pecuniary profit ; his idyl having brought him one hundred and seven thousand francs. I keep subject to your order Taine's three thick volumes on the history of English Literature. The style is of a somewhat studied elegance, but very pleasant reading.

LONDON, *British Museum*, *July*, 1864. — From eight o'clock in the evening until midnight my life is passed at dinner parties, and the morning in looking at books and statues: or I work at my great article on the son of Peter the Great, which I am strongly inclined to entitle, "The Danger of being a Fool;" for the moral drawn from the work is that intellect is a necessity. You may find here and there something to interest you; notably, how Peter the Great — a detestable man and surrounded by detestable *canaille* — was deceived by his wife. I have carefully, and with some difficulty, translated his wife's love letters to her lover, who was impaled for his pains. These letters are really better than could be expected from the age and the country in which they were written; but love works wonders. The misfortune is that she knows nothing of orthography, thereby rendering her meaning somewhat obscure to a grammarian like myself.

Nothing is talked of here but the marriage of Lady Florence Paget, the beauty of London, the last two seasons. It would be impossible to find a prettier face on a more delicate figure, too slight and small for my special taste. She was noted for her flirtations. Mr. Ellice's nephew, Mr. Chaplin, of whom you have often heard me speak, a tall young fellow of twenty-five, and with twenty-five thousand pounds per annum, fell in love with her. She trifled with him a long time, finally became engaged to him, and, it is said, accepted from him jewels and six thousand pounds with which to pay her mantua-maker's bills. The wedding day was arranged, and last Friday they went together to the park and the opera. On Saturday morning she left home alone, and proceeding to St. George's Church was married to Lord Hastings, a young man of her own age, very ugly, and possessed of a slight fault — a passion for cards and wine. After the ceremony they started for the country, and at the first station she wrote to her father, the Marquis of Anglesey: "Dear Papa — As I knew you would never consent to my marriage with Lord Hastings, I was wedded to him to-day. I remain yours, etc." She also wrote to Mr. Chaplin: "Dear Harry — When you receive this I shall be the wife of Lord Hastings. Forget yours, very truly, Florence." Poor Mr. Chaplin, who is six feet high and has yellow hair, is in despair.

MADRID, *October*, 1864. — It is terribly cold and damp, and every one is ill, the bad weather having come upon us with excessive violence, according to the custom of this country, where gentle transitions, of whatsoever nature, are unknown. Imagine the misery of people who live on an elevated plateau exposed to every wind of heaven, their only stove being a *brasero*, a very primitive contrivance, giving one the choice of being frozen or asphyxiated. Civilization has made great progress here, but without a corresponding improvement. The women have adopted your absurd hats and wear them in the most uncouth fashion. The bulls are worthless, and the men who kill them are stupid and cowardly.

CANNES, *January*, 1865. — What do you think of the Pope's encyclical? I delight in reading the letters from the Bishops. There is a Bishop here, a man of wit and good sense, who veils his face. There are few attorneys more subtle than these gentlemen; but the most ingenious is M. D——, who makes the Pope say precisely the contrary of his encyclical and he may possibly be excommunicated at Rome. It is vexatious to serve in an army the General of which exposes one to defeat. Do they hope at Rome that the Marches, the Legations and the County of Avignon will be restored to them by a miracle? The misfortune is, that the world is so stupid that to escape the Jesuits it may be necessary to throw ourselves into the arms of mere blusterers.

The number of English here becomes more alarming every day. A hotel as large as that of the Louvre has been built on the sea-shore, which is always filled with these Islanders. One can no longer walk without meeting young Misses in Garibaldi *caracos* and hats with impossible feathers, making a pretense of sketching. There are croquet and archery parties of a hundred and twenty persons. I regret the good old times when one never met a soul.

Do you know that I received compliments from every quarter on my appointment as successor to M. Mocquard? I believed nothing of it, but by dint of seeing my name in the newspapers of various countries I began to be uneasy. With my disposition you may believe how well the position and I should agree!

Imagine my reading Lamartine's "Entretiens," in which I fell on a life of Aristotle, wherein he states that the retreat of the ten thousand took place after the death of Alexander. Would it not really be better worth while to sell steel pens at the gate of the Tuileries than to utter such enormities?

CANNES, *April*, 1865. — Your friend Paradol is Academician through the will of the burgraves, who for this purpose obliged the poor Duc de Broglie to return to Paris in spite of his gout and eighty years. It will be a curious sitting. Ampère once wrote a very bad history of Cæsar, and you may imagine all the allusions that M. Paradol will take occasion to make to this work, now forgotten by every one save the burgraves. Jules Janin remains outside of the door, as also my friend Autran from Marseilles, who, assuming the clerical, was abandoned by his religious friends.

You have heard, perhaps, that Mr. William Brougham, brother of Lord Brougham, and his successor in the peerage, has been caught in the fact in a very ugly matter of cheating. It causes great scandal here among the English colony. Old Lord Brougham puts a good face on it, and is, of course, a perfect stranger to all such villainy.

To teach myself patience, and to woo sleep, I am reading a book by Mr. Charles Lambert, who demolishes holy King David and the Bible. I find it very ingenious and rather amusing. Serious and pedantic books at which ten years ago no one would have dreamed of glancing, have now, thanks to the clergy, become popular and widely read. Renan has gone to Palestine to make new studies of landscape; Peyrat and this Charles Lambert are writing books still more serious and learned which sell like bread, my bookseller tells me.

LONDON, *British Museum*, *August*, 1865. — I have been here about six weeks, catching a few days of "the season," and have undergone some terrible dinners and two or three of the last routs. Lord Palmerston strikes me as having grown singularly old, notwithstanding the success of his elections, and it seems to me more than doubtful if he be equal to the approaching campaign. His retirement will insure a fine crisis. I have just passed three days with his probable successor, Mr. Gladstone, who did not amuse, but interested me, for I still find great pleasure in observing varieties of human nature, and here they are so different from our own as to excite an inexplicable wonder that within ten hours' distance bipeds without feathers should so little resemble those of Paris. In some respects Mr. Gladstone appears to me a man of genius, in others a child. There is in him something of the child, the statesman, and the *fou.* Five or six deans were at his house, and every morning the guests regaled themselves with a little prayer in common. I did not attend that of Sunday which must be something very curious. What surpassed everything was a sort of half-cooked roll that is taken hot from the oven for breakfast, the digestion of which gives one infinite trouble the rest of the day. In addition to this we had hard *civrn*, that is to say Welsh ale, which is very celebrated. You doubtless know that only red hair is worn. Nothing could be easier in this country, and I am quite sure it is not dyed. Not a single horse is to be seen in Rotten Row ; but I rather like a great city in this state of semi-death. I profit by it to see the lions. Yesterday I passed an hour at the Crystal Palace watching a chimpanzee nearly as large as a child ten years old, and whom it so strongly resembled in its actions as to humiliate me by the incontestable relationship. I begin to tire of London, and thought for a moment of going to Scotland, but I should have fallen among sportsmen, a race I abhor.

PARIS, *September*, 1865. — I passed through Boulogne, which has improved both as to houses and inhabitants. I saw many fishwomen prettily dressed ; but what Englishwomen, and what *pork pie* hats ! These ladies should be warned that when lining the quay they make a great exhibition of their garters to steamer passengers coming in when the tide is low.

I am not dissatisfied with my article on "The History of Julius Cæsar." As the task was imposed on me, submission was unavoidable. You know how very highly I think both of the author and his book, and you also appreciate the difficulties besetting the critic who would deprecate the imputation of sycophancy and yet say nothing unbecoming, I have extricated myself pretty well, I hope. My text is, that the Republic had served its purpose, and that the Roman people were going headlong to the deuce when Cæsar stepped forth to save them. The thesis is true and easy to maintain, and I have merely written variations on that air.

I went yesterday to see Princess Murat, who has nearly recovered from her terrible accident, which she describes very graphically. She saw her coachman, a Swiss colonel, thrown high into the air, and four hours afterwards she found herself in bed, with her head the size of a pumpkin. During this interval she walked and talked, but she retains not the slightest remembrance of what passed from the moment of her fall. I hope, and it is probable, that in the moments preceding death there is also a loss of consciousness. I found Madame de Montijo recovering from the effect of her two operations. She extols highly her oculist Liebreich, who appears to be a great man.

PARIS, *October*, 1865.— Their Majesties have brought me back in a good state of preservation from Biarritz, where I passed my time as delightfully as possible. We had a visit from the King and Queen of Portugal. He is a timid German student; the Queen is charming, resembling the Princess Clotilde, but *en beau;* an improved edition. Her complexion is of that pure red and white, rare even in England; true, her hair is red, but of the very deep shade, now the fashion, and she is very affable and engaging in manner. They had with them a certain number of male and female caricatures, who were apparently collected for the occasion from some *rococo* shop. My good friend the Portuguese Minister led the Queen aside and made some complimentary remarks about me, which Her Majesty immediately repeated to me with much grace. The Emperor presented me to the King, who shook hands and looked at me with two great, round, astonished eyes that nearly made me fail in proper salutation to His Majesty. Another personage, M. de Bismarck, pleased me much more. He is a tall German, very polite and far from *naïf*. He is apparently utterly destitute of soul (*gemüth*), but all mind. He made a conquest of me. He brought with him a wife with the largest feet beyond the Rhine, and a daughter who walks in her mother's footsteps.

The Legitimists are in a nice state of uncertainty since the death of General Lamoricière ; and to-day I met an Orleanist of the old school who was equally disconsolate. How little it requires to be a great man now !

You cannot imagine the gossip caused by Princess Anna's marriage, nor the anger and comic rage of the Faubourg Saint-Germain. There was not a family having an unmarried daughter, who did not cherish designs against the Duke de Mouchy. The great question now agitating them is : "If they make visits shall we send them our cards ?" On the other hand there is now in Paris a young lady with several millions in her pocket, and some fifty more in expectancy. She is a very pretty and rather mysterious person, the adopted daughter of M. Heine, who died this year, and her origin is an enigma ; but on the strength of her millions the finest names of France, Germany, and Italy are ready for every absurdity. These adopted children are favorites of the goddess Fortune. The Greeks call them "children of the soul" — is it not pretty ? Have you read Victor Hugo's "Chansons des rues et des bois ?" Can you tell me if you perceive a difference between his former verses and those of to-day ? Has he suddenly become insane (*fou*), or has he always been so ? I incline to the latter view. We have only one man of genius remaining : M. Ponson du Terrail. Have you read his *feuilletons ?* No one else writes of crime and assassination with such skill as he exhibits. I quite revel in it. Were you here I should try to shake your orthodoxy in making you read a rather curious book on Moses, David, and St. Paul; not idyls after Renan, but dissertations somewhat too much interlarded with Greek, and even Hebrew. It is well worth reading, however, though the story of the Yankee, who, wishing to make a novel, makes a religion, and a flourishing religion, is only a stale invention.

CANNES, *January*, 1866.— How does it happen that with your taste for travelling, and having, moreover, the care of souls, you do not pass your winters at Pisa, or some other place where the great arbiter of human health is visible, Monsigneur the Sun? I am confident that but for him I should long since have been several feet under ground. All of my contemporaries are hastening to precede me. The past year has been severe upon a little circle of comrades who for several years have dined together once a month, and of which I am the sole survivor. This is the grave reproach that I address to the Great Mechanician — why do not men fall together, like the leaves of a season? Your Father Hyacinthe would not fail to utter some nonsense in reply: "O man, what are ten years, a century!" etc. What is eternity to me? The few days comprised in my span of life are of more importance to me. Why are they made so bitter?

You tell me nothing of Ponsard's piece, "Le Lion Amoureux." He has preserved the tradition of Corneille's verse rather emphatic, but grand, sonorous, and chaste. I imagine that people of society admire it as they admire M. Babinet's science, or the sermons of Abbé Lacordaire, the moment they were persuaded that it was genteel.

SAINT-CLOUD, *August*, 1866.— The Emperor has quite recovered from his illness, and has resumed his usual mode of life. It appears to me that everything tends to peace. It is very evident that M. de Bismarck is a great man, and so well prepared that it would be unwise to provoke his hostility

We shall have to swallow a few mortifications perhaps, and we shall continue to digest them until we are provided with needle-guns. It remains to be seen what the German parliament will do, and whether their advantages may not be lost by a few stupidities.

You asked me whence I derived my knowledge of the gypsy dialect: from M. Borrow, whose book is one of the most curious that I ever read. What he relates of the gypsies is perfectly true, and his personal observations agree perfectly with my own, except on one point. In his character of clergyman he was naturally deceived in matters respecting which I, as a Frenchman and *laic*, have a clearer insight from personal experience. It is exceedingly singular, however, that this man, gifted in languages to the extent of speaking the Cali dialect, should possess so little grammatical perspicacity as not to see at a glance that many words unknown in Spanish have remained in this dialect. He asserts that only the roots of Sanskrit words have been preserved.

BIARRITZ, *September*, 1866. — Four days of the week we have rain, the remainder being suffocatingly warm, accompanied by a horrible sirocco; but the sea is much finer here than at Boulogne, and figs and ortolans aid us in sustaining the burden of life. The other day we made a charming mountain excursion to see two famous grottoes on the Spanish border, in one of which we found twenty contrabandists, who sang Basque choruses, accompanied by a little sharp flageolet that has a very wild and agreeable effect. The music is full of character, but sad, like all music of mountaineers. As to the words, I only understood "*Viva Emperatriça.*" Our guide was a singular man, who had made a large fortune by smuggling. He is the king of these mountains; every one obeys his orders. While we followed the open paths with difficulty, it was fine to see him galloping among the rocks, clearing all obstacles, calling to his men in French, Spanish, and Basque; never making a false step. The Empress commissioned him to watch over the Prince Imperial, whom, on his pony, he led through almost impassable roads, having as much care of him as of a bale of contraband merchandise. We stopped an hour at his house at San, where we were received by his daughters, who are well educated, well dressed and not at all provincial, differing only from Parisians in the pronunciation of *r*, which with the Basques is always *r-r-r-h.*

PARIS, 1866. — While at Biarritz a discussion arose one day as to the perplexing situations in which one might be placed, as for example, Rodrigo between his papa and Chimene, or Mademoiselle Camille between her brother and her Curatius. The same night, having taken some over strong tea, I wrote fifteen pages, depicting a situation of this kind. The story is perfectly moral *au fond*, but there are details of which Monseigneur Dupanloup might disapprove. It is not, I think, the worst thing I ever wrote, although written very hastily. I read it to the lady of the house (the Empress). There was then at Biarritz the Grand Duchess Marie, daughter of Nicholas, to whom I had been presented some years previously. Shortly after the reading I was visited by a policeman, announcing himself sent by the Grand Duchess. "What is your pleasure?" "I come on the part of her Imperial Highness to beg you to wait on her this evening with your romance." "What romance?" "That which you read the other day to Her Majesty." I replied that I was Her Majesty's jester, and that I could not work elsewhere without her leave; and straightway I hurried to tell the Empress what had passed. I expected that it would at least result in a war with Russia, and was not a little mortified at being not only authorized, but entreated to go in the evening to the Grand Duchess, to whom the policeman had been assigned as a factotum. Nevertheless, to console myself I wrote a letter to the Grand Duchess in rather strong terms, and announced my visit to her. On the way with the letter to her hotel, I met in a little side-street a woman, who, the wind being high, was in danger of being blown into the sea, her petticoats having been caught up by the wind, and who, blind and giddy with the noise of the crinoline, and the dread of the possible consequences, was quite overwhelmed with embarrassment. I ran to her assistance, had much difficulty in aiding her effectually, and then only did I recognize the Grand Duchess. The gust of wind spared her some little epigrams. Besides, she showed herself a very good Princess to me, and gave me excellent tea and cigarettes; for, like almost all the Russian ladies, she smokes. Her son, the Duke of Leuchtenberg, is a very fine fellow, with a good air, is amiable, reads Schopenhauer, holds to the positive philosophy, is a little of a Republican and Socialist, and a nihilist into the bargain, like Tourguenieff's Bazarof; for princes in the present age do not think that the Republic progresses with sufficient rapidity.

July, 1867.—I have not been dazzled by the Exposition. I saw some fine Chinese objects too dear for my purse. Some Russian carpets, already sold. You appear enchanted with the bazaar, and if you will some morning be my guide there, your enthusiasm may awaken mine. The Japanese pleased me very much. Their skin, the color of *café-au-lait*, is of an agreeable tint; but as well as I could judge from the folds of their robes, their limbs are as small as the slats of chairs, which is a pity. As I noted the crowd of loungers surrounding them, I could but think that Europeans would have less self-possession in presence of a Japanese public. Imagine yourself, *you*, being exhibited at Yeddo, and a grocer saying: "I should like to know if the hump this lady wears beneath her dress is really a part of herself!" Come soon and give me your opinion about the Sultan and the Princes who had the privilege of looking at you for three hours. Would it not have been better to bring me the bouquet yourself? You pained me by sending it.

I fear that this shooting of Maximilian will ruin our affairs, which were proceeding satisfactorily. It is a sad pity.

The Pacha of Egypt has made two visits to Mademoiselle ——, which I dare not relate to you, although they were very curious. He has been reconciled to his cousin Mustapha, but they have not yet been induced to take coffee together, each one being persuaded, in view of the progress in chemistry, that it would be dangerous.

Something beautiful was lately brought to me ; a shield with *fleur-de-lis*, setting a miniature portrait of Marie Antoinette, probably made at Vienna before her marriage, and given to the Princess de Lamballe. The back had contained hair, now lost. After some resistance I allowed myself to be conquered, and purchasing it sent it at once to Her Majesty who is making a collection of everything that ever belonged to Marie Antoinette. It will certainly be one of the prettiest souvenirs, is undoubtedly authentic, and was long worn by Madame de Lamballe. For myself I have a horror of these sad antiquities, but one cannot dispute tastes.

PARIS, *October*, 1867.—You speak, dear friend, of a vegetable life, which in truth one would prefer to lead in this age ; but the world moves, and human vegetables are as unfortunate as those who live at the foot of Etna ; from time to time a stream of fire descends on them, and nearly always they are enshrouded by sulphurous vapor. Is it not deplorable that Pius IX. and Garibaldi, two fanatics, should throw everything into disorder through their obstinacy ? One thing that demonstrates the morals of the present day, is, that the persons who blame the sending of our troops to Rome, say, when reminded of the treaty of September : "What matters a treaty ? M. de Bismarck does not adhere to them !" I am inclined to steal their watch and tell them that precedents for stealing watches may be found. The most distressing point in all this is, that we have renewed our pledge, for how long a time I do not know, to protect the Pope, who does not feel the slightest gratitude. All that is said for and against the temporal power is so silly, so absurd, that I blush for my century. Another subject that makes me furious is the project for the reorganization of the army. All the well-born young men are dying with fright at the notion of fighting for their country at any given moment, and say that this vulgar method must be left to the

Prussians. Imagine for a moment what will remain to the French nation should she lose her military courage!

I am still suffering, breathing with difficulty, and on the eve of breathing no longer. M. Fould's sudden death has grieved me very much; it was the serenest that could be wished; but why so quick? He wrote eighteen letters the morning of his death, and had previously seemed perfectly well. He had apparently not moved in bed, and no contraction of his features was observable. It is just such a death as was that of Mr. Ellice, and is what the English call "visitation of God."

CANNES, *December*, 1867. — I am uncertain how long I may be able to remain here; it depends on the Pope, Garibaldi, and M. de Bismarck; I, like the rest of the world, being somewhat in the hands of these gentlemen. I am really alarmed by the political situation, and in the general tone of the press and public speakers find a reminder of 1848 — strange and angry agitation without apparent cause. The nerves of all are on the stretch. M. Thiers, after passing his entire life in political conflict, is seized with nervous trembling because a Marseilles lawyer utters platitudes that only deserve to be smiled at. Most vexatious of all is this M. Rouher, who wishes to out-Herod Herod, and uses expressions the reverse of politic, from which every Minister should abstain.

I know of nothing more shameful than Garibaldi's conduct; if ever a man was under obligation to kill himself, assuredly it was he. To go off to Caprera after causing the death of some hundreds of simpletons, appears to me the height of disgrace for the revolutionists and the English noblemen who thought this animal something other than a dancing jack. It is annoying, also, that the Pope is thoroughly convinced that he owes nothing to us, and that it is Heaven that has done all for love of his *beaux yeux*.

What shall I say to you of the policy of M. Ollivier and *tutti quanti?* In vain do they turn elegant phrases and affirm that they are thoroughly satisfied; they seem to me merely second-rate actors, who play the first *rôles* in a manner that can deceive nobody. We are daily becoming smaller. The only truly great man is M. de Bismarck.

A propos; might it be true that he spent the secret-service money? I consider the purchase of the journals very probable; but as M. de Bismarck will not send his receipts to M. de Kerveguen, I suppose that these gentlemen will come off with honor.

CANNES, *February*, 1868.—I am sometimes the greater part of the day unable to breathe; not a sharp pain but a teasing discomfort that acts on the nerves. I am more and more melancholy, and yield to gloomy forebodings. I do not succeed in accustoming myself to suffer, and am irritated by it, which only adds to the evil. I am reading an over-long and badly written book, the author of which, however, appears to be honest, and relates what he has seen and heard: it is Dixon's "New America." His reflections must be passed by, for he is somewhat silly. He saw the Mormons, and what is even more curious, the republic of Mount Lebanon; that and Fenianism give an idea of America which Talleyrand's *mot* defines precisely.

I am delighted that my article on Pouchkine should not have wearied you. I have not the works with me, and the verses quoted are those that I learned by heart during the time of my great Russian enthusiasm. There are many Russians here, and I commissioned a friend to procure me the volume of Pouchkine's detached poems if it could be found in the Muscovite colony here. He made inquiry of a very pretty woman, who, in place of the verses, sent me a huge bit of fish from the Volga, and two birds from the same region, all cooked within a few metres of the North pole. They were pretty good. The fish must be a fine fellow of some five or six feet, to judge from my specimen slice. This lady, Madame Voronine, has a charming head, her husband the unmistakable look of a Calmack. The lady at first refused him her hand. He put a pistol to his head, missed fire, and for his pains she married him. As for the Englishmen and Englishwomen, never has there been so great a number with impossible hair and toilettes, red stockings, parasols, and paletots lined with grebe skin. Among other extraordinary Englishmen there is the Duke of Buccleugh, who has a horn in the middle of his forehead, and his son inherits the peculiarity. It projects from the skull, and will end I fear in playing them an ill turn.

The discussion on the press disgusts me. Every one lies too much, and not an idea is suggested that has not already been twenty times expressed in better terms. It strikes me that the level of intelligence is greatly lowered, as well as that of honesty. It is all very sad. I saw yesterday a friend just returned from Montana, who tells me that the Garibaldians were well whipped, and that they were a singular mixture of vile rabble and the flower of aristocracy.

MONTPELLIER, *April*, 1868. — Dear friend, I suffered so intensely before coming here as to lose all courage ; it was impossible to think, still more so to write. Chance brought to my knowledge a physician of this place who treats asthma by a new method, and since my trial of it during the last five days, my condition seems to be ameliorated, and the physician gives me hope. Every morning I am placed in a great iron cylinder that resembles, I confess, one of the monuments erected by M. de Rambuteau. There is an arm-chair within, and glazed apertures give sufficient light by which to read. The door is closed, the air of the cylinder is compressed by means of a steam-engine, producing the sensation of needles penetrating the ear, to which one becomes accustomed after a few seconds, and what is of more importance, one begins to breathe with wonderful ease. At the end of half an hour I fell asleep. The physician, who has nothing of the charlatan about him, thinks my case by no means desperate.

Have you read Abbé Dupanloup's letter ? The soul of Torquemada has entered his body, and he will burn us all if we do not take care. I fear that the Senate will do, and say everything calculated to make itself ridiculous and odious. You would not believe what terror these old generals, who have already passed through so many perilous adventures, now have of the devil. I do not know whether Sainte-Beuve is in a condition to speak, as the journals state; I doubt it, and moreover am by no means certain if he would deal with the question in the best way; I mean to ward off this bombshell. His duty is to speak his mind boldly, regardless of consequences, as he did on the subject of Renan's book. All this irritates and torments me.

Château de Fontainebleau, *August*, 1868. — I have been here a fortnight finding idleness to be a good thing for body and soul. The trees and sky are a perpetual delight. There are not more than thirty persons at the château, the only ones not in waiting, besides myself, being some amiable cousins of the Empress; gentlemen and ladies whom I knew at Madrid. I have made a copy of a portrait of Diana of Poitiers after Primatice; she is represented as Diana with her quiver, and she undoubtedly sat for the picture. as from the head to the feet it is evidently a likeness. Moreover, if I may dare to say it, the examination of the legs proves that she gartered below the knee according to the fashion of the time, which is now abandoned, as I hear. I will show it to you, as it is a portrait of historical importance.

I dined yesterday with Sainte-Beuve who interested me exceedingly. Although he still suffers he has charming wit, and is assuredly one of the most agreeable talkers whom I have ever conversed with. He is greatly alarmed by the progress of the clericals, and takes the matter to heart. I believe that the danger does not lie on that side.

So poor Rossini is dead. His friends say that he continued to work, although not wishing to publish the result of his labor; but that appears to me highly improbable; for the immense value that he placed on money would have induced him to publish. He was one of the most *spirituel* men I have ever known, and nothing more marvelous has been heard than the song of Figaro, from the "Barber of Seville," as sung by himself. No actor was comparable to him. The past year has been fatal to great men. Lamartine and Berryer are said to be dangerously ill.

CANNES, *February*, 1869. — I am sad and suffering, not the least amendment! On the contrary the doctors have not even succeeded in alleviating the painful spasms that seize me from time to time. We have a magnificent sea and sky, and these influences that formerly restored me to health no longer avail. What must be done? I only know that my desire for the end is unceasing.

I have been reading with much interest "The Memoirs of a Scotch Peasant," who by dint of intelligence and labor became a man of letters, a professor of geology and a person of celebrity. Unfortunately he cut his throat a short time ago, overwork having, without doubt, entirely worn out his brain. His name is Hugh Miller. It seems to me that everything is going to ruin. There is no longer a Spain, soon there will be no Holy See. The loss will be more or less great according to men's ideas.

PARIS, *June*, 1869. — The disturbances that are of nightly occurrence on the Boulevards, and which recall the fine days of 1848, contribute not a little to sadden me, and I exclaim with Hamlet: "Man delights me not, nor woman either." What most afflicts me in these disheartening affairs is the profound stupidity. This nation, who believes and styles itself the most *spirituel* on earth, testifies its desire to enjoy Republican government by demolishing the booths where poor people sell newspapers. It cries "*Vive la Lanterne!*" and it breaks street lamps. It makes one hide one's face. The danger is that there is a sort of emulation for stupidity as for everything else, and between the Chambers and the Government, God only knows what may be done!

I pass my time in deciphering letters of the Duke d'Albe and Philip II., given to me by the Empress. They both wrote like cats. I begin to read Philip quite fluently, but his general still perplexes me. I have just read one from him addressed to his august master, written a few days after the death of Count Egmont, in which he is moved to pity by the fate of the Countess, who has not a morsel of bread after having had a dowry of ten thousand florins. Philip says the simplest things in an involved, long-drawn style ; it is very difficult to guess his meaning, and it seems to be his constant aim to confuse his reader and force him to take the initiative. They were certainly the most odious couple of men who ever existed, and unfortunately neither was hung, which is not to the praise of Providence. I have also received a very curious book from England, in which it is claimed that Jeanne la Folle was not crazy, but a heretic, for which reason mamma, papa, her husband and son came to a clever agreement to keep her in prison, with, from time to time, a little torture.

PARIS, *June*, 1869. — I am reading Renan's "Saint Paul" with difficulty. Decidedly, he has a monomania for landscape ; and instead of keeping to his text he describes the woods and fields. Were I an *Abbé* I should amuse myself by writing a review of it. Have you read the harangue of our Holy Father the Pope ? I am quite sure that we are about to have in words and deeds enormities for which there will not be enough roasted apples. Alas ! things may end in still harder projectiles. What a misfortune that the modern mind should be so vapid ! Do you believe that it was ever before so much so ? Doubtless there have been ages when people were more ignorant, more barbarous, more absurd ; but there were here and there some great geniuses as a compensation ; whilst now, it seems to me, there is a universal depreciation of intellect.

Some one has sent me Baudelaire's works, which have infuriated me. Baudelaire was insane ! He died in the hospital after writing verses that gained him Victor Hugo's esteem, and which had no other merit than that of being prejudicial to morals. Now he is regarded as an unappreciated man of genius !

PARIS, *August*, 1869. — I passed a month at Saint-Cloud in tolerable health, the open air renewing my strength, but on my return was seized with distressing oppression, when my physician from Cannes arrived with a newly discovered remedy of his own that relieved me ; this was eucalyptus pills, the eucalyptus being an Australian tree naturalized at Cannes.

At Saint-Cloud, by command of the Empress, I read "The Bear," now called "Lokis," meaning bear in *jmoude*, before a very select audience, including several young ladies, who appeared to see no harm in it ; this has encouraged me to make a present of it to the "Review," since it causes no scandal. Tell me exactly what you think on the subject, holding the balance even as to the *pour et contre*. The progress in hypocrisy during this age must be taken into consideration. What will your friends say ?

A few days ago I dined with the innocent Isabella, and found her superior to my anticipations. Her husband, who is very small, is a polished gentleman, and paid me many well-turned compliments. The Prince of the Asturias is a very nice lad, with an air of intelligence. He resembles ——, and the infantas of the time of Velasquez.

The Emperor's illness is not serious, but it may be prolonged and there may even be a relapse.

I design writing a life of Cervantes to serve as preface to a new translation of "Don Quixotte." Is it long since you have read it, and does it still amuse you ? I find it entertaining, for which I can give no valid reason ; on the contrary, I could offer many that would prove the book to be bad ; nevertheless, it is excellent.

CANNES, *November*, 1869. — I breakfasted yesterday at Nice with M. Thiers, who is much changed physically since the death of Madame Dosne, but not at all so morally, it seemed to me. His mother-in-law was the soul of his house ; she drew people to his *salon*, and understood how to make it attractive to politicians and others. In short, she was queen of a court composed of very heterogeneous elements, which she had the art of turning to the profit of M. Thiers. Now, solitude has begun for him ; his wife will interest herself about nothing. In politics I found M. Thiers still more changed; he has regained his senses in perceiving how extreme the folly with which the country is possessed, and is ready to combat it again as in 1849. I fear that he deludes himself somewhat as to his strength. It is much easier to burst the bags of Æolus than to mend and make them air-tight. It seems probable that we are coming to a fight; the *chassepot* is omnipotent and can give the populace a historic lesson, as General Changarnier said; but will it be used to good purpose? Personal government has become impossible, and parliamentary government without good faith, without honesty, and without men of sagacity, seems to me no less impossible. In short, the future, and I might say the present, looks very dark to me.

CANNES, *January*, 1870. — To-day I am suffering less, and avail myself of the respite to write to you. I am much discouraged; I have tried every remedy, but the suffering still returns with such intensity as almost to banish sleep. I not only do not eat but have a horror of all nutriment. I can hardly read, and often cannot discern what is before my eyes. Such, dear friend, is my situation. I am certain that it is a slow and very painful death that is approaching. I must make up my mind to it.

Politics, which I no longer understand, offer no agreeable distraction. It appears to me that we are striding towards a worse revolution than the one that we passed through so gayly twenty years ago. I should be glad were the performance a little delayed, that I might not be a spectator.

So you have had a disturbance as stupid as its instigator (Victor Noir). We offer but a sad spectacle in our abuse of liberty and parliamentary government. It is impossible not to be struck with the truly laughable audacity with which, in the Chamber, the most monstrous *spropositi* which no one would venture to enunciate in a drawing-room are presented and supported. This representative *régime* is hardly an amusing comedy; every one in it lies shamelessly, and yet allows himself to be caught by the most plausible speaker. There are even people who believe Cremieux to be eloquent, and Rochefort a great citizen. People were stupid in 1848, but they are infinitely more so now.

CANNES, *May*, 1870. — My health is irretrievably destroyed. I cannot yet accustom myself to this life of suffering and privation; but whether resigned or not I am a doomed man. Wishing to make an experiment and ascertain if I could bear the journey to Paris, I lately went to Nice to pay some visits. I thought for a moment that I should commit the indiscretion of dying at the house of some one with whom I was not sufficiently intimate to take that liberty. I envy some of my friends who have contrived to leave this world suddenly, without suffering and without the tedious warnings that reach me daily. The political commotion of which you speak has also invaded this petty corner of the world. I have seen here very clearly how stupid and ignorant the men are. I am convinced that very few of the electors have understood what they were doing. The Reds, who here are in the majority, have persuaded the imbeciles, still more numerous, that there was a project to impose a new tax. The result is good. (The vote for the plebiscite.) "It is well cut, the question now is to sew it up," as Catherine de Medicis said to Henri III. Unfortunately, I know few persons in this country who are skillful with the needle. What think you of my friend M. Thiers, who, after the history of the banquets of 1848, begins anew the same tactics? It is said that magpies are never caught twice in succession by the same trap; but men, and clever men, are much more easy to ensnare.

PARIS, *July*, 1870. — One must be in vigorous health and possess nerves of exceptional strength not to be affected by the events now crowding about us. There is no need to explain to you all that I feel on this subject. I am of those who believe that this thing could not be avoided (the war with Prussia). The explosion might have been retarded, but to exorcise the animus of it was impossible. Here, the war is more popular than it has ever been, even among the *bourgeois.* They brawl loudly, 't is true, a bad thing; but they enlist and give money, which is the one essential. The military are full of confidence; but when we remember that the whole future is at the mercy of a bullet or a ball, it is difficult to share their trust.

PARIS, *August,* 1870. — It would not be well for you to come to Paris just now. I fear that in a short time only sad scenes would greet you. Only men given up to dejection, and drunkards shouting the Marseillaise are seen. Great disorder everywhere. The army deserves all praise, but it appears that we have no generals. All may yet be retrieved, but for this a miracle must supervene. I am not more ill, only overwhelmed by the situation. I write from the Senate, where we do little save exchange hopes and fears.

PARIS, *August,* 1870. — Affairs seem to assume a somewhat brighter aspect these few days past, yet I see everything *en noir.* The military are sanguine. The soldiers and the *Gardes Mobiles* fight bravely, and it appears that Marshal Bazaine's army has accomplished prodigies although always opposed one to three. Now, to-morrow, to-day perhaps, we may expect another great battle. The late actions have been appalling. The Prussians make war by massing men (*coups d'hommes*), and until now this method has been a success; but it seems that the carnage around Metz was such as to give them food for thought. It is said that the young ladies of Berlin have lost all their waltzers. If we could reconduct them to the frontier, or bury them here, which would be better, even then we should not be at the end of our calamities. This horrible butchery, it is useless to dissemble, is only the prologue to a tragedy of which only the devil knows the *dénoûement.* A nation is not shaken as ours has been with impunity. A revolution must follow, whether we are victorious or defeated. All the blood that has flowed or that shall flow, will inure to the profit of the Republic — that is to say, to organized disorder.

Adieu, dear friend. Remain at P——, where you are safe. We are still quiet here; we await the Prussians with much cool ness, but the devil will not be the loser. Once more — Adieu.

CANNES, *September* 23, 1870.[1] — Dear friend, I am very ill, so ill that writing is a difficult matter. There is a slight improvement. I will write to you soon, I hope, more in detail. Send to my house at Paris for the "Letters of Madame de Sévigné" and "Shakespeare." I ought to have sent them to you before my departure. Adieu. *Je vous embrasse.*

[1] The last letter — written two hours before his death.

TWENTY-FIVE YEARS OF MY LIFE.

BY

ALPHONSE DE LAMARTINE.

TRANSLATED BY LADY HERBERT.

TWENTY-FIVE YEARS OF MY LIFE

BOOK I.

I.

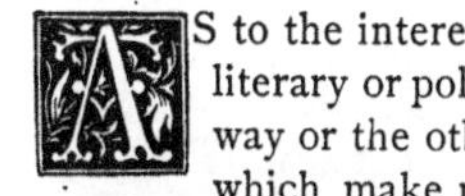

AS to the interest which these memoirs will have in a literary or political sense, I do not exaggerate it one way or the other; but the following are the reasons which make me think I shall at least be forgiven for their publication.

I was born in the very midst of the French Revolution — a time of passion, folly, and fury of parties on all sides. My first recollections are of a father in prison; of a mother a captive on parole in her own house, under a revolutionary guard; of the songs of the "Marseillaise" and the "Ça ira," sung in the streets, and echoing, as it were, the anguish in the bosom of the families around us; of the dull *thuds* which followed the stroke of the guillotine in our public squares; of the march of half-scared troops all day long on the highway. I used to sing myself the songs I heard others sing — poor, little, unintelligent echo that I was of a world into which I had just entered amidst smiles and tears! My poor mother used to look at me sadly enough. One day a change came: the soldiers overpowered the demagogues; the guillotine was swept away, and my own family could breathe freely again. We went to seek a humble shelter among our faithful peasants in the country. Little by little we obtained the kind of security granted to proscribed persons. Year after year my sisters came to brighten the home, which our devoted servants always maintained on the most comfortable footing; and here I grew and throve in the midst of our people.

My mother taught me the existence of that mysterious and Divine Being who is Justice, Power, and what we call Providence. This was to me a great joy: my little mind had been always working; now I had found a key to the problem of life — the only real and true foundation — in a word, I believed, and prayed. My heart opened to these pious influences; the spirit of a man began to develop itself in me; in a word, the child was being matured. Then came my school and college life, when rude hands fashioned me, in sad contrast to the gentle, loving training of my home. I passed through this ordeal, and came out of it transformed but not improved. I was an excitable lad, like a will-o'-the-wisp, with no very fixed ideas, and willing enough to float down the flowery stream of life. The Revolution broke out again, and I looked upon it as solving for me the mystery of the future. I went into the army: I loved the Bourbons, and thought I would die to serve them. But when peace came I was soon sick of a military life. Napoleon returned, and there was an end of my dreams of glory. I accompanied the Bourbon princes to the frontiers of France, but I did not go beyond — I felt that I belonged to my country above all else. Then came the bloody field of Waterloo: the 20th of March was avenged, and the Bourbons were reinstated. I again took my place in their guard, both from a feeling of honor and of fidelity. But I did not remain there long: I could not stand a life of inactivity and of discipline without glory; so I again became a vagabond and a wanderer on the face of the earth. Travelling not only dispels our *ennui*, but interests and fills the heart. I led a life of pleasure and of love for several years; then followed sadness, dissatisfaction, and remorse. I resolved at last to do something, and went into diplomacy, for which I felt I was well qualified. Not long after I married a good and accomplished woman, who brought me back to all virtuous and domestic habits, and I became once more satisfied, calm, and happy.

The Revolution of 1830, which drove the elder branch of the Bourbons into exile, induced me to share their fate, in spite of the wishes of the Orleans princes, whom I was very willing to respect, but whom I could not serve. I started for the East, and for two years diverted my mind by travelling in Turkey, the Archipelago, the Holy Land, Syria, and the Lebanon. I came home. My reputation had grown during my absence. I found myself elected a member of the Senate. I resolved to abstain from party votes or passions, and to devote myself entirely to the good of my country ; thus giving up any chance of promotion or public employment, but preserving my own principles and self-respect. I conquered at last a certain position for myself, but with difficulty. Certain literary successes at this time added slightly to my reputation. After ten years, party strife and passions got the upper hand. The very men who had brought about the Revolution of 1830, and the Government of the Orleanists, turned against their own work. I opposed them vigorously ; but I refused everything save the pleasure of defeating and overthrowing them. I could not bear that my indignation should be attributed to any other feeling than one of right. I repudiated all idea of intrigues and revolutionary banquets. I struggled at one and the same time against the coalition and the royalists of 1830. I had the happiness of being understood by the country and the King, who sent for me and begged me to take office. I refused, though with respectful firmness. I chose to have no *rôle* but that of a volunteer: all for my country, nothing for myself. The crisis became imminent: there were risings in various places ; the Ministers lost their heads ; the coalition disbanded itself ; the King lost his presence of mind ; the people were in a ferment. At last the Revolution, with which I had nothing on earth to do, was declared. I was only mixed up in it during the last few hours, after the flight of the King. I appeared like Fate, to repress, and, if possible, keep it within bounds. It has been said and written that such and such a faction or secret society brought it about. This is not true. I can appeal to the ocular testimony of thousands — not in defence of myself, but to bear witness to the fact that, finding the Revolution inevitable, it was I who organized it; and unless we had been content with utter anarchy, what else was there to be done? I asked it of the whole of France. It was a bold step; but it was a necessary one. The alternative was only a continued and aggravated anarchy. *Felix culpa!* The Republic once proclaimed, I found the means of moderating its action. France behaved admirably. For four months we governed in the midst of the storm, without what one may call a government at all. Afterwards everything was changed. I refused what was offered to me, and returned into obscurity. I had not the vanity to pretend to that to which neither my birth nor my talents entitled me. I bore without complaint fifteen years of unjust reproaches and of continued misfortunes, under which I am now sinking. I worked on courageously, however: I am working still. These events may interest my readers — I write them in good faith. May God be my helper!

II.

I was born at Mâcon, a pretty little town of Lower Burgundy, in 1790. My grandfather was a man of high rank. He was a fine-looking old man, but one who cared for nothing but the pleasures of society. He had served for a long time in the cavalry during his youth — without, however, rising above the rank of captain — which was the custom among the gentry of the provinces in those days. He was very rich. His principal estates were in Burgundy, and in the neighborhood of Mâcon; but he had also property at Péronne, Champagne, Monceau, Milly, and Ursy, near Dijon. In Franche-Comté, which was the home of his wife, he had also a beautiful estate, near St. Claude; the Forest of Fresnoy, of which the wood would now be worth many millions, but of which I witnessed the sale as a boy for about 60,000 francs to an old farmer, out of sheer disgust at having a few leagues to go for its superintendence; also a property at Villars, which he gave to one of my aunts ; that of Amorandes, with the ruins of a fine old castle ; that of Poligny ; and last, not least, the valuable manufactories of Morez, which had been begun and worked by himself. He rarely went to visit his outlying properties. His usual home was the Château of Monceau, near Mâcon, of the origin of which I know nothing, but which I have a good deal enlarged, and which is still in my possession. Monceau was then a fine country-house on the road to Cluny, with imposing looking gardens, terraces, and lawns on the one side, and on the other a quantity of outbuildings and vineyards, with the houses of the vinedressers and laborers, which gave it the stamp of opulence and plenty. In the midst of all my debts and difficulties, I jealously guard this last remains of the fortune of my ancestors, so that I may at least die where my fathers have died. In my grandfather's time there were at Monceau large vineyards, fine houses, extensive silkworm plantations, a pretty theatre, plenty of visitors, and stables full of horses for the owner and his visitors. It was his favorite summer residence. The views on all sides are magnificent. After passing through a long avenue, bordered with rich vineyards, the eye follows the road, which opens into a beautiful and fertile valley, the blue smoke from the shepherds' houses rising here and there among the trees, and adding to the beauty of the view.

After being set at liberty, my grandfather never went back to Monceau. Age and heavy cares induced him to remain with his wife and children in his town-house at Mâcon : everything around him had become sad. In the evening some old friends or relations, and one or two proscribed priests, would steal through the badly-lighted corridors, and take their places almost silently at the whist table ; for the Revolution had not interrupted the nightly rubber. But they played secretly ; and when the game was over, they lighted their little paper lanterns and disappeared through the narrow streets of the old town to their poor lodgings, and went to bed noiselessly, for fear of awakening the suspicions of jealous or ill-disposed neighbors : it was still the reign of terror.

The family party in the Hôtel Lamartine at this time consisted of my grandfather and grandmother, who had borne him six children; the eldest son, a man of great merit and ability, and of studious habits, who had shared his father's imprisonment, although holding himself advanced liberal opinions. But it was a wise, just, and moderate liberality, the natural result of his distinguished education. My grandfather could not endure the new law which had just then come into force, whereby this, his favorite and eldest son would share equally with his other children, instead of inheriting the whole of his property, as in former times. My grandmother, who had been born at Besançon, could not either accustom herself to the idea that he would only have his share, and that the others would "rob" him, as she called it, of that which was his right by birth, thanks to some unheard-of change in the civil code. The second son, the disciple and friend of M. de la Fayette, who had procured him a canonry, with the reversion to a bishopric, had not yet returned from the pontoons of Rochefort, although his release was momentarily expected. The third was my father, the Chevalier de Lamartine, who likewise had only just escaped from prison, and who had been married for two or three years. My grandfather had given him a nice little detached house for his wife and children, which communicated with the family mansion by a long covered passage. Three daughters, all nuns or *chanoinesses* — Mlle. de Lamartine, Mlle. de Villars, and Mlle. de Monceau — turned out of their convents by the Revolution, and obliged to seek a shelter in the home of their childhood, took care of their parents, with a timid and obedient tenderness which was touching to watch. At the top of the house, looking on the garden, was another apartment, occupied by a dear old aunt, the only sister of my grandfather, who was called Mlle. de Luzy. She had been for thirty years Superior of the Ursulines at Mâcon. Driven out of her convent, like all the rest, she had been received with open arms by my grandfather, and lived very happily in her retreat, in spite of her age and infirmities, and was carefully tended by one of her nuns, a sister named Nanette. My nurse used to carry me to her room regularly every day. Even to this hour I have an indelible recollection of these two women, who held a large place in my heart. Goodness is always fascinating to a child: holy faces, whether of children or of old people, have the same charm. It is the beauty and purity of childhood in both cases. Dear aunt Luzy! dear sister Nanette! before I knew what it was to feel, I loved you!

III.

I lived for several months in this way. Then came a day when I was startled by seeing my aunts in tears, and I was told to be very quiet, for my grandmother, who was upwards of eighty, had just died. My grandfather, who was also ill, had me brought and placed upon his bed to give me his last blessing. He had composed some pretty verses on my birth; I found them not long ago, in my mother's writing-table. He was very fond of me and so he kissed me tenderly, and gave me some bonbons. Little as I guessed it, this was our last parting: he died two or three days after. I see him still: he was a magnificent old man, with his high forehead, and soft, long, white hair. He had been one of the handsomest men of his time, when he was in the army, and when in garrison at Lille, under Louis XV., he had been a great favorite with Mlle. Clairon, who had just made her *début*, and was greatly struck by him. I have often seen the remains of his magnificent camp equipage, with its beautiful silver plate and silver warming-pan, and all the luxury of the young noblemen of his day. It was the bivouac of this reign; yet it did not diminish the valor of our troops at Fontenoy. Two of my uncles were killed by the English battery, and the third was knighted and received the Cross of St. Louis.

IV.

My grandfather being dead, the division of his property followed. It was a long and thorny task. The new law, abolishing primogeniture had scarcely been called into existence

The peasants, those sons of the soil, did not understand it; they felt it was contrary to their conscience, and so carried it out as inefficiently as possible. No lawyer could make the father of a family understand that he had not a right to deal as he pleased with his own property; and that by giving his eldest son the largest portion he thereby robbed the younger ones. An abstraction of right, or equality, has little chance of prevailing against nature.

My father was summoned to receive his share, but he never would consent to it. The habit of respecting the wishes and intentions of his father was to him a higher law than any written code. To profit by the new act would have seemed to him a positive sacrilege. He had received as a *dot* on his marriage a little property called Milly, worth about 250*l.* a year, and that sufficed for his humble wants. He declared that he was satisfied with this poor portion of my grandfather's magnificent inheritance, and renounced all further share. So he remained a poor man; but he won the love and admiration of the whole family. The rest of the property was divided by lot, which gave rise to long and painful discussions; but at last all was amicably settled. My eldest uncle and aunt, who were both unmarried, had the estate of Monceau and the vineyards in Champagne. My uncle, the Abbé Lamartine, had the Château of Ursy, in the midst of the forest of Burgundy, near Dijon. The house and gardens were magnificent, and the solitude complete. This suited my good old uncle, who would not, to please the Revolution, give up his priestly functions; but abjuring all society for the sake of peace, was content to live as a hermit according to his own convictions. I have always loved and venerated this uncle, who was a real St. Evremond in our family. When I grew older I was frequently his guest, and always happier with him than with any one else. Madame de Villars, the *chanoinesse*, who had made a vow of poverty, obtained a dispensation from the Pope, on the condition of being simply a distributor of her income, and became the proprietress of the rich property of Péronne, where she always lived in summer. She kept her promises to the Church with scrupulous fidelity, and became the generous benefactress of the whole neighborhood. She was handsome and clever, thoroughly versed in habits of business, and was of great use to my father on several occasions. Mlle. de Monceau, who had all her life been rather childish, lived with my father and mother. She was always treated as one of the children of the family, and by her large income added to the comfort and happiness of our home. The shares having been thus adjusted, every one went to take possession of his property. The Hôtel de Mâcon alone was kept as a common home for us all to pass the winter together.

V.

I was just beginning to see and understand something of outside things when my father and mother carried us off — a whole tribe of children, in a long file of bullock wagons — to establish us and all our worldly goods at Milly. Our dear mother was in the first carriage with two of my sisters on her knees, and another at her breast; a quantity of loose packages filled up the lumbering vehicle. My father went on foot as a sportsman, carrying his gun, cheering my mother, and helping the carriage when it got into any bad ruts. Two dogs in a leash followed him, and then two more wagons full of maids and nurses and household goods of every description, going at a foot's pace. Then came a carriage containing Mlle. de Monceau and her maid. All this formed a regular procession of old-fashioned equipages rolling and tumbling about in the mud, for the public roads in those days were execrable. The cries of the drivers, the lowing of the bullocks, the clamor and fright of the women servants, and the hearty laughter of the children at each fresh misfortune, made up a picturesque scene, which was partly amusing and partly touching. We did not arrive at Milly for five or six hours, although it was hardly more than twelve miles.

Milly was then a poor little village built on the ridge of a hill planted with vines, at some distance from St. Sorlin, which was the rural capital of the country.

VI.

Ever since the spring, my father had come to Milly from time to time to prepare the house for his family. The revolutionists had, to a certain degree, spared the old place, and contented themselves with turning the drawing-room into a dancing saloon on Sundays for the benefit of the neighboring peasantry. The sabots of the dancers had broken the old encaustic tiles into a thousand bits; not from pure mischief, but simply from a sort of pleasure at profaning a nobleman's house. We stumbled among the broken fragments of pavement until a workman had clumsily repaired it with large square common bricks. There was not much more damage done. The vines continued to bear and the fruit trees to blossom, so that the traces of the Revolution in Milly might be said to be restricted to the ball-room. Every one — father, mother, aunt, children, and servants — had soon found his or her place in the house. Our only furniture were a few beds, tables, and chairs. The kitchen, soon filled by the peasant women, once more sent up the cheerful smoke from its wide, ingle-nooked chimney. The nurse and children walked and played in the corridor. My father spent his days in hunting or shooting on the mountains. My mother was occupied in writing, in the care and superintendence of the house, or in visiting the sick and suffering, with whom she at once made friends, and was beloved as readily as she herself loved all around her.

VII.

Do you wish for a description of these my first happy days at Milly? The account of one day will serve for all the rest.

No sooner had the first rays of the sun lit up my mother's room, than my father, who was a very early riser, went out walking. A maid used to fetch me and put me into my father's place, by the side of my darling, gentle mother, who used to kiss and pet me, and then teach me to lisp my little prayers. I did not know very well the meaning of the words, or understand what that Invisible and Omnipotent Power was, called

God; but I knew I was doing like mamma, and that was more than enough for me. Most good things are done from imitation. To try and be like what one loves, that is the first instinct of man. At any rate, it was mine. Reasoning one may dispute, but not that which has become a habit. My father was not a very religious, but he was an honest and an honorable man. The love and respect of his wife, whom he adored, made him pious almost in spite of himself.

After prayers we went to breakfast, I on my nurse's knee, off the vinedresser's soup, which I used to think the best in the world. Then I trotted off into the vineyards to play with my companions (the children of our peasants), or else, like them, to keep the goats and sheep in the mountain forests. We used to return when the bell of the old steeple rung the midday *Angelus*. Then a fuming hot soup with bacon and vegetables awaited us round the homely wooden table; a repast which I infinitely preferred to the pure white tablecloth and more delicate dishes served to my parents. I remember even now with appetite the little two-pronged, twopenny forks which doubled into our pocket clasped-knives, and with which we used to pick out and eat the bouilli of our soup, in little bright red or green varnished earthenware bowls! Soup has ever since appeared a luxury to me. A cabbage or celery leaf, with a radish, just stirred in what is called "tea-kettle broth," with a bit of black bread, this is the true food of the country peasant. My simple life made me relish the homely fare of the cottager as much as a child who had known nothing else. When I grew older, and was no longer allowed to run wild, and the age of lessons and school came, I was obliged to give up this simple food of goat's cheese, cabbage, onions, and the like, and made to eat meat, which disagreed with me so much that I had a regular illness in consequence; and, ever since, I have never lost the early tastes contracted at that time. Even when we dined up-stairs, my mother never could persuade us to eat anything but vegetables.

After dinner, my father used to go back to his shooting on the mountains, sometimes alone, at other times in company with one of his head vinedressers, of whom he had made both a guide and friend. This man, who was in every way superioı to his class, was called Claude Chanut, and became quite a favorite with us all.

VIII.

Sometimes it happened that we passed the whole winter at Milly, as in a kind of domestic convent, completely snowed up, but visited from time to time by certain old friends of my father's, who were living in hiding, as it were, in the neighboring villages. First, there was the doctor of the canton, who lived with his wife at St. Sorlin, with a son, who became my great friend, and a daughter, whom I should have fallen in love with, if I had been of the right age. Then there was the Chevalier de La Cense, a retired officer in the Guards, living with his sister, Mademoiselle de Moleron, in the same village, a cheery, jovial, good-natured man, whose arrival brightened the whole house. Then there was M. de Vaudran, of the Bruys family (one of twenty children, all distinguished in their different careers), living at Bussières, in the parish of Milly. M. de Vaudran, who was an old friend of my father's, had been secretary to M. de Villedeuil before the Revolution, and initiated into all the political secrets of the highest society in Paris. He was a Royalist of the good old school — moderate, impartial, and just towards every one, even towards the men who had mingled in the Revolution, without having imbrued their hands in crime and blood. He took pity on my somewhat neglected education, and gave me my first writing-lessons on a little table in the dining-room, for which I have remained eternally grateful to him. His three sisters — simple, gentle, loving, agreeable women, and great friends of my mother's — often accompanied him to Milly. Although obliged, from political circumstances, to live continually in the country, and only associate with people of a humbler class, the natural distinction of their manners, and the companionship of their brother, who always spent part of the year with them, gave them a high-bred tone which could not be mistaken; and their entire absence of affectation made their reception of friends in their own home most pleasant; while their natural grace and dignity gave a special charm to their conversation.

The Curé de Bussières, their near neighbor, young, handsome, mundane, amiable, and of elegant and refined habits, was full of respect and deference for these ladies, and he was also a favorite shooting companion of my father's.

IX.

At a quarter of a league from our house, buried in the wooded gorges of the mountains of St. Point, was a site which has enshrined itself in my memory and imagination forever. I mean the village and château of Pierreclos — the habitation of the old Count de Pierreclos, whom I have before mentioned. Walter Scott has nothing more romantic or original in his descriptions of the nature, habits, and dwelling-places of the Scotch lairds. Now for a description of the château itself, its inmates, and the life they led there.

We used to go and dine there every Sunday after high mass; that is, at a quarter before twelve. After having clambered on foot to the summit of the Csaz mountain, which threw a long gray shadow over the Milly valley behind my father's garden, a steep and rapid descent to the right brought us into the Pierreclos valley. A rough path, full of rolling stones, but shaded by old walnut-trees, led us by several barren hamlets to the head of the valley. There the aspect of the scenery changes; the hills, covered with vineyards, slope down towards the rich meadows, irrigated by bright and rushing streams, and shaded by poplars cutting the sky-line, like the cypresses of the South. Very soon the valley widens, and the eye is lost in a distant vapory forest of pines and beech. The background is formed of dark mountains, covered here and there with snow, which lies in deep patches in the hollows. After having walked on a little way on the high-road, we used to perceive a mass of smoke and vapor coming out of the mouths of the village furnaces, which blackened even the walls of the old steeple of Pierreclos. But it was church-time, and we hurried into the chapel, where the priest was saying mass. The old lord and his family occupied a bench to the right of the altar. The family consisted of the master of the château, a gouty old man, but with a proud and determined countenance, who looked down with a sort of insolence on his old vassals; his brother, M. de Berzé, who bore the name of the old Gothic château of which we spoke just now, between Milly and Cluny; his five daughters, all very pleasing-looking, both in face and figure; and a young son, of about the same age as myself, with whom hereafter I was to be bound in the ties of a warm friendship. As soon as we appeared they made room for us in the church, and we were soon kneeling in our proper seats. The mass being over, the peasants separated. The old lord mounted his horse (with the help of his servants), and rode up to the castle by a steep paved road. We followed on foot with the rest of the family, and winding through the vineyards, soon arrived at the iron gates of the château. Nothing could be more imposing than its appearance as you entered. A vast courtyard, which led you through a high subterranean passage, or covered way, to the keep, from which you suddenly emerged into an open sunny space brilliant with flowers, growing up to the very foot of the steeple of the old chapel, which was built on a high terrace to the extreme left of the castle. Then the ground suddenly fell, like a drop-scene in the opera, and revealed to you a mass of towers and pinnacles and quaint Gothic windows and ornaments, the whole lit up and illuminated, as it were, by the setting sun.

X.

On first entering the large courtyard, I was struck at the sight of a new building not yet finished, on the windows of which the workmen, in fact, were still at work. It was evidently intended to replace the old Gothic castle, which, being mainly composed of keeps and square towers, circular staircases, irregular turrets, and pointed roofs, was more picturesque than comfortable, and rather gave one the idea of an aerial village. This old fortress, in reality, had been built on the edge of a promontory, and followed the sinuosities of the rock both above and below, from the summit to the valley. The upper part formed an oval terrace, upon which all the doors opened, whether of the kitchens or drawing-rooms.

XI.

The apartments with the exception of a great stove in an angle of the dining-room, and a magnificent fire-place of black marble in the drawing-room, large enough to burn whole trees at a time, had the appearance of rooms recently restored after a fire of the day before. The mortar scarcely filled up the spaces between the stones ; and the walls, guiltless of white-wash, seemed never to have been smoothed by the mason's trowel. The flames had licked the paint off the ceilings, which bore the traces of an incendiary fire, seemingly scarcely put out.

"Look !" exclaimed the old Count, showing me the marks of the above-mentioned destruction ; "look at the traces of the passage of those brigands ! Here was the torch of one, there the hatchet of another, a pickaxe was the tool of the third. Ah ! the rascals ! I know them well ; and never in my life-time will I suffer the remembrance of these horrors to be effaced."

In truth in 1790, in the famous and inexplicable day called *du Brigandage*, this grand old castle had been completely ravaged, and nearly burnt to the ground, by the peasants from the mountains, who had determined to avenge the supposed wrongs of the villagers, and took advantage of the unpopularity of the owner, who was hated by the people, to carry out their nefarious designs. The pillage and devastation were indeed complete.

His wife and daughters were saved by the fidelity of two or three of their tenant farmers, and concealed in the neighboring forest. The Count and his son escaped by a miracle, and swore to be avenged. His eldest son emigrated the next day. As to the old Count himself, he returned after a time to his ruined home, and went on living there till the day when they came to carry off the cannons of his terrace to Mâcon, at the same time that his whole family were thrown into prison by the agents of the Revolutionary government. My father, who in 1790 was on leave at Monceau, armed and mounted the young men of Mâcon, and pursued the incendiaries to the Château of Cormatin, killing several in an engagement in the neighborhood of Cluny, and hanging others on the trees by the roadside, — a service never forgotten in the grateful memory of the old Count. The insurrection was at an end, and order was everywhere restored, until the day when the Government, in its turn, had given the signal for persecution, and imprisoned, as we have said, the whole family as Royalists.

XII.

The head of the family had been formerly captain of cavalry during the Seven Years' War. He had been taken prisoner by the Prussians, and used to tell us how the Queen of Prussia, delighted with his good looks and cleverness, used to knock every morning at his door in the corridor, calling out, "Count Pierreclos! get up, and follow the King's hunting party! Your horses are waiting." "At these words," he added, "I gladly rose, and started for Sans Souci, where we used to eat delicious sour-krout." The Queen of Prussia was always brought into the conversation.

On returning from Potsdam, he sent in his resignation, and married a young girl of good family from the neighborhood of Lyons. She bore him five or six children, and they lived constantly in the Château of Pierreclos, the old Count being the object of the timid fear of the peasantry, and the ridicule of the middle classes. He was not a bad man at all, but absurdly vain and boastful, with a good heart at bottom, though often violent and rough in his manners. His wife had died during their imprisonment. The eldest of his sons had emigrated; the youngest who was called the Chevalier de Pierreclos, was a boy of my own age, brave, clever, and intelligent, left to nature and with scarcely any education; but giving promise of what he afterwards became — a brilliant adventurer, like the

Chevalier de Grammont, a hero of the civil wars, of romantic love affairs, of duels, horses, and all that is comprehended in the old term of a "free lance." We were intimate from children, and shared in all boyish sports.

His sisters, older than himself, were handsome, *piquante*, and original. As they had no mother, they had consequently little or no education, properly so called; they, in fact, brought up one another. There was certainly in the château an old aunt, the only sister of the Count, a clever woman, and as strange as himself; but who could only have taught cards to her pretty nieces, that being the one occupation of Madame de Moirode from morning till night. She used to come into the drawing-room at eight o'clock in the morning, and sit on a curtained seat, like Madame du Deffant! Then lowering the curtains round her on three sides, to keep out the draught, she would offer cards to all comers: brothers, sisters, nephews, nieces, friends — no matter who! playing without a moment's intermission from one meal to another; resting for a few minutes, perhaps, in the middle of the day, and beginning again with any new-comers till supper-time.

The Chevalier de Berzé, an old cavalry officer like his brother, the Count de Pierreclos, ran through his whole fortune very early in life, and now had accepted the posts of agent and gardener to the family. In the drawing-room his only functions seemed to be to provide fresh cards, and to bring in fresh logs for the fire. He was a thoroughly good-natured, "serviceable" fellow, ready to do a kind turn to everybody, and universally beloved. I saw him live, grow old, and die, like a living piece of furniture, having no idea in life but that of saying "Yes" to everything proposed by his brother; of bringing the finest melons from the garden to the dining-room, the most beautiful flowers to his nieces, and fresh faggots for the inexhaustible fire-places in both apartments.

XIII.

But when the time of the vintage drew near, everything assumed an aspect of work and life and gayety, which metamorphosed the whole country. The peasants loaded their carts with water thoroughly to cleanse the deep wine-presses which were to hold the grapes. The bullocks, coupled together and harnessed at dawn, lifted their intelligent heads and velvety eyes under the heavy yoke ; or else ruminated, by the side of the pole, the armfuls of hay which the children gave them. The women, lifting us up in their arms, would help us to scramble up by the axle of the wheels into the vat. This was a large, oval kind of bath, in which the vine-dresser goes to the vineyard, and which he there fills with great bunches of cut grapes to bring them back to the wine-press. Then we were lifted out by the workmen, and our places filled by the contents of their baskets. A quantity of sticky flies and wasps, drunk with the juice of the grape which had already begun to ferment, fell with the fruit into the vat, but either instinct or satiety prevented their stinging us.

Thus we went joyfully from one vine to the other, helping to cut the rich bunches and fill the baskets or bins of one set of reapers after the other. The cleverest and handiest girls from the neighboring villages formed themselves into bands, slept in the barn at Milly, and were hired as cutters by the owners of the vineyards. They used to walk singing, their pails on their heads, or their baskets on their arms, behind the one who served as guide in the narrow paths between the vines ; and then placing themselves by twenties or thirties, each at the foot of a vine stock, would quickly clear the whole stem with careful, skillful hands, of its rich white or blue burden, squash them in their fingers, and throw them into the bins, which the boys would then carry off to the carts. The very vineyards seemed to sing as their rich produce fell under the scissors ; the earth, as it were, rejoiced at her spoil. We, children, used to follow the carts dripping with their juicy burden ; our little pinafores all stained with the blood of the grape, and meeting with joyous cries each fresh band of workers. The joy ran like the wine from hill to hill. Then we helped to empty the grapes from the vat to the wine-press ; or gathered bunches of fresh grapes to refresh the tired bullocks, whose carts creaked under their heavy load. Then we would count the number of bins, and run to tell our father, who would calculate the numbers of tuns of wine which would be the final result, and which, in reality, formed our whole income for the year. A few days after, the same work was begun again, until the leaves of the vine, all yellow and seared, had no more fruit to conceal; until, in fact, the vintage being over and the barrels filled to the brim with wine, the vines were left desolate, the goats picked off the few remaining leaves, and the once busy paths were still as death.

XIV.

Then began the spinning of the flax and hemp in the evenings at home ; or else the cracking of the walnuts, which was the last gay work of the season for the villagers. The mistress of the house, by the light of a rustic lamp called a *creuse-yeux*, gathered round the large kitchen table, children, servants, visitors, and neighbors. The men went to the cellar and brought out huge sacks of nuts, of which the husk, already half rotten, was easily detached from the shell, and threw them on the floor. Every one, armed with a hammer, set to work on a heap of this rich fruit before him, to crack the nuts carefully, and take out the kernel (if possible entire) and put them in little heaps, either for sale or for the oil mill. Gay laughter and innocent conversation echoed from one end of the room to the other, and made the work seem like play. When all was done, dancing began, and generally continued till midnight.

It was the same with the weaving of the hemp and flax, which used to occupy the winter evenings in the great barn until the tow merchant came round and bargained for the long hanks of yarn and vegetable silk, the produce of which was the gain of the wives and daughters and women-servants of the house, and often served to keep them in clothes altogether. We used to take our share in all these works with our servants and peasants, as was the custom in those primitive days. The presence of our gentle mother was a check on any light or improper word or action; for she had won the respect and love of the whole neighborhood.

XV.

Our conversation at these gatherings was generally on the subject of the good or bad crops; the price of wine or wheat; the marriage of this or that village lad or girl; the wages of the women-servants, which generally consisted of ten crowns (thirty francs) a year, six yards of unbleached linen for shifts, two pairs of *sabots*, a few yards of stuff for petticoats, and five francs as a present on New Year's Day. These were the current wages of servants in those days. They are now at least ten times as much; but I doubt if the people themselves are one whit richer or happier. Money only represents, under one denomination or other, a certain amount of wants. All is equal, except in the mind of man.

Very often, on coming out of some sanguinary revolutionary crisis, very terrible at the time, perhaps, but quickly forgotten, the talk among the elder men became political — that is to say, military. Itinerant hawkers used to come round to our doors, crying out, "Great battle between the French, under command of General Bonaparte, in Italy, and the English or Germans" (or else it was "Moreau on the Rhine," or "Massena in Switzerland," or "Macdonald in Suabia," or "Hoche in the Palatinate," or "Marceau in Germany"). Then the peasant would rush out of his cabin, while the hawker unrolled to his admiring eyes highly-colored portraits of heroes, and he listened with all his ears to the startling tale of battles won, and heroic escapes, or glorious death-scenes; and bought for a penny the true (?) history of all these feats of arms. He would then nail them up on his wall, or get his wife to sew them on the serge curtains of his bed, where they remained for himself and his family as a true history of France and of her doughty deeds to all time.

The first political enthusiasm with which I was myself fired was in the village square adjoining our own courtyard. There was a young man named Janin, a little better educated than his neighbors, who taught the village children the elements of reading and writing. One day he stepped out of the cabin which served as a school, and sounding a drum and a clarionet of which he had somehow become possessed, he quickly attracted all the boys and girls in Milly; to whom he commenced showing off a quantity of pictures of military heroes, which he had obtained from one of these hawkers, who was standing by his side. "Look," he exclaimed, "at this picture of the battle of the Pyramids, gained by General Bonaparte! He is this little dark, thin man, whom you see here mounted on a horse as yellow as gold, which is rearing and plunging, with his long sabre in his hand, before that mass of cut stone which is called the Pyramids, and who is saying to his soldiers, 'From up there, forty centuries look down upon you.'"

But his eloquence was rather lost on his audience, who did not understand a word of it, and preferred Augereau galloping on a white charger and crossing the Rhine with one bound, as if he had been carried on the wings of Victory herself; or Berthier, tearing a swan's quill from his floating plume to write the staff orders with a pensive countenance. But Kléber, with his drum-major's figure and size, carried the day, and excited the enthusiasm and plaudits of the whole hamlet.

The hawker passed the morning selling these pictures of national glory from house to house, with Janin to explain the subjects of each. His enthusiasm spread the excitement over the whole country, and no one shared in it more vividly than myself. It was thus that I first began to understand what was meant by military glory. A horse, a plume, a sabre were henceforth to me symbolical of great things. The people were fired with a military ardor, which lasted a long time. All through the winter evenings nothing was talked of but the hawker, and Janin was continually summoned to explain again the text of these wonderful, and of course *truthful* pictures.

XVI.

Time went on, and I was eleven years old. My father began to talk seriously of sending me to school; but it was difficult to decide, because, since the Revolution, no public school existed, if we except certain private houses, more or less famous at Paris or at Lyons, and a College of Jesuits (who were then called *Fathers of the Faith*), whom the uncle of Bonaparte, Cardinal Fesch, protected on the frontiers of Italy, in the little town of Belley, in Bugey. My mother very much wished that my father would decide on sending me to this college, which had a very high reputation for piety and learning. The greater portion of the noble families of Piémont, Lombardy, Turin, Alessandria, and Milan, sent their children there. But my mother was opposed by all the rest of the family, who wished me to go to a private house in Lyons, called the house of *La Caille*, at la Croix Rousse, and which also was well spoken of. My uncle, M. de Lamartine, did not much like the Jesuits; my father was indifferent, but above all wished to please his brothers and sisters, on whom my future fortune depended. So that he ended by saying "Yes," and my mother rather sorrowfully took me to Lyons.

XVII.

How sad was my departure from Milly! It was the first deep wound my heart had received, and I felt it bitterly. How broken-hearted I was at saying good-by to the old servants, who all loved me, and I them, and especially Janette, a charming and beautiful girl from the mountains, whom I cried terribly at parting with, and whom I left equally bathed in tears! Janette came to kiss me in my little bed, and I started for Lyons as if it were (as in reality it was to me) for the other world. From that hour Milly, its rocks and vineyards, its peasants and servants, and all belonging to it, seemed to be graven in my memory as a warm and living thing which formed part of my very self. Alas! I have had to part with it all since, down to the very stones. And when I pass by the road, I turn away my head, that I may not see it, and do not look round till the ruined steeple and vine-covered hills have altogether disappeared from my sight.

BOOK II.

I.

THE family coach brought my mother and myself the next day to Lyons. We stopped at Madame de Roquemont's, a good and tender-hearted woman, and a cousin of my mother's, who loved her like a sister.

She lived in the Rue St. Dominique, near the Place de Bellecour, which had been ruined at that time by the pickaxes of the Revolutionists. Opposite Madame de Roquemont's house was a wholesale bookseller's, named Leroy. He had a large family of children, one more beautiful than the other, who spent most of their time on the balcony opposite my room. Amidst these living flowers there was one, a girl of twelve or fourteen, whose like I have never seen before or since. She had the most delicate features, blue eyes, skin as white as the finest Chinese paper, and an expression of such deep thought and feeling, that it remained indelibly impressed on my dreams. Her long fair hair fell in heavy curls on her neck and shoulders; while her beautifully slight and graceful figure, her dreamy, earnest face, and her white forehead, leaning on the edge of the balcony, made such an impression upon me, that although I was then only eleven years old, I have never forgotten it all my life. I used to spend hours watching her behind the glass panes of my little window, and every turn in her face seemed to me more lovely than before. Perfect beauty defies oblivion. Whenever I have wanted to paint a faultless or divine being, superior to every one else on earth, I have always had *her* in my mind. Man, after all, rarely invents anything — he remembers.

This incomparable child married, a few years after, a M.

Pelaprat, a financier of Lyons, who was doubtless won by her charms and exceeding beauty. She had several children, all worthy of their mother, and, among the rest, the Princesse de Chimay, whose enchanting face had the same type. Twenty years ago a singular thing happened to me with regard to this lady, and which, until now, I have never mentioned to a soul. One day I was waiting in an anteroom at Paris, where one often met persons whom etiquette prevented one's speaking to without an introduction, and there came in a very pretty person from eighteen to twenty years of age, who sat down at the farther end of the room. At first I did not dare speak; but as our time of waiting seemed to be indefinitely prolonged, and we were *tête-à-tête*, I ventured at last to say some insignificant words. Our conversation became more easy as we went on, and at last I ventured to ask her her name. "I am the Princesse de Chimay," she replied. "I thought so!" I answered joyfully. "How so?" she asked with surprise. "Because I knew your mother thirty years ago."

In truth, certain charms are hereditary, and can never be mistaken.

Madame Pelaprat, who established herself later in Paris, was an object of respectful admiration to Napoleon himself. When he returned from the Isle of Elba to Lyons he asked to see her, and she came to the archbishop's palace where he lodged. I suppose he thought her beautiful eyes would bring him luck! They say he received her as if she had been a goddess; but he had himself lost his "prestige," and the great man had dwindled into an unprincipled usurper.

II.

During my stay at Lyons, I witnessed a strange act of humility in Madame de Roquemont — a humility which at that time I did not understand, but of which later I saw all the beauty and greatness.

M. de Roquemont, a Norman gentleman of high birth, had taken refuge in Lyons during the Revolution, and determining not to be dependent on others, had embarked in the agency of an Italian commercial house. His wife, who was related to a noble Italian family, named Dareste, encouraged him in this undertaking without any false shame ; not in the interests of their children, for they had but one little girl, but to be able to live comfortably themselves, and, above all, to help the number of *émigrés*, who, like themselves, had lost their all in the Revolution. During this time, a member of the Dareste family, a clever, calculating man, bethought himself of proposing a tax upon tobacco, and communicated his ideas to the Government. This tax, which was eventually to bring in so many millions, at first only produced a few centimes. The collection of this duty was vulgar and humiliating, from the contact it entailed with the consumer. Madame de Roquemont, through her relationship to the inventor, had obtained permission to collect this popular tax in her shop. Sitting behind the counter, I saw to my amazement this noble lady, with her distinguished air and manners, open her door to the poorest and lowest workmen of the town, called *canuts;* ask them, with the greatest civility, what quantity or quality of tobacco they required; open the different canisters, and weigh out each little parcel or pinch herself; receive the farthing or half-penny in payment, and seat herself again with as much dignity as if she were selling pearls or rich jewels in an Oriental bazaar. It struck me the more as, until then, I had always looked upon such employments as servile and unfit for persons of gentle birth. But when I found out (as I did later) that Madame de Roquemont employed all the profits of this business in bringing up a number of little orphans, whom I saw daily well clothed and fed at her table, I understood the whole beauty of her self-sacrifice, and felt that I had before me the example of a woman as saintly as she was nobly born, and that what all the world despised was in reality what did her the most honor. Her charity had overcome all feelings of human respect, and she went on with her business till her death. Even now her name is never mentioned in Lyons without tenderness and respect.

III.

She herself took my mother and me to the Croix Rousse. It was a terrible moment for me, and still more for my poor mother. The great house (which had been an old convent) where we stopped, was called the Pension "*Pupier*." One heard a sort of buzz of voices even before entering the door. This door had a grating in the middle, through which one looked into the courtyard. Dante's Gate of Hell would not have appeared to me more terrible. I felt the words which I did not then know: *Lasciate ogni speranza voi che entrate!* All my courage forsook me. The walls seemed to me those of a prison — the faces those of jailers. I saw about two hundred boys in the playground which we crossed while following the porter to the reception-room; and they looked at me with a wicked or mocking expression of face, as much as to say, "So much the better; here comes a new victim, who will be as miserable as ourselves." The grand air of Madame de Roquemont and the graceful beauty of my mother, however, rather imposed upon five or six of the elder ones, who took off their caps, and respectfully ranged themselves on one side of the wall to let us pass, looking at me in the meanwhile with a sort of kind compassion. At last we arrived at the parlor of the establishment, as it was called. It was a very large, barely-furnished room, where the Misses Pupier received visitors, or the parents of the pupils. There were four people in this room to whom the establishment belonged since the death of M. Pupier the founder. These four associates were Miss Pupier the eldest, a bony woman of thirty or forty, who was the housekeeper: she was neither pretty nor ugly, and looked neither good nor bad. One saw at a glance that the soup was her business, and economy her darling virtue. The next was a tall, ill-made woman, on the eve of her confinement, married to a M. Philippe, who was also one of the firm. The said M. Philippe, who was, virtually, the principal professor or head master of the school, was a clever, well-educated man, but violent in the extreme, and one who inspired nothing but fear and repugnance in the minds of his pupils, in spite of a soft outside manner which deceived no one. The fourth was a priest, named M. Croizier, a good and gentle old man, caring little for the interests of the house, but holding a class in which he was universally beloved. The establishment did not in any way give one the idea of a college, but simply of a house of business. Nor did anything remind one of the "family" tone so much vaunted in the prospectus, unless it were the baby which Madame Philippe was on the point of bringing forth to the world! After having talked for some time with these four important personages, when my mother had insisted greatly on indulgence and gentleness toward me on the part of my new masters, the moment of parting came. My mother burst into tears, and I did the same; till Madame de Roquemont gently drew her away; the heavy iron outside door was shut, and I was launched into the playground, very much as a condemned criminal is launched into eternity. I could not say a word, but sat on the base of one of the columns of the cloister which surrounded the court, and I continued gazing through my tears at the hill of St. Foy on the other bank of the Saône. Some of the students who were from Mâcon, and among the rest MM. de Veydel, the sons of a lawyer there, who had arrived a few days before, came up to try and comfort me. I clung to them in my sorrow — an unfortunate thing for them, as you will see.

IV.

I was placed in the lowest class of the school, but I did not stay there long, and very soon had distanced all my companions. The healthy country life I had led had strengthened my mind as much as my body. I was old for my age. I rose rapidly from class to class, and soon became one of the head boys. After some months of captivity, the longing to leave my prison made me push forward more and more in my studies. But I was always equally miserable: Milly, my mother, my father, my sisters, my dear nursery maid Janette, my friend

Claude Chanut, my dogs whom I loved nearly as much as the people — all seemed to have an equal share in my longing dreams. All my hopes were in the future; the present was hateful to me. The violence of M. Philippe, who was continually punishing and beating pupils whom he chose to call refractory, filled me with disgust and hatred of the man. What a difference between him and the tender reproaches of my father, or the tears of my mother, if we had committed any boyish fault! I recollect I used to pass whole hours, during the playtime, looking sadly and wishfully at the beautiful hills of Beaujolais, and fancying what every one was doing at home at such and such an hour. All my dreams were of Milly.

But one day brought my disgust at the whole thing to a climax. A young man of Mâcon, named Eugène Siraudin, three or four years older than I, proud, brave, strong, looking every one straight in the face and fearing no one, had committed some slight infraction of rule in the German class, and had refused to kneel and beg pardon publicly of the professor. M. Philippe was summoned, and we were called in to be spectators of the punishment about to be inflicted. M. Philippe going up to him ordered him to kneel and make his excuses to the good old German master, whom we all liked, though he had been the involuntary cause of this scene. Siraudin, rising from his bench, said he was innocent of the fault laid to his charge, and positively refused. M. Philippe insisted, and threatened to force him to obey. The poor German, in despair, threw himself between them, declaring he was satisfied that it was a mistake. We all joined in the protest; but M. Philippe, roughly pushing aside the professor and unintentionally throwing him down on the slippery floor of the schoolroom, seized Siraudin by the hair and flung him under the table at his feet. Siraudin was sixteen, and a capital wrestler. Furious at this unmerited act of violence, he rose instantly, red with passion, and flying at the throat of M. Philippe, threw him in his turn under the table, and seizing the great mass of fair hair which adorned the professor's head (for they wore wigs and pig-tails in those days), held him by main force down to the floor. M. Philippe, in struggling to free his head, left his wig in the hands of his adversary and a great white place in his bald head was exposed to the eyes of the whole school. Siraudin triumphantly holding up the wig, shook it in our faces with a fierce and ironical laugh. All the students who hated M. Philippe, rejoiced at his defeat, although none dared move or share in the struggle. The two enemies exhausted with passion again held one another in a ferocious embrace, each trying to knock the head of the other against the flag-stones of the hall, whèn the poor old German professor, fearing the death of one or the other, threw himself with all the weight of his enormous body on the interlaced arms of both, and so contrived to separate them. No sooner had he regained his breath, than a terrible cry from M. Philippe summoned all the servants from the kitchen to the assistance of their master. Three or four cooks, armed, like the executioners of former days, with spits and frying-pans and other cooking utensils, rushed to the rescue and endeavored to secure our companion who fought like a lion. At last they overpowered him, and, at the voice of M. Philippe, threw him out into the street to the mercy of the elements. The house reëchoed with the cries of the women, who, of course, took the part of the brutal pedagogue against the courageous martyr, as we considered our friend ; and the rest of the day was spent in looking after his wounds. As for myself, the impression left on my mind by this barbarous scene (the blows, the cries, the struggles, the hair which flew about the room, amidst torn books and broken benches and tables) was such, that a horrible shudder came over me which changed my sadness into hatred, and I vowed that I would no longer remain in the house. However, in order to insure the success of my plan, I felt that I must hide my rage for the moment in my heart, and try and obtain some accomplices. From this moment I began to plot my escape. I said to myself : "I will no longer stay in this shambles, which is more like a slaughter-house than a school. I will go back to my mother and to Milly. I would rather be the companion of "Turc" in his kennel (that was the watch-dog in the courtyard at home) than the favorite of this brute of a master." Resolutions of this sort, once firmly taken, are catching. My indignation was soon shared by the Veydels, whom I have before mentioned as being natives of Mâcon, and sons of an old friend of my mother. I often walked with them, and we concocted together the best means of carrying out our plan of escape.

One day, soon after the struggle in which poor Siraudin had been well-nigh murdered by the head-master, they took us to a wood called La Caille to celebrate some feast or other. This wood was the great place of meeting for the silk-workers of both sexes in the neighborhood of Lyons. Our boyish eyes were witnesses of plenty of scandals there ; it was not, in fact, at all a fit place for any young persons to go to. In the midst of the wood was a long avenue, which was the scene of our games. What those games were, and how little humanity or delicacy was shown in their selection, may be judged of by the following description. We had been told this day that a new sport was prepared for us which would exercise our bodies and (of course) improve our hearts. A long string was stretched from tree to tree across the avenue. To this string a goose was fastened by the feet, its long neck and head hanging down, and its great wings palpitating with fright. We were each blindfolded and given a naked sword, and the one who succeeded in cutting off the unhappy bird's head was to have the prize. He who only mutilated its wings, or legs, or neck, was to be content with a green crown. We were ordered to applaud this barbarous sport ; but my disgust kept me silent. Brought up to love animals, and to think it a sin to give wanton pain to any living thing, I could find no words to express my loathing at this horrible amusement. One of the Veydels was chosen, armed with the sword, and had his eyes bandaged. I drew close to him and whispered in his ear, that he had only to strike hard in the direction of my voice, which would be close to M. Philippe, and that then probably *he* would receive the cut intended for the poor bird. It happened as I had expected. M. Philippe received a slashing blow; but, unfortunately, only his hat suffered, and a great cry arose from the students at the pretended awkwardness of Veydel. He was led back to the path and his eyes unbandaged, when he appeared very penitent for the mischance. But the horrible games continued until the poor goose was nothing but a bloody trunk still quivering on the cord.

I went up to the Veydels, and gave vent to my fury. "How frightful an education this monster is giving us!" I exclaimed. "What would our parents think of such lessons and such examples? To torture a wretched bird in this way for no earthly reason but cruelty, and give it no chance of escape — can we doubt that if our families knew of it they would instantly remove us from such hideous influences?" I saw that my words had had their effect. "Well," I continued, "don't let us hesitate any longer. It is of no use to write, for our letters are always read before they are sent. But let us go ourselves, and report to our parents the real state of things. If they blame us, we have the massacre of our friend Siraudin, thrown more dead than alive into the street, to plead as our justification." "That is quite true," they replied. "Now let us separate," I continued, "lest we should be observed. Let me choose the day and the hour. Get together whatever money you may have, and carry it always about with you in your pockets. Then watch me, and be ready at a moment's notice to follow me."

We went back to the college with this understanding, and no one had overheard our conversation.

V.

Two days after, the opportunity presented itself. I was ready, so were the Veydels; and I had only to give the signal. It was playtime, and after breakfast. The boys were scattered in the rooms, in the corridors, and in the courtyard. Some were playing at ball, others at racket. The Veydels, at my signal, followed me into the hall, of which the iron-grated door opened into the street. "Let us pretend to be playing at tennis," I whispered to them, "and when the ball shall have passed the door, which I will leave open as if by accident, rush out as if to rescue it; I will run after you as hard as I can toward the wood. If they see us, they will fancy that I am running to help you to catch the ball. Then we will go slower, and take the road which leads to Fontaine. There we will stop for dinner, and a little carriage will take us in two days to Mâcon."

I opened the door accordingly, and the game began. There were only one or two fellows in the corridor who were watching us play. I threw the ball into the street, the Veydels rushed after it as if to catch it; I followed; and then we all three took to our heels and ran as hard as we could in the direction of the wood, only looking round from time to time to see if we were followed. Our *ruse* had been successful; no one had thought of us at all, or, if they did, it was to imagine the ball had spun farther than we expected, and that we should return with it immediately.

VI.

At the bottom of the hill, we stopped to take breath and hold a council of war. "So far so well," I exclaimed to my companions. "Now let us change our course, and endeavor effectually to cheat our pursuers." We had one sure and faithful guide, which was the Saône, gliding like a bright blue ribbon between the two shores. We left the wood, therefore, and followed a path which led us up higher and higher on the left bank of the river, from whence we could see everything without being seen. We walked quickly but in silence. After having marched for two hours, we found ourselves at the village of Fontaine, which supplies Lyons with flour. We began to feel very hungry, and so resolved to enter the little town; but fearing discovery if we stopped at an inn on the Lyons' side, we walked up the High Street till we found ourselves in a little clean café at the other end, where we ordered dinner and a carriage to take us on to Villefranche. A nice looking servant girl showed us into a tidy little dining-room; and the smell from the kitchen, where a fine Bresse *capon* was roasting on the spit, warned us that we must either break the law of the Church or of nature, for it was a Friday. After a moment's hesitation nature gained the day, and we agreed to eat the chicken. We had heard our mothers, who were very pious, say that when travelling one might eat meat without scruple, provided one did not do it from contempt for the laws of the Church ; so our consciences were at ease. Hardly had we sat down to eat, however, than we heard a great noise at the front door of the inn. The door opened, and M. Philippe himself entered, wiping the perspiration off his forehead. Turning to the mistress of the house he merely said, "That 's right, put another cover here, and I will dine with these gentlemen." Whilst speaking he threw a wicked and satisfied look at us, which you may imagine pretty well spoiled our appetites. However, our pride made us resolve not to appear ashamed or troubled. We pretended to laugh at our little adventure, and to eat our uncanonical dinner with apparent gayety. Some bad jokes were made by M. Philippe himself on the *capon*, but we felt that the worst was to come.

The dinner being over, M. Philippe summoned a policeman, and made us march before him through the wood back to the college. We looked down certainly, but we maintained a calm and quiet countenance for fear of being taken for prisoners. In an hour or two we arrived at the door of L'Enfance. M. Philippe went in first, leaving us in the charge of the policeman, hoping to prepare a public humiliation for us. Accordingly we found all the students ranged in a double file to receive us, and M. Philippe gave the signal for hissing. But no one responded. Not a sound was heard from any of the boys — only a suppressed look of pleasure and excitement ; so that our entry had more the character of a triumph than anything else. M. Philippe, more furious than ever, placed us in separate prisons. My two companions were put in a low dark room on the ground floor, where they only remained two days, having consented to ask pardon publicly, and so were forgiven. But as for me, who was looked upon justly as the most guilty, they knew they need not expect so prompt a repentance; so I was shut up in a little room under the leads, where I had, certainly, plenty of time to reflect on my fault. But though I was only twelve, the feelings of honor I had inherited from my father made the very idea of denying the facts utterly out of the question; and in reality I considered my punishment rather a glory than the reverse. I threw myself on the bed, for I was very tired; but I did not shed a tear. I thought to myself, "I shall have plenty of time, at any rate, to plan a better way of escape." Unfortunately, for the moment, all means of doing so had been taken away from me. My door was fastened outside with a padlock. My food was brought to me daily, but with precaution. They had taken away my coats, so that it was utterly impossible for me to escape without detection. Every day the more good-natured among the professors and the best disposed among the students, were sent to talk to me and try to make me repent. I was glad to see them, and was touched by their kindness; but they gained nothing. I was firmly resolved not to yield, or remain in that house. A whole month passed in this way. I studied, read, wrote, and dreamed; but my resolution was unalterable, and no power on earth could have moved me.

VII.

The vacation time approached. My family, who had been informed by M. Philippe of my transgression and its punishment, were in despair at my obstinacy. At last my mother arrived herself, and to her I told all. She took me away with her instantly to Milly, when I became the gentle, loving child I had been before. It was then determined to find another school for me. To send me to the Jesuits' College at Belley had always been my mother's wish; she ended by gaining over my uncles and aunts to her views. My father yielded, and my mother took me toward the end of October to this, the place of her predilection. I was as happy and bright as if she were taking me to a *fête*. My deliverance had been accomplished.

Our road wound up a steep hill to the château of M. d'Angeville, an old officer in the Spanish service. He was the father of M. d'Angeville, a distinguished member of parliament since 1830, and of Mlle. d'Angeville, who first among women accomplished the ascent of Mont Blanc. From hence the view is magnificent. The town of Belley, with its imposing spires and steeples, lies at your feet. A little farther on, the strong castle of Pierre-Châtel stands out bleak and gray against the sky; while the blue Rhone winds through the distant plain, and foams on the strand of Dauphiny.

We met M. d'Angeville (the father) coming out of his castle on horseback and cantering toward the town. He stopped and bowed, seeing by my boyish face and the expression of my dear mother's, that she was evidently taking her son to the college at Belley, which had already acquired a great reputation among all pious parents. Having ascertained his name, my mother at once handed to him a letter of introduction which she had from M. de Cordon. He read it, and his face, which had been kind before, became radiant. "The Hotel Chevalier is the best in the town," he exclaimed. "I will go on and get everything ready for you;" and so saying he touched his beautiful Andalusian pony with his whip, and galloped off to announce our arrival.

We went slowly down the steep hill and entered the Faubourg de Belley. The first great building on the right was the Jesuit college, called that of the Pères de la Foi. A large courtyard, from whence issued a confused sound of merry voices, divided it from the high-road. "There are your future companions," said my mother. "To-morrow I shall introduce you to them." At the angle of the college was the church, with a fine architectural façade. The door was open toward the street. The church was divided in two by a kind of raised platform, the upper part being for the scholars and professors, the lower for the townspeople. My mother stopped the carriage and told me to come in with her for a few moments. I knelt by her side while she prayed with her whole heart. I saw the tears coming into her beautiful eyes as she prayed, and although her lips gave no sound I knew she was praying for me, and thanking God who had enabled her to bring me to such a safe home. She made me repeat a few little prayers too, though I was too confused to take in the sense of what I said. Then we got into the carriage again and soon arrived at the hotel which M. d'Angeville had told us of, and where he himself was at the door to receive us, and to show us into a very pretty and comfortable apartment. Madame de Chandor, his cousin, came directly after dinner to invite us to dine with them the next day; so that we already felt we had found friends. In the evening the Père Génisseau, who had been informed of our arrival, came to call upon my mother. He was very kind and very merry. His business was to manage all the temporalities of the college, see the parents of the students, and in fact attend to all the external work. He was also steward of the house. He bought the bread, wine, meat, milk, and vegetables, and had the power of selecting and dismissing the servants and workmen. As there were upwards of four hundred persons in the establishment the labor was immense. He was always on horseback, dressed half as a religious and half as a secular, with a black great coat, high boots, a riding whip, and a round hat. His character and face corresponded with his functions. Always civil, good-natured, gay, prepossessing, and cheery, he was a first-rate intermediary between the world and the convent. He understood and loved children, for whom he had always a kind word and a merry laugh. My mother was touched by his manner. It was agreed that I should enter the college the next day, and be presented to the superior, the Père Debrosse.

VIII.

The following morning accordingly I was duly installed. The Père Debrosse was a fine looking man, and what is called "very good company." He was not clever, but governed the house by his sound common sense. He was a perfect model of virtue, piety, and modesty. He received my mother with marked respect and attention, but asked very few questions about me. It struck me that my antecedents were of little interest to him, and that he trusted to the good set among whom I should be placed, to the rule and to the excellence of the professors, to bring me back into the right way even if I had strayed from it. The conversation was long but not at all severe. He then made us over to the Père Génisseau that we might see the house and garden in all their details. Everything was in perfect order. In the school-rooms we heard the murmur of voices repeating the lessons in class, the calm voice of the professor predominating from time to time. The dormitories were large and airy; the refectory beautifully clean and nice, without being luxurious; the courts were finely sanded; the gardens shady and well kept. A ménage, a *salle d'armes*. and a tennis-court, were included among the means of exercise and amusement for the students. Nothing seemed to be too dear to answer this purpose. Evidently profit was the last thing thought of in this establishment — only the moral and physical welfare of the boy.

I went back with my mother to the Hôtel Chevalier, and we went to dine with M. d'Angeville and Madame de Chandor. I do not know how it happened, but a chance word, which I heard pronounced by the ladies, and of which I did not even know the sense, made me feel that my reputation (such as it was) had preceded me. "Oh!" exclaimed Madame de Chandor to my mother during dinner, "the good fathers are enchanted at the gift you have bestowed upon them in the person of your son, for they say he is a true *matador*." This Spanish word, which signifies the feller of the monster in the bull-fight, made me lift my head a little higher. "They already look upon me as somebody," I said to myself, when the word had been duly explained to me after dinner.

My mother stayed some days at the hotel to accustom me to our approaching separation, and to recommend me to the kindness of the best persons in the town. I went with her to see the Château de Pierre-Châtel, which was then a state prison, and which made a very painful impression upon me. We also made several expeditions to some of the most beautiful sights in the neighborhood, and were more and more struck with the wild beauty of the country.

When my mother at last was obliged to go home, I was already accustomed to my new position. It was a sad moment; but I was not now, as at Lyons, without hope. I seem even at this moment, to see her carriage toiling up the steep hill on the road which led back to Mâcon, by the gorges of St. Rambert, as I watched her white handkerchief, which she was waving from the window to wish me a last good-by. All that day I was sad; but my companions did not laugh at me, or intrude on my sorrow.

IX.

The next day I had already found friends. I chose them by their faces, an instinct which has rarely deceived me. The first were Italians from Turin, Alessandria, and Asti — Sambuy, Alfieri, Ghilini. They were all three of noble family in their own country. The neighborhood of Piedmont, the political sympathies of their parents, and the wealth of their families, had made them choose this Jesuit college in preference to any other. All the religious traditions of their nation flourished here. Alfieri, a tall and handsome youth, like his uncle the poet, was son of the marquis of that name, who was attached to the royal household of Savoy, and afterwards became ambassador (after the Restoration) to the Bourbons. He transmitted to the good Pères de la Foi the necessary sums for their luxurious establishment in France. Alfieri, with whom I have always maintained the same intimate relations, became president of the Piedmontese Senate during the late revolution. He owed his influence no less to his ability than to his high character. Sambuy, springing from a military race, followed the same career under Bonaparte, and greatly distinguished himself. As for Ghilini, his destiny was written on his face, which was the sweetest and most pleasing one possible. It was impossible not to fall in love with him at first sight. His mother and sisters could not have had bluer eyes, or a whiter and more transparent skin than his, or a more modest and grave expression of countenance. He was chosen as page to the Neapolitan Cleopatra — the beautiful Princess Borghese, at Turin. I do not know when he was called home by the Great Reaper; but he was the choicest flower ever culled on the slopes of the French Alps. A good many young men of Brescia, Bergamo, Bologna, Florence, and even Rome, joined their set. The college, in fact, was cosmopolitan.

X.

At the end of a few days my choice was made, and my first friendships became irrevocable. Boys choose, as I have said before, by instinct, which is as rapid as the eye or the ear. The Fathers tried me in one class after the other, to ascertain my mental capacity. One day I was higher, and one lower, in my work. It was difficult to know how to place me. In some things I was far above my age; in others a very child, and my inattention often discouraged my masters. At last I was put in the third or middle class, a sort of half-way position, in which one could be a child in the study of language and a man of taste in poetry and rhetoric.

One of the Fathers soon attracted me to himself. He was a man of good family, who was a priest in dress and in piety, but in other ways a man of the world; his name was the Père Béquet. I have never known his origin; but his high birth revealed itself in his delicate features, beautiful hands, aristocratic manners, keen and yet gentle look, and sweet voice, which made him loved and preferred to all the rest. He was not a bit of a pedant. His tone in class for young and old was that of a father of a family teaching his own children. He would joke even when pointing out a fault, and none of us ever saw him out of temper. His corrections, when necessary, were those of a mother. If they had cost us humiliation or tears, I believe he would have blushed and cried himself. The hour of his class was a real delight to us all. We did our work, but he always contrived to make it interesting, and often amusing. He often made us laugh, but we did so quietly, not to wound his high-bred sensitiveness and good taste by our roughness or rudeness. Every one in the class of the Père Béquet seemed insensibly to take their tone from him. His piety was attractive even to the most careless of us. When it was his turn to say mass, he said it with a tender recollection and devotion which was more edifying to us than half a dozen sermons. We seemed to feel as he felt, and his face was our best lesson. When the religious office was over, he resumed his bright playful manner with us directly the solemn shadow of God had left his face, and he was only all the more ready to enter into our feelings and amusements ; so that it was impossible to associate anything gloomy with his religion. He loved God with all his heart, but as a tender Father and Brother and Spouse, and he made us do the same. In playtime, or in the garden, or in our walks, he would pick out the best of his pupils, and talk to them familiarly and intimately on all sorts of subjects ; so that he became our great friend as well as our master, and one to whom we were not afraid to open our whole hearts. He thus formed and moulded us to his will, and communicated to his class a delicacy of feeling, a sense of honor, and a refinement of taste, which made us feel like a kind of confraternity. I need not say that I at once attached myself to this man with all the enthusiasm of my nature. In the Père Béquet was centred, in fact, the whole teaching of the college. As he became the vice-principal, and thus followed us in our studies up to the higher classes of rhetoric and philosophy, we had no other master for three years ; and the fruits of his teaching were shown in what I might call the graces showered on this portion of our lives. He would have been a perfect Fénélon for the education of a prince ; he remained by chance, or rather, as we felt, by the providence of God, a Fénélon to a mountain college. When the order was suppressed in France, Fouché fancying that the Jesuits were dangerous to the empire, his superiors recalled him to Belgium. No minister was ever more mistaken. So far from inspiring us with a spirit of hostility or opposition to the government, or with a taste for republicanism, their lessons and example tended only to give us a stronger love for monarchy, religion, and the empire. Bonaparte was deceived by his police minister. His uncle, Cardinal Fesch, was preparing for him good and loyal subjects — Fouché, soldiers, and Saïds. Fouché, unhappily gained the day!

XI.

The professor of physics and mathematics was a man who had joined the society from piety, and in gentleness and goodness resembled our dear Père Béquet. His name was Dumouchel. He had enough intelligence to see one thing through nature and science — and that was God. But he saw Him without a shadow of superstition, as the cause is judged by the effect. Mathematics were his forte; he never disputed — he proved all that he asserted. He was not a priest.

There was another professor, whom I have not yet described, but a man of a totally different stamp. He was called the Père Varlet, and was of the stuff of which the old monks were made. He was very well informed and clever, but austere and silent — his life was one long meditation. He had been appointed not only to the chair of rhetoric, for which he was quite unfit, but to be the habitual confessor of the students — an unfortunate selection. He acquitted himself scrupulously and severely of this duty; but his conscience was as fearful as our own. He was certainly a good man, but too silent and reserved to win our confidence. I recollect one spring when I had been ill, the doctors ordered me to take long walks in the neighboring woods. Father Varlet was one day told to take me with him on an expedition he was to make, for some reason or other, in the mountains. As he walked along, he said his office or prepared the lessons for his class, but never spoke a word. It was in the month of May; the country was exquisite with the breath of flowers which scented the whole air; the ground seemed a perfect mossaic of color. I loitered behind the Father, gathering these floral treasures till my hands could hold no more, and came back loaded to the college. The rushing mountain streams had sprinkled them with water, which looked like dew, and I was in the seventh heaven of delight! The Father did not deign even to look at them. To one of his ascetic temperament, my enjoyment of these minute beauties of Creation was almost a crime. Not one word of admiration could I extort from him on the subject of my floral treasures — unless they had been consecrated on the altar at Mass or at Benediction, they were to him but worthless weeds. We used to return very late to the college, after three or four hours of solitary walking, during which time we had not exchanged a single word.

This went on for two months. At the end of that time I was cured, but very much bored. The spring-time of this holy man had no flowers but in his psalms.

XII.

Although our superiors endeavored as far as they could without injuring private friendships, to avoid dangerous intimacies and secret conversations, although they preferred in our walks and games the number *three* to the number *two* — because three is always innocent and two is sometimes suspicious — we soon began to single out one or two amongst our companions and form little groups of intimate friends out of this great and mixed society. My first acquaintances were chosen from their age or place in the class next to me, but very soon I selected two with whom my sympathies and tastes were most in unison. The first of these was Aymon de Virieu. He was the son of the Marquis de Virieu, a member of the constituent assembly; inclined to be a revolutionist in 1789, but a counter-revolutionist in 1790. Then, in 1792, he commanded the Royalist cavalry at the siege of Lyons, and disappeared in the retreat without anybody being able to discover his body. He was evidently a warm-hearted, brave man, full of talent and courage, but of an excitable temperament, which, in the state of parties in France at that time, led him one day into one extreme, and one day into another. He was at one time closely connected with Mirabeau, then with the Court, but especially with Mounier and Lally-Tollendal, who sent in their resignation after the 6th October, and who contented themselves with writing against the Revolution without fighting against it. The Marquis de Virieu at first took refuge in one of his estates in Dauphiny, but when the Royalist troops besieged Lyons he could not resist joining them, and was killed in the struggle. It is difficult to do him full justice, his antecedents being ultra revolutionary, while his later life was just the reverse. But he was always a deeply religious man, and had a strong feeling for the maintenance of the aristocracy. His dream of reform was, in fact, confined to the nobility, and he had not calculated on its ultimate consequences. His opinions may be judged of by those of his son.

Virieu had two sisters, one married to M. de Quinsonnas, a most amiable person and the mother of several children, who are now rich and well-known in Paris. The other was Mlle. Sétphanie de Virieu, a charmingly pretty, clever girl, who never would marry that she might not leave her mother. She had a wonderful talent for painting, and her pictures seemed to grow under her hand as rapidly and eloquently as her speech. Her sketches were admirable and life-like; once taken by her you became immortal. Her talents were only equaled by her goodness. She lives now alone and solitary, in a château of her mother's in Gascony.

As to Virieu himself, the idol of his mother and sisters, he then lived in the province of Dauphiny on a property called Grand-Lemps, which had been the favorite residence of his father. He was about fifteen when I first knew him, and consequently a year or two older than I was. His features were not beautiful but very remarkable. His forehead had those bumps which phrenologists look upon as indicating certain great qualities. His fair hair, which curled over his forehead, gave him the look of an old Roman bust. But the wonderful part of his face were his eyes, which no one could look at without being startled. It seemed as if wit and genius poured out of them as from an inexhaustible source. His nose did not correspond with the rest of his face; the nostrils were too open, and gave him an ironical expression. But his fine and delicate mouth, with its short and arched upper lip, redeemed what was wanting elsewhere, and gave, like the eyes, a character of wonderful distinction to his whole countenance. His character was as varied as his features. He was an enigma to most people, but that made him all the more interesting. He was a mixture of Rabelais and Socrates. What was on the side of Rabelais as a child, amused and yet made one anxious for him. What was on the side of Socrates attracted one irresistibly. He always appeared to me in this light, and if I was repelled in one way I adored him in the other. For the same reason people said of him "that he had sugar and salt on his lips," but nevertheless I failed in separating myself from him, and we became fast friends.

As for me, it was evident that I made a different impression upon him, and that I helped to modify his nature in the right direction, and to bring him back to the religious teaching of his youth, more, perhaps, than approved itself to his reason.

But he died thus, and I thanked God for it His strong sense of right had sufficed to bring him back to his childhood's God. But at the time of which I am now speaking, he was still halting between two opinions, and that annoyed me. All arguments with him ended in a joke, whereas I could never bear to laugh on serious subjects. My mother had taught me not even to laugh at myself, but to realize that I was the work of God's hands, and, therefore, responsible to Him in all things. My face became grave and displeased when Virieu adopted a mocking, doubting tone in speaking of religion. This annoyance on my part, which I took no pains to conceal, influenced him, though insensibly. He was at first puzzled, not seeing how he had saddened one whom he heartily loved. Afterwards he understood me, and corrected himself as much as his nature would allow.

XIII.

The other friend I chose was a young man of Chambery, Louis de Vignet, a nephew of the Comte de Maistre. I did not then even know the name of a family with whom I have since been so closely connected. Louis was my first acquaintance amongst them, and he also was older than myself. We were not the least alike in character, but our minds had a great deal in common. It was in this way that we came to sympathize so much with one another. He was inclined to be sad and reserved. I was bright open and communicative. Although he was not yet arrived at the age when the passions devolop themselves, he had the silence and expression of a man already overwhelmed with suffering of this kind. His face was like that of Werther; his pale high forehead, and the black clustering hair which shaded it, gave him the look of an Italian; his eyebrows were strongly marked, and added to the depth and sadness of his eyes. His closed lips seemed to be afraid of compromising him by any light or careless speech. His figure was tall and slight. He was thoughtful and grave, and his head, which he naturally held down, showed the working of a mind far in advance of his age. No one could see him without remembering him. He made at once on me the same strong impression which he did on every one else. At first, I looked upon him with the respect of an inferior to one infinitely above me in everything. I tried to understand him, but I did not dare speak to him. He, on the contrary, sought me; and his conversation interested me the very first day more than that of any one I had ever heard. His mind, in fact, had a power and an originality which far surpassed his masters. He seemed sometimes to despise them. But when in composition, or in an examination, he was anxious to justify our high opinion of him, he used to come out like thunder from a cloud and surpassed every one. It was, in fact, almost impossible to come up to him. I was, in one sense, his rival; but I was ashamed of being compared with him. His superiority seemed to me to be so incontestable, he was so richly gifted in all ways, that I accepted my inferiority without envy and without pain. He was already great in everything, whereas I was only growing.

In the first school in which he had begun his studies, he

had acquired certain advanced ideas and thoughts which were very unlike those of a boy. In religion especially, he was a free thinker. At a time when we, children, had hardly begun to think at all, he considered himself an Atheist, though he did not dare to own it. I found that on this account his influence was dreaded and himself suspected by the masters. It is curious that my first ideas of incredulity should have come, as a boy, from one of this very family of Le Maistre, from whom afterwards were to emanate my strongest religious impressions. This proves how the thoughts of one single family, multiplied by five or six clever men, become a power in the world. Louis de Vignet was often out of humor — this sometimes affected our intimacy — yet I never was myself out of temper at that time. When he came out of what we used to call his "black fits," he found me just as he had left me. But take him all in all, he was certainly the greatest man I ever came across during my college life. He changed afterwards, and in some ways for the better, and died Ambassador at Naples.

XIV.

I have now described the two natures to whom chance or instinct had linked me at a period when intimacies often decide one's future character: Virieu, the type of the aristocracy, and Vignet, of genius. But there was one more who has recently died, Guichard de Bienassis, who was a complete contrast to the other two.

He was the only son of a good and amiable widow called Madame de Montlevon. M. de Montlevon was a man of a certain age, who had married, late in life, a woman of inferior rank. She had borne him this one son, and he had left her all his fortune, which consisted of a little château called Bienassis, situated in Dauphiny, at about half a league from the town of Crémieu. This house, which later became our headquarters, was built on a solitary hill, flanked by two towers and backed by a beautiful wood. A pretty stream shaded by weeping willows ran through the garden. By and by I shall describe its inmates.

Bienassis, who bore the name of his castle, was then half noble by his father, and half of the middle class through his mother, but he decidedly preferred the latter. He was a thorough child of Nature. He had found a little room in the castle which his father had converted into a library. This room was kept locked by Madame de Montlevon, but the key was hung in her bedroom. A young girl of fifteen, who was half-maid, half-companion, to Madame de Montlevon, was very fond of Bienassis, and at his request used to bring him very often this fatal key. He used to go by stealth into the library and carry off a provision of books, which he hid under his mattress. It need not be added that he chose those which were the most attractive, and yet the most dangerous at his age. The "Confessions" of J. J. Rousseau, so enticing at fourteen; Helvétius, so tiresome but so calculated to destroy all faith in a child's mind; Raynal, that bloated philosopher, who mistook declamation for elegance and affectation for feeling; Faublas's "Liaisons dangereuses," and other novels of the same kind, where vice parodied virtue, and riotous liberty, love. These, and works like these, had done their best to deprave this good and simple nature. He had become thoroughly imbued with these false sentiments and this mock wisdom. But when the true chord had been struck by J. J. Rousseau, his enthusiasm reached its height, and his admiration became a worship. The different passages which he knew by heart, and which he repeated to us with delight, used to enchant us. We would have given all we possessed for the key of the little sanctuary into which he had dived to such good purpose. Thus our group was composed of Virieu, the skeptic; Vignet, the incredulous; I, pious by instinct, but ignorant; and Bienassis, whose susceptibilities had been excited by these readings to an alarming extent. It was evident that some strong element was needed to direct four minds in such a state of doubt and ferment. This element was found, and I will tell you how.

XV.

One lovely spring day when all the country was radiant with flowers and sweet smells, and when the windows of our class-room, opening on the garden, let in great puffs of soft air, redolent of honeysuckle, and roses, and pinks, and verbena, our professor suddenly stopped in his thorny translation of Ovid, shut up his Latin dictionary, and taking up a book in a stitched cover which lay on the table beside him, he said softly to us: —

"Now, young gentlemen, I give you a holiday, and entire liberty to all of you who wish to enjoy this beautiful day. For you who are older, and who perhaps find greater pleasure in books than in games, I am going to ask your permission to read to you some pages of a new book, which I have just received from Paris. The author's name is M. de Châteaubriand. He is just come, not from a polytechnic, or normal or military school, but from the virgin forests of America. He had been sent there as one of a regiment of Vendeans, a battalion of emigrants, in fact, of the army of the Great Condé. Listen, or not, as you please. The waters and the woods will be silent, and the celestial spirits will give ear, for it is their Creator who speaks. Try only to understand the nobility of his language." This preamble struck us all immensely. We listened with all our ears. The good Father struck his hand on his book, and began with these words: —

"There is one God. The fool alone hath said in his heart 'There is no God.'" The simple grandeur of the ideas and the simplicity of the words laid hold of our imaginations, the solemn voice of the Father, the tears which seemed to be swelling up in his throat and trembling in his tone, the novelty of the style and the holiness of the author's dreams, completely captivated our imaginations. We heard for the first time what we had never realized before, the beauty of truth, the sentiment of greatness, the workings of the heart in the harmony of language — there was no need to tell us to keep silence! The end of the class coming only too soon, we rushed upon the professor imploring him to read just a few more pages; but he was inexorable, and we had to go out with all the unsatisfied longing which that wonderful volume had awakened in us. We talked of nothing else, and the promise to read us some more if we were diligent was the most infallible encouragement to work which our professors could have suggested. I was certainly the most touched, because the three notes of my existence, religion, melancholy, and family love, were likewise the key to Châteaubriand's divine genius. The next day, having accompanied my companions to the park of a beautiful country-house where we often went, belonging to a Colonel Maupetit, and the conversation having fallen on the "Génie du Christianisme," they asked me, "Well; what do you think of it?" "I," I replied, "I am enchanted, but not convinced." "And why not?" retorted a young man from Grenoble, who was afterwards drowned when bathing in the Isère. "Because it lacks, according to me, the principal element of perfect beauty, which is *nature;* it is beautiful, but it is too beautiful!"

These words pleased my audience, who thought them just; and in fact, I could not find any better explanation of my feelings about this book even now.

I passed a first-rate examination and obtained a quantity of prizes towards the end of the year. Vignet shared them with me. My mother had come to assist in the distribution, and be present at the solemnity. We acted a little play. Vignet and I had the first parts, and were loudly cheered. I returned home in triumph. The carriage could not hold all my (already faded) wreaths and my prize books, which, fortunately, were more lasting treasures. Milly soon made me forget all these follies. I found there Charles Chanut, my old friend, and Janette, my faithful love, and the simple tastes of my childhood resumed their full sway.

Bienassis made his mother write to mine for leave to come and spend a few days with him at his château in the neighborhood of Crémieu. Virieu was to join us from his home at Grand-Lemps. I obtained the desired permission and started joyfully. I never shall forget the day that I arrived at Bienassis, where my two friends had preceded me. No sooner did they see me from the tower of the castle, than they fired a *feu de joie* and waved flags and handkerchiefs from every window. I hurried my driver, and was soon in the arms of my friends. Madame de Montlevon received me like a mother. One saw that her boy was her idol, and certainly he was master of the house. We were very soon initiated into all the corners of the house, the orchard, the gardens, the fountains, and even the forest. We came back to dine at the castle, where every delicacy of the season awaited us. After dinner we went up-stairs and Bienassis brought us the fatal key, which a too good-natured person had lent him; we followed him in silence to the library, and there found ourselves in what appeared to us a paradise of thought. Each one chose the book most suited to his taste; I pounced upon the "Confessions of J. J. Rousseau," so full of beauty and of villainy. We plunged in silence into that sea of troubled waters, not knowing whether to be most shocked or astonished at what the head had dared to conceive, and what the pen had had the equal courage to record. We each of us carried off our favorite volume in our pockets to read at our leisure in our own rooms, or in the shade of the woods. We had gone into this fatal room innocent as children; we came out of it with the guilt of men. A turn of a key had given up to us the tree of the knowledge of good and evil. The two fruits were in our hands, it was for us to choose. We still had a sense of right; but we needed an experienced eye to make a selection for us out of such dangerous materials, in which curiosity and pleasure were our only guides. We had, it is true, a feeling of remorse at eating this forbidden fruit, but this remorse vanished in presence of the new passion which this kind of miscellaneous reading had developed in us. We were like bathers, who, at the first plunge into the sea, feel a kind of shiver at the waves, and then realize only the voluptuous freedom of the element. With these feelings we left the hidden library of Bienassis, where every species of corruption had been thus unconsciously revealed to us.

XVI.

After passing some days at Grenoble, whither we went from Voreppe and Voiron, we returned to Bienassis by the Lyons road. We were welcomed back as if we had been the sons of the house. The fatal key of the library was again lent by our accomplice. We found it simpler to leave the door open and hang the key as usual in Madame de Montlevon's bedroom. Her age and infirmities prevented her going up-stairs, so that we thus escaped her maternal vigilance. We read everything that we ought not to have read. Our life was perfectly delicious, and we prolonged our stay till nearly the end of the holidays. On our way back we stopped a day or two at Grand-Lemps, the austere house of Madame de Virieu and her daughter. It was a convent in a house of exiles. We respected its silence and shared in its prayers. It was like a home of the early Christians. Mademoiselle Stéphanie de Virieu, by her grace and beauty, no less than by her great talents, reminded one of those holy Virgins who sanctified the homes of the first martyrs in the time of the Roman persecutions. She was like a flower on a tomb, whose sweetness embalmed the air around her, and softened the sad recollections of her pious mother. This ascetic life made us ashamed of the bad books we had been devouring at Bienassis. Thus the world appeared to us under two contrary aspects. On the one hand, the giddiness of passion and skepticism in Madame de Montlevon's library; on the other, sorrow, piety, and mourning in the drawing-room of Grand-Lemps. These were the two distinct impressions which remained on my mind after my return home.

XVII.

I returned troubled but not altogether perverted to Milly. The genial piety of my family did not fail to bring me to repentance. The Pères de la Foi made me forget the library in Dauphiny. The first days of November I found myself again at Belley. This was a year of good and holy impressions. My imagination, touched by the example of my mother, and by the holy lives of the Fathers around me, took a complete turn. I realized, for the first time, the delights of religion, and might easily have been led on to positive fanaticism. If I were to live a thousand years I should never forget those days of conscientious study, those hours of fervent prayer, and those nights spent very often altogether in meditation; or the delight which I felt in the consciousness that I was accomplishing all my duties as in the sight and in the very presence of God. Yet I lost nothing of my usual gayety. On the contrary, no one can tell with what delight, that winter, I skated over the marshy flooded meadows, in the midst of ice and snow, flying rather than skating, through the clear frosty air; or how in the spring, seated in the shade of our favorite avenue, I breathed the soft sweet air and lifted up my heart to God in pious ejaculations, thanking Him for the peace of mind and conscience He had given me; while no sound disturbed the stillness around me, save the music of the scythe through the long thick grass, and the monotonous creaking of the wheels which bore home its fragrant load of hay down the hill-side. No, nothing will ever come up to these delights. The angels alone can have similar joys and similar feelings. I dreamt but of heaven and of God. I was good, and therefore intensely happy, except for an occasional longing for my home and family. I can imagine nothing more perfect.

This state of mind lasted for three years, with no other interruption than a course of study which had become play to me; excursions at the end of each scholastic year, which were always triumphs; and holidays at Milly, Bienassis, or Grand-Lemps, which were unmixed felicity although only, as it were, an essay of life. But in spite of my enjoyment, the love of liberty would sometimes overpower all other feelings. I could not help dreaming now and then of a life of entire independence. The Government of Napoleon strengthened these ideas; for every day there were rumors in the college that the Fathers were to be expelled, and that a quarrel had broken out on their account between the Emperor and Cardinal Fesch, the result of which would be that they would have to give up their admirable college, and send us all home.

XVIII.

What had been rumored came to pass. I then saw how governments are often deceived by their ministers. Bonaparte expelled the Fathers as enemies, and yet they were his best friends.

I left the college, as usual, loaded with academic honors, with a mixture of regret and yet joy in my heart, and I composed some verses of "Adieu" on my departure which are published in my works.

BOOK III.

I.

Hardly had I returned to Milly than I felt what a difficulty a young man of my age and class must be to my father and mother. What was to be done with a youth too old to remain idle, too distinguished in his studies not to be ambitious, and too aristocratic to serve the new Government? The *embarras* was great, and helped to strengthen my besetting sins of indolence and indecision. I should not have minded going into the law courts, where many of my companions were learning to become future counselors or judges; but the pride of my family revolted against the law as a profession. To join the army, which I should have preferred, would have involved me in the service of the present dynasty, which my parents might recognize, but whom they would not allow me to serve. To be auditor of the Council of State (which was offered to me) would result in my being forced to be a flatterer and a tool of the Imperial *règime.* Not one of these positions was possible to one of my birth, society, or antecedents; so that there was no alternative but to wait.

II.

Things remained in this state of indecision during the autumn and winter which followed my leaving college.

But, at the end of the following year, my father and mother took us to pass the winter at Mâcon, in a large house which they had just bought, and in which we installed ourselves. There I first learnt to understand what was meant by a serious passion. It was my first real love. Now, it appears to me to have been only the shadow of it; but the impression it left on my mind was deep and lasting. The lady who awoke this feeling in my heart died not long ago; therefore I can speak of her without fear; and, indeed, there was nothing in the smallest degree to throw a shade on her memory in the reciprocal affection of two children, for such we both were.

III.

There was, then, at that time in Mâcon, a young girl of fifteen or sixteen, of whom all the town spoke in raptures, not only on account of her great beauty, but of her singular talents and modest grace. Her name was Mlle. P. On her mother's side she was noble: on her father's of the middle class; so that both held her in equal honor, and she was received with the most flattering distinction in both sets of society. She had one brother, a vulgar, commonplace man, who seemed to have united in his own person all the defects of the father; whilst his sister had reproduced all the beauty and refinement of the mother, who, in fact, only cared for her. The father never appeared in the drawing-room; he lived alone in his own apartments. The son mixed with the lowest set in the town. Everything was as aristocratic about the wife as it was plebian about the husband. There were, in fact, two houses under the same roof; and, in visiting the mother, you were not *censé* to know the father, although he was a man of the strictest probity and honor. These contradictions rarely occur but in small country towns.

IV.

Mlle. P. wore on her face the signs of this strange destiny. She had the most delicate and beautiful figure which any sculptor ever idealized in a sylph. She danced as the dragon-flies skim over the water, her feet scarcely touching the ground. At every ball at which she was present, when the orchestra struck up a waltz, a circle was sure to be formed round her; the women to envy, the men to rave about her; but she never seemed to be conscious of it. This wonderful grace was part of her very nature. Her little oval head resting on her small white neck was beautifully formed. Her eyebrows were finely marked, and her long eyelashes shading her soft downcast eyes, made her look like a statue of Purity. Her half-shut eyes, her little half-open mouth, her delicate features, and her clear and transparent complexion, gave her face an expression which it was impossible to forget.

It was thus that this beauty suddenly appeared to me, and love first said to my heart "*Here I am.*" I felt a longing desire to go out of the ball-room and breathe the cold fresh air on the borders of the Saône. I did so, and came back when the orchestra struck up a second waltz — then went out — then came back again, till my friends burst out laughing at my proceedings, and called out to me, as I was disappearing a third time, "Stop! Mlle. P. is going to dance." She heard them, and cast a grateful glance at me in passing, as much as to say, "I saw you, and I shall think of you even when waltzing with another." Every time she passed me, she gave me the same kind, fixed look. That is how our acquaintance began.

When the ball was over, I staggered out like a drunken man. I followed a whole troop of young men who escorted her to her door. I saw that, after having wished them good-by, she still sought some one else. I did not dare advance, or go back. I stopped still. The door, which opened on some turning steps, as is often the case in Mâcon, was suddenly thrown open, and threw her back down the first step. Her mother uttered a cry of fear. I rushed forward and caught her, as she was falling, in my arms. Directly after I wanted to retire, but her mother called me back. "Ah, sir!" she said, "you must give us leave to express our thanks; come in; and as our introduction has been so obliging a one on your part, I must insist on making your acquaintance, and my child will promise you the first dance at the next ball." I followed her into the drawing-room where she gave us tea, and I asked permission to come the following day and inquire after the young lady. Her mother granted it with great kindness, her daughter thanked me with a look. I went out of the house mad with joy. For a long time I watched, from the angle of the quay, the lights from her window, which gradually went out; and I felt that that beautiful pure child was dreaming in her little bed. Did she think of me? I wondered. I came home very late and alone; but I could not sleep; my heart was too overflowing with happiness.

V.

The next day, when the *salon* of Madame P. opened to receive her friends, I was one of the first arrivals. I found Mlle. P. alone. She was evidently as much afraid of missing my visit as I was of not finding her. Thus our two hearts understood each other without a word; the same electric spark of sympathy ran through us both. The mother came in soon after, and received me as if I had been an old friend of the family. She did not visit my mother, for they were not in the same set of society. She knew her, however, by sight, and had that affectionate respect for her character which every one felt in the country. But the pride of my uncles and aunts would not have permitted the mixture of the old nobility with the new *régime*, or allowed them to be invited to our house. We only met, therefore, at the balls of the Prefecture, or at the *fêtes* occasionally given in the Town Hall, when there was, of course, a mixture of classes.

VI.

Madame P. was proud of her daughter. She had given her the education of an artist. She had learnt every possible accomplishment, especially dancing; that silent art which suited the dangerous times in which we lived, when an imprudent or incautious word might have had serious consequences. In those days a good dancer was as much esteemed as a clever orator or writer is now. Mlle. P. was really a modern Terpsichore. Her tall and elegant figure, the perfect suppleness and grace of her movements, the beauty of her arms, the delicacy of her feet, the soft languor of her expression, captivated every one even before she moved; but, when she began to dance, her lightness was such that she seemed hardly to touch the ground.

Her mother never took her eyes off her child. You saw that she was wrapt up in her, and that she was in fact the pride of her life. She had heard people speak of me as having had a brilliant career at college, of which not only my family but all Mâcon was proud. She was consequently flattered that I should have become the admirer of her daughter. She treated me as somebody and something above the rest; and flattered my self-love almost to the extent of compromising her charming child. In the very first conversation we had together she took care to make me understand that there were but two beings among the young people of Mâcon whom she considered worthy of attention — her daughter and myself: the one for her beauty and talents; the other for my birth, and for the superiority I had shown to all my academical rivals. She thus, as it were, set us apart, in a little world, to ourselves — a position which we were nothing loth to accept. At our very first meeting our eyes had said the same thing to each other, and we did not want even her mother's help to fall in love! Henceforth there was a sweet mystery between us; that is, we adored each other, and despised every one else. Her mother was a sort of accomplice, as she had been, from the first, our confidante. I very soon became the friend of both, and the *habitué* of the house. All the town seemed to me to favor my suit. Every one was full of the passionate affection which had broken out between the queen of the balls, Mlle. P., and the young student from Milly, who had so distinguished himself at college, and had fallen in love at first sight. Men smiled and women sympathized in our wooing. My family only either did not or would not see what was going on; and I took care not to enlighten them.

There was a lady in Mâcon, Madame L., who was noted for her beauty, but of a rather doubtful reputation, and who had married, late in life, an old Knight of St. Louis, who was a near relation of my father's. She kept open house, receiving every evening a large and somewhat mixed society, among whom Madame P. and her daughter were always found. When eight o'clock struck, Madame L. used to retire to her own apartments ; but the party went on, and Madame P. and her daughter and a good number of young people stayed chatting till midnight, or else got up some music, with that easy, happy familiarity which is the result of intimate acquaintance on all sides. One heard bright jokes and merry laughter all round ; but the happiest were those who, like me, leaning over the piano, listened breathlessly to the touching voice which spoke words understood only by ourselves. Such were our happy evenings ; and, when we parted, it was sadly, perhaps, but full of hope for the morrow. We did not use to say much to each other, but our silence was understood, and without words we knew at what hour we should pass by a certain street the next day, at what precise time we should meet in the green paths of St. Clément, and exchange a look — without stopping to speak, or awakening the suspicion of indifferent people ; sure of one another, and reckoning on making up for our silence by a long talk in the evening. Until then it was joy enough to have seen each other, if but for a moment. When a ball drew near, the consultation as to the dress to be worn, and the color of the bouquets to be chosen, was quite sufficient to satisfy us. Each understood the other, and our hearts needed no further symptoms of a love which knew no bounds. Her mother did not attempt to interfere with us. I saw, on the contrary, that she enjoyed it. As to the father, he never appeared, either in his own house, or in any other society. He was constantly at magistrates' meetings, or in his own quarters ; and only saw his child's dress as she crossed the road to go to the ball, of which she was the chief ornament.

VII.

Thus passed this happy and mysterious winter, which appeared to me to last but a day.

However, spring came, and the first green of the meadows gave a tender shade to the willow leaves by the river side. Walks outside the town, in which we always contrived to meet, had replaced the musical *soirées* at Madame de L's. A young lady of Mâcon generally accompanied Mlle. P., and by her amiable conversation enabled me to have many a *tête-à-tête* talk with her whom I loved. We profited by these moments, which friendship had so good-naturedly contrived for us; and it was very rarely that we met any one, or were interrupted. However, once or twice we met a man standing at the corner of the hedge close to the charming village of St. Clément, and he always bowed and looked at us with a certain amount of curiosity. This gentleman, whom I only knew by name, was, however, well-known in the town. He was an old friend of the family of P., and lived, since the Revolution, on a pretty little property in the village of St. Clément, where he was looked upon as a speculative philosopher, given chiefly to agriculture and contemplation. I appeared to be a special object of his attention, which rather annoyed me and made me anxious. I fancied that the rumor of my attentions to the young lady had reached him, and that he perhaps wished to judge by my appearance, if I were a man calculated to make her happy. I did not dare own my fears, however, to her who was the cause of them. But, before long, I did not rail to be enlightened on the subject.

Some days after, Madame P. told me that M. F. C. had the custom of giving a little *fête champêtre* every spring to her daughter and herself in his orchard at St. Clément; that his wife helped him to do the honors with her beautiful flowers, and her fresh eggs and cream, which were noted all over the country; that he had written to propose the following Sunday in the afternoon for their visit; that, having seen us together several times, he had ventured to ask me to join them, and had begged her to be the bearer of the invitation. I was delighted to have my share in this little family gathering, and concluded, in consequence, that I was not displeasing to their old friend and counselor. I saw that Mlle. P. was equally pleased, and prepared myself joyfully for the Sunday's *fête*. Madame de L. and Madame de X. were also invited; but I was the only *man* admitted, which filled me with hope.

VIII.

At last the Sunday came, and Madame P., her daughter, her two friends, and I started separately for St. Clément, not to attract the attention of the Mâcon gossips. We met in the steep and narrow path which led to M. F. C.'s villa, about half a league from the town, and in a few minutes found ourselves at the door. Mons. and Madame F. C. were waiting for us on the threshold, and received us as if we were the only guests they expected in the course of the year. Their first kind words were for me. "Young man," said the philosopher, "you are welcome to my hermitage ; and, as you are the friend of these ladies, you must look upon us likewise as your friends, for we have none dearer at Mâcon.' Then, taking the arm of Mlle. P., whilst his wife took the other ladies into the house, he led her and me all over the gardens, kiosks, and orchards of his pretty home, and made us eat the strawberries and cherries which grew in his beds in such wonderful profusion. "What a delicious place ! " we exclaimed, "and how one would like to live here forever ! " "Yes," replied the old man, smiling ; "but to be perfectly happy there must be *two*, must there not, for nature only seems to grant happiness to man on that condition ? " Mlle. P. blushed and looked at me as she hung down her head. I colored too. But our host did not seem to perceive it, and went on gathering some beautiful large gooseberries, and throwing them into her lap, while our talk became more and more intimate, till at last on suddenly turning a corner, we found ourselves opposite a thatched summer-house, where the luncheon was already prepared. We went in with him, and exclaimed at the beauty of the fruit, the richness and thickness of the cream, the great cheeses of St. Clément, the delicate cakes, so exquisitely light and varied, and all made by his wife ; and at the good wines, both white and red, which were the produce of his own vineyard. "Let us sit down, dear children," said the old man, "whilst we are waiting for those ladies ; let us have a little comfortable chat. Now tell me young man, what do you like best in my country retreat?" he added, with a kind smile. "I can feel nothing but the happiness of being here, sir," I replied. Mlle. P. looked at me again and colored. "But," he continued, one sees the sun this year everywhere. So you do the running waters, and the shady nut avenues, and the flowers and the fruits. Can you not find all these equally at Mâcon?" I smiled, and replied, "Yes, certainly, one can find these things elsewhere." "Well, then, it is not this which makes you so happy that you feel that you cannot be more so! What is it, then? Now to enable you to find out, I am going to leave you for a few moments, and go and seek those ladies. You shall tell me when I come back. And he went out with an air of secret satisfaction, and left us together.

IX.

As for me, I was certainly a thousand times happier than I had ever been in my life, but also a thousand times more timid and embarrassed. My looks, my sighs, and my attentions had often told her the state of my feelings; but I had never ventured on any actual avowal of my passion till this old man, as it were, forced it upon me. Covering my face with my hands, I remained silent.

"Let me go!" exclaimed the poor child, her shaking voice betraying her emotion; and she got up to escape. These words broke the spell, which seemed to enchain my speech. "Oh, no!" I at last cried, throwing myself at her feet. "You shall not go till my heart has spoken. Do not look at me; but let me only say that what makes me so intensely happy here is neither the sun, nor the trees, nor the flowers, nor the waters; but simply that I am here with *you*, and that I can at last tell you how I love you." A soft sigh was my answer. "Let us go," she repeated; "though I have said nothing, you will understand me." We went out after this double avowal, both of us scarlet with emotion, and soon met the old man, talking in a low voice with Madame P., who was leaning on his arm. We turned away, but he had seen our troubled faces, and understood all.

X.

When we returned to the house, we found the rest of the company. Madame F. C. made us see the inside of her house, the library, the drawing-room, the court-yard, the pigeon and chicken-houses, until our emotion was a little calmed, and then they came to announce that the luncheon was waiting in the summer-house. A silent joy filled both our hearts, which were overflowing with tenderness and trust. At last we felt sure of our mutual love. The old man seemed as happy as we were. He talked to us all the time about the happiness of his country life, alone with the only human being he cared for, and who was his wife. Mlle. P. looked at me from time to time with a soft smile. I felt I had nothing more to wish for here below. I came back in the evening, walking before Madame P. and her friends, and telling her daughter all the thoughts of my heart — thoughts which I did not know I possessed till then, and which she alone could have inspired. Everything now was understood and clear between us, and we had only to wait till circumstances should enable us to consummate the happiness the first germs of which had been revealed to us in the summer-house.

XI.

A few moments later our hopes were rudely dashed to the ground. I had gone home with them, and we were sitting side by side on a sofa, whilst her mother was dressing in an adjoining room, of which the door opened into the drawing-room. We spoke low ; for who likes such confidences to be overheard, however innocent ? The mother, who thought our silence strange, suddenly and softly opened her door, and whilst I (who had my back turned to the door) was whispering my fond hopes into the ear of her daughter, I felt a heavy hand laid upon my head ; whilst, with the other arm, she violently pushed her child away from me. " Is this the *réticence* which you had promised me, and in which I was such a fool as to confide ? Leave my house this instant, sir ; and you, mademoiselle, take care never to appear without me in a room where this young man is present. You are both unworthy of my trust!" I sprung up, humbled and indignant, at this unexpected outburst. Taking my hat, I prepared to leave; but protesting against this unfair imputation on the purity of her child. The poor girl herself burst into tears, and indignantly repelled her mother's unworthy suspicions. Madame P. saw she had spoken precipitately, and coloring, made some excuse. After a time we made it up. We promised to hold our tongues, and be only to each other as a very dear brother and sister. Our love remained the same as ever — the dream of two young pure hearts, who had nothing to reproach themselves with but love.

XII.

It was, however, impossible to stop the gossip of the town, and the affair soon came to the ears of my family. My mother spoke to me about it. I answered by asserting that I never could love a more accomplished or charming girl. She was wise, and agreed with me as to the superiority of Mlle. P.; but she represented to me, tenderly yet firmly, that we were both too young to think of settling in life, and that we must wait many years before it would be prudent to think of marriage. This answer calmed and quieted us, without extinguishing our mutual passion. Not to argue or positively refuse, but to counsel hope and patience, is the wisest remedy for the insane desire of extreme youth. I felt that I must have some change of scene and thought. My family were of the same opinion, and arranged it as if by chance.

The daughter of Madame de Roquemont (that cousin of my mother's of whom I have before spoken) had just married at Lyons. The honeymoon was to be spent in Italy. Certain business reasons served as a pretext for the young couple to visit Milan and Leghorn, where their parents had correspondents in certain commercial houses. It was settled that I was to accompany them. Three months before they had come to Mâcon to see my mother, and now they returned to arrange about the time of our departure.

XIII.

This journey to Italy was an immense joy to me. I left my love, it was true, but only for a few months, with the certainty that she would remain true to me, and with her equally firm persuasion that I should return with a heart as devoted to her as ever. The trial was short; the happiness certain. So I gave my whole mind to learning Italian, and devoted myself especially to Tasso, Ariosto, Alfieri, and others. Towards the end of that spring we parted. I had a perfect thirst for travelling. It seemed to me like the passion of the Infinite, which had no limits. Each new country appeared as a new world added to creation. My delighted curiosity seemed to grow at every turn of the wheel.

At last we got to Leghorn, on the borders of that exquisite Mediterranean — a visible infinity to infinite thought!

My travelling companions having the intention of spending some months here, took a house; while I went to a hotel in the next street, from whence I came every day to dine with the family. I passed several months in this way, hard at work all day at the Lingua Toscana; and all the evenings at the theatre or the opera; but I found time to write to my mother, and that with all the pride of my newly acquired knowledge. I may say that this time was my honeymoon of thought: my enthusiasm had found a new element on which to feed. I wrote also occasionally to Mlle. P.; but, at the risk of shocking my readers, I must own that my passion for her had a good deal cooled, and at last froze, like a globe which is removed from the sun. I had a pleasing remembrance of her, but that was all; my new passion for travelling had extinguished my rural flame of St. Clément. The remarkable faces of the Italian women had not perhaps more beauty than Mlle. P., but of a far more sensational kind. And then they were Tuscans, and their beautiful tongue seemed to me to have the accent of heaven itself.

XIV.

The month of October drew near when we were to start for Rome and Naples. But letters from Lyons changed the plans of my companions. It was decided that they should return home at once, without proceeding any farther on that delightful tour which we had planned together! The blow was terrible; but I soon determined that their plans should not affect mine. I wrote to my father begging his permission to continue my journey, saying that I was only a few steps from Rome, that dream of my youth, and very few more from Naples, the centre of all human delights; that it would be too cruel to dash the cup from my lips, which I had only just begun to taste: that I had enough money to spend the winter at Rome; that, in the spring, I should obtain from M. Dareste de la Chavanne (a relation of my mother's living in Italy) the sum necessary to go on to Naples; and that, therefore, I was going to take his permission for granted and start for Rome where his answer would find me. It was a bold step on my part; but, after all, not an unreasonable one.

Having written, I waited a few days for a reply; determined, however, that, should it be in the negative, it would arrive too late; and then started joyfully back to Florence, to make the necessary arrangements for my solitary journey to Rome.

XV.

There were only two regular ways of travelling at that time in Italy — by post or *vetturino;* but the former was beyond my means, and the latter was too hopelessly slow. Sometimes one had to wait five or six days before the driver had made up his party; and then, going on always with the same horses, which had to stop and bait continually on the road, you were an age reaching your destination.

From time to time, however, you could get a place in the mail-cart; and that I determined to try for. A man named *Tagglio Vino* offered me a place in one of these conveyances; we were to sleep for two or three hours in an *osteria* in the mountains; but to reach Rome in four or five days. I agreed to be ready the following evening at night-fall in one of the faubourgs of Florence; and accordingly, at the given hour, Taglia Vino and his carriage made their appearance.

I found four persons already settled inside, but my curiosity as to my fellow-travellers had to wait till daylight, for they all went to sleep soon after we started.

The first was a young man towards whom every one showed great respect. Taglia Vino knew him and called him "M. Le Duc," and was constantly on the watch to do him some little service. This care seemed to me to be needful; for though the weather was excessively cold, and we had to cross the snowy mountains of Camaldoli, he wore the thinnest possible coat, with short breeches, silk stockings, and thin shoes, as if he had just come out of a ball-room. The very sight of him froze me; but he did not seem to feel it, and continued his journey with great gayety and good humor. The second was a young man with a charming countenance, who appeared to be the son of the actor Davide, an old and well known singer, who was very famous at that time in Italy. You will very soon see why I said *appeared to be the son.* This young man had the long hair of a woman hanging over his shoulders; his features were soft and delicate, but his black eyes brilliant and bold. I could not help lowering mine when he looked at me. The third traveller was Davide himself, a cheery, fat, jolly old man, a good and rather comical talker, and reminding one of Lablache. Everything he said began with a joke and ended by a hearty laugh. No one could help liking him.

We were very soon all four fast friends. The pretended son of Davide seemed to be particularly attracted by me. He always followed me when we got out of the carriage to walk up the hills, and explained the country to me which he knew thoroughly. At Terni he pointed out the remains of the magnificent Roman bridge the arches of which unite the hills of Clitumna to the Roman Campagna. When we first caught sight of the Eternal City on her Seven Hills, the Duke, Davide, and his companion urged me to go and lodge with them in the Via Condotti, at the inn where they generally stayed, and which was the *rendezvous* of the greater portion of the French, German, and Swiss travellers. I accepted their proposal with joy; it made me feel at once at home, and as if my companions and myself had become one family; Taglia Vino even was less of a driver than a friend.

At last, towards evening, we perceived, above the fogs of the Tiber, something immense, which seemed to float in the heavens and which reflected the last rays of the setting sun. It was the dome of St. Peter's. The night was closing in when we reached the Piazza del Popolo. The Via Condotti was to be our destination; they gave me a very pretty room, and the Duke went to the opera to see his illustrious parents; Davide and his son were lodged in an adjoining apartment. I could not sleep for thinking of Rome: it was, however, very sad and very desolate just then. There was neither Pope nor Cardinals; Bonaparte had made a clean sweep of them all. The Pope was at Savona.

XVI.

The next morning on going down to breakfast, I found the good Davide and his companion, the latter transformed into a beautiful woman. Her name was Camilla; she was a singer in Davide's theatre, whom he took about with him from kindness, so that she might be under his care and protection.

"One's clothes do not change one's heart," said Camilla to me, smiling at my astonishment. "Only you will no longer sleep on my shoulder, and, instead of receiving flowers from me, *you* must get *me* some." Davide and his pupil spent several weeks at Rome. Camilla knew the town by heart, and used to take me at the best hours for seeing this beautiful city — the morning under the dome of the stone pines in the Pincio; the evening under the shade of the grand colonnade of St. Peter's; by moonlight in the solemn inclosure of the Coliseum; and in the glorious autumn days to Albano, Frascati, or the Temple of the Sybil, echoing with the foaming cascades of Tivoli. Camilla was bright and gay, like a figure of eternal youth amidst these vestiges of bygone times; she danced on the tomb of Cecilia Metella; and while I was sitting dreaming on a funeral mole, her beautiful but somewhat theatrical voice echoed through the Palace of Diocletian.

In the evening we returned to the city, our carriage full of flowers and fragments of marble, and rejoined her old companion Davide, whose affairs kept him at Rome, and who took us to finish our day in his opera box. The fair singer, who was a good deal older than I was, had no other feeling for me than a kind of brotherly liking. I was much too shy to show any other; but, besides, I did not feel any more affection than herself in spite of her beauty and my youth. Her man's dress, her easy familiarity, the male sound of her contralto voice, and the freedom of her manners, gave the impression of her being simply a handsome young man, whom I could treat as a companion and a friend. When Davide left the hotel in the Via Condotti, I went to seek a lodging for the winter elsewhere.

XVII.

I had taken an Italian professor, who had been introduced to me by a German of great distinction, the brother of M. de Humboldt and an eminent diplomatist, who dined at the same *table d'hôte* as myself in the Via Condotti. This old professor was called Giunto Tardi. He was a very handsome man, and had married a Russian widow lady. He had been named consul at Rome during the short-lived reign of the Republic, which the French soldiers had quickly crushed. Giunto Tardi had gone quietly back to his position as a Roman citizen; but his moderation and justice, during his short tenure of office, had given him a high place in the esteem and consideration of his countrymen. He lived as a poor man, but much respected in the town which he had governed, and maintained himself by teaching rich strangers his native language. I took him not only to teach me Italian, but as a master of literature, and we became great friends. I shall have occasion later to mention his brother, who bore the same name, but who was a distinguished painter. I was his guest for a few days, and he set me the example of every Christian virtue.

XVIII.

M. de Humboldt, the Prussian diplomat, was a man whom I thought far superior to his brother, the author of "A Journey to South America," and "Cosmos," whom I also knew but esteemed less, in spite of his great name and reputation. A clever man he was ; but without much real merit ; it would be difficult to cite anything remarkable in his works, except his adulation of French philosophers and heroes of various shades of opinion, as he had discovered that theirs was the only real European glory. People speak of him as "the friend of Arago," "of Châteaubriand," "of Napoleon," "of Louis XVIII.," etc., &c. ; he always, in fact, worshipped the rising sun, and managed to get a reflection from its rays. This reflection (accumulated during thirty years) made him appear to many as a bright light, while he was in reality only a flashing fire-work.

When one considers his extraordinary reputation and the mediocrity of his talents, one is bound to acknowledge that he was a master of *savoir faire.* His brother, on the contrary, was a frank, modest, and clever statesman. He flattered none, but won the good-will and esteem of every one. This is the feeling with which he inspired me at eighteen, and I have seen no reason to change my opinion since. The other obtained his reputation by a cheat, which is worse than not having deserved it.

XIX.

When Davide, Camilla, and M. de Humboldt were gone, I stayed alone in Rome with no other companions than the monuments and ruins, which Camilla had made familiar to me, and my Italian master. I asked the latter if he would allow me to make acquaintance with his brother, to which he consented. I went daily to see him. His studio was an isolated convent in an obscure corner of Rome. He sold me a charming picture of the Cascades of Tivoli for a few Roman scudi.

It is a model of beauty and patient skill. I still have it at St. Point, and look at it whenever I wish to remember those happy, peaceful days.

Another artist, a lady named Bianca Boni, did a beautiful copy of Guido for me which I have never parted with. It is a Virgin, but with an exquisite expression. The features are angelic, and the forehead, mouth, and neck are positively radiant with light. Her eyes are looking upwards, as if they could not think of sublunary matters. A large blue veil falls over her head, hides her hair, and falls on her shoulders. Everything in this composition is ideal, chaste, and pure; it is better than a woman, and more than an angel; it is the Virgin before the Annunciation.

I had my picture taken by Bianca for my mother; and as she was young, gentle, and very attractive, I was fool enough to fall in love with her, and let her see it. She was furious, destroyed the likeness she had taken of me, and sent me back the money she had received for the portrait. I wrote a humble note of excuse and apology, and left the sum again at her door, telling her that I had been justly punished in being deprived of the work of her hands; but that it was not just that she should lose the price of her time which was so precious to her; and so implored her to receive back the money. But she was inexorable, and made me feel that these great Italian artists are likewise women of high and unimpeachable virtue. I distributed the money she would not accept among the poor. Such was the result of my first adventure in Rome. Bianca Boni inspired me ever after with a respect which was worth a good deal more than my stupid affection.

The old painter, brother of Giunto Tardi, was another object of my esteem; I might almost say, of my veneration. He rarely left his studio but to go to mass with his wife and daughter, a young girl of sixteen, as virtuous and good as himself. Their house was a species of monastery, where work was only interrupted by a frugal repast and by prayer.

BOOK IV.

I.

ONE day, at the *table d'hôte* of the Via Condotti, I became acquainted with a young Lyons merchant, who, after a time, proposed that we should go together to Naples. This young man was gentle, good, and well educated. I accepted his proposal, and had no occasion to repent it. He was a very agreeable companion, and we started in his own carriage.

We slept at Terracina, the brigands having made night travelling too perilous. We went on the next day, and suddenly heard a succession of shots fired in an olive wood on our left. Soon we came upon a carriage half burnt lying in the middle of the road, which was that of the courier from Rome to Naples. The bodies of two travellers were lying dead on the roadside, and a wounded horse lay in the middle. Some soldiers were guarding them, while others were pursuing the assassins, and firing on them as they fled from rock to rock of the mountains above us. We were very much shocked, and continued our journey not a little saddened by the scene we had just witnessed.

II.

We arrived at Naples as the night fell; the noise and bustle of the streets and public thoroughfares positively deafened us; while the sea was lit up by the reflection of the countless lights which burned in the shop windows, or in the niches of the Madonna. We drove through the street of the "Florentines," which crosses that of "Toledo," and stopped at an hotel well known to my Lyons friend. After the silence and stillness of Rome we seemed to have passed into a new world. The next morning I was woke by some monks who sang verses in our honor, and brought us magnificent fruits from Castelamare, and other presents from the convent, for which, however, we had to pay handsomely. Then I got into a little carriage and went all over this enchanting town. I was quite delighted. No city had ever produced such a magical effect upon me; Rome was a monastery, Naples the Garden of Eden.

Nature and man seemed to have combined to produce this most perfect spot. From the moment of my arrival I was scarcely myself; I was boiling all over with emotion, and could not stay still in one place. I rushed off to the post-office; they spread out a quantity of letters on a board before me. I found one addressed to myself, which was given to me readily enough when I had paid the postage. It was from my old friend M. de Virieu, to whom I had written from Rome. He replied that he was just starting from Grand Lemps with his mother's consent, and with a letter of credit on Rome and Naples, and that he should join me almost as soon as I had received his letter.

In fact he arrived a very few days after. He met me at the hotel Fiorentino, where I had prepared a room for him, and where we became intimate with a young Calabrian gentleman, who initiated us into the mysteries of gambling. This was the first time that that wonderful temptation had assailed us. At that period in Naples the great game was the *trenta e quaranta*, played in a public room at the end of the Via di Toledo. This young Calabrian was married, but as inexperienced as ourselves. We used to spend hours in losing or spending a few *carlini*.

III.

I had all this time a kind of compunction about certain letters of introduction which my mother had given me to M. de la Chavanne, director of the tobacco manufactory at Naples, and which I had hitherto neglected to deliver. Liberty without control seemed to me infinitely pleasanter. At last, however, I felt I could no longer delay my visit. I inquired for his house and was directed to a magnificent establishment dedicated to St. Pietro Martyro, in the most noisy quarter of the town. It was just midday; I climbed up a magnificent staircase of one hundred and twenty steps till I got to the fifth or sixth story. Below was a large garden surrounded with arcades. These arcades and the lower story of the house were filled with vats, workshops, and other things belonging to the state manufactory. I took in every detail of this picture, which remained indelibly impressed upon my mind, as it led to one of the great events of my life, and in fact was to bring about a decisive change in my existence.

Arriving out of breath at the top story, I rung at a great door which gave entrance to a large and long cloister, out of which opened different doors to the right and left. At the end of this gallery were three large windows called *finestrati*, which threw a brilliant light on the cloister itself. A number of young girls crossed and recrossed this place every moment, carrying I knew not what in their aprons. I found afterwards that these children were employed in choosing the finest tobacco leaves for the manufacture of cigarettes. I was far from imagining that one of these very girls would soon become *Graziella*, change her occupation, and influence forever my future life. I did not dare own the truth when in 1847 I wrote the novel of "Graziella," which had such a success because every one recognized that it was true to nature. I had from vanity altered the first few pages, but all the rest was exact. Now I am going to make a full confession of the whole facts, and give you the true history of "Graziella."

IV.

At the end of the cloister to the right, I perceived an open door and a good many servants, going backwards and forwards, carrying plates and dishes, while inside the room I heard the clatter of knives and forks. I saw I had inopportunely chosen the time of M. le Directeur's breakfast; but it was too late to go back; I had already sent in my card and was announced.

No sooner had he heard my name, than M. de la Chavanne rose and received me with open arms, exclaiming, "He is the very image of his mother!" He embraced me with the greatest warmth and tenderness, and made me sit down on a sofa under the window which lighted the breakfast-room. I found out that this house had been a monastery, and that we were in the room of the old superior of St. Pietro Martyro. Two other persons were breakfasting with M. de la Chavanne: one from twenty to twenty-five years old, named Antoniella—a pleasing person but with nothing very striking about her; she was evidently on intimate and confidential terms with the director, and had, as I afterwards found, the superintendence of the young girls employed in the cigar manufactory; the other was a most charming girl, but of her I shall speak later. Our conversation, in which neither young lady took a part, turned entirely on my mother and her family. M. de la Chavanne declared that he would never allow me to remain in a hotel at Naples, and that he would give me a charming little room in his house looking on the sea. He got up to show it to me, and I found a most comfortable room with a camp bed and a winding staircase leading up to the flat roof of this immense convent, from whence there was a glorious view of the sea, with Capri, Sorrento, and Vesuvius. A trellised wall sheltered a portion of this beautiful terrace from the wind; so that you were at the same time warmed with the genial Italian sun and your head shaded from its rays. I came down quite delighted with my little apartment, promising myself the pleasure of occupying it as soon as possible.

M. de la Chavanne, of whom my mother had often spoken to me, was a man of between forty and fifty years of age, and of remarkable goodness; his frank, cheery face and cordial manner made one love him at first sight. He was tall and large; his honest blue eyes looked you straight in the face, and his mouth alone would have told you his character; it was the very type of benevolence and sweetness It was really impossible not to love him. He had served valiantly with his countrymen against the army of the Convention at the siege of Lyons. This seige had ruined him, and he had sought refuge in Italy. Here Murat, king of Naples, had given him the directorship of the state tobacco manufactory, a lucrative and honorable post. He established himself at Naples, and became rich and happy. He had left his wife and several sons in France, whom she had brought up admirably. From time to time she came to see him; he loved her devotedly, and was equally loved by her; the necessity of being so often separated from her was the only thing which ever embittered his life. He lived at Naples as an exile; but as one who endeavored to forget it by active work for those dear to him. He was adored by all the French in Naples and by the Neapolitans themselves, who knew him by the continual kind services which his position enabled him to render them. He was always kind and generous, fond of young people, and ever ready to contribute to their amusements. Such was the man into whose home I had thus been admitted, and I could have found no one so worthy of my esteem and affection. In taking leave of him, I felt the attraction which he universally inspired, and promised to return in a few days and take advantage of his generous hospitality. I had not then scarcely realized the secret and invincible charm which strengthened my resolution; *i. e.* the thought of seeing once more the fascinating face I had had a glimpse of at his table.

V.

On returning to Virieu, to whom I had to break my approaching separation from him, in obedience to my mother's wishes, I went to the post and there found a letter directed to me in an unknown writing from Mâcon, which I opened with a trembling hand. It was from the old man of St. Clément, the friend of Madame P., and ran as follows: —

"SIR, — Your age and position made me believe that your affection for Mlle. Henriette P. (of which, as an old friend of her family, I had heartily approved), would result in a union which would secure your joint happiness; your departure and prolonged absence have given rise to certain doubts and scruples in my mind. Mlle. Henriette is very young, and so are you; you are not yet your own master, and you cannot answer for the wishes of your parents. I am, therefore, charged to tell you, in her mother's name, that proposals of marriage have been made to her by another person, whose character and fortune promise her that which, I fear, it would not be in your power to give her for many years. Be so good, then, as to examine your own heart and conscience, and to let me know whether you still have the same feelings for this young lady as when you left Mâcon; and if her family may expect from you as favorable settlements as those which are now offered her elsewhere. We wait for your answer, and remain," etc.

VI.

This letter, which was evidently written with the concurrence of Madame P., if not of her daughter, troubled me very much. I took some days to think about it. I certainly was anything but free to choose; I had nothing, or next to nothing, of my own. I could only love her; but I could not, without great imprudence, answer for the consent of my family to a union, which I was not quite sure now of even wishing for myself. So I wrote a frank and prudent letter, explaining my position, and virtually leaving the decision in the hands of Mlle. P. herself.

I learnt soon after that she was about to marry her other suitor. I regretted her; but I felt that her parents were right not to sacrifice the future of their child to an illusion of seventeen. Thus ended my first love dream, which was only a short but delicious bit of imaginary happiness.

I did not see her again for thirty years, when we met, with some regret perhaps, but with no bitterness. There are passages of this sort in most men's lives, which seem to be but dreams of our first youth. Mlle. P. was one of those fancies. She was very happy in her married life, and was united to one who was far more worthy of her than myself. I was still a child, and scarcely knew my own mind. But I wished to be sincere and loyal.

VII.

After having passed a day or two longer with Virieu in our hotel, I went to live with M. de la Chavanne. It was only a few doors off. I used to part with Virieu at night, sure to meet him early the next day; so that he became reconciled to our short separation. M. de la Chavanne was not at home when I arrived at his house. I was received by his old Neapolitan cook, and by that charming child, Graziella. She opened the door of the little room assigned to me, undid my portmanteau, and placed my things in the drawers, even kneeling down to take the creases out of my clothes. Every movement of hers was full of grace; only she seemed to me more shy and pale than the day I had seen her at breakfast. I scarcely dared raise my eyes to look at her, and felt distressed at her waiting upon me in this manner; but we scarcely exchanged two words. I felt as if she were one of my sisters, who had come as usual to do little things for me on my return from a long journey. The simplicity of her manner and dress added to my illusion.

VIII.

After settling me in my room, we went back to the drawing-room, where she took up her work, and we began to talk a little. Antoniella came in from the large workroom, where she had been superintending "her children," as she called them, in the cigarette factory. Then came in the master, and the breakfast. We sat down to it as before. "Now I must introduce you properly to one another," exclaimed M. de la Chavanne gayly. "This one is Antoniella. She is a good child, and very useful to me in the factory. She chooses, admits, or sends away the novices of my convent, who number some hundreds, and who are employed not exactly in saying their prayers, but in making cigars and cigarettes. She knows all the poor people and lazzaroni of the place, and finds out which of them have too many children to support, and wish to get work in my establishment. She manages all this quite admirably, and lives with me, as you see, like my daughter, to receive and transmit my orders. Everybody is pleased and satisfied with her — employers and employed. My little workwomen are like her own sisters or children. She watches over them like a mother, and reports to their families if there be any cause of complaint in the workrooms; and so she helps me to keep perfect order and peace in the establishment. They call her in Naples '*la madre delle cigarette.*'" At these words, Antoniella burst out laughing, and M. de la Chavanne, glancing at her with his kind, paternal face, smiled also. "Now," he continued, "as for this little girl" (pointing to Graziella, who colored up to the eyes), "who is still a child, Antoniella is teaching her French, that she may be some day my interpreter between the administration and the directors. who are our countrymen. She is called Graziella, and is the daughter of a poor fisherman in the island of Procida, who has a whole tribe of children. She only receives the pay of a cigar workwoman, but she transmits it regularly, at the end of the month, to her mother, *La Procitana.* She does not, however, work with the rest but lives with us, so as to be under the immediate care of Antoniella, who is her friend and protectress. She superintends the house under her directions, and transmits my orders to the servants, who are Neapolitans, and whose *patois* she alone understands. She is still a child, as you see; but a good child, and beloved by everybody. I treat her more as a father than as a master. She orders everything here, and is our aide-de-camp, or rather, our mouthpiece. Ask for whatever you wish. She is at your orders; only do not look at her dress, which is that of the children of Procitana, of the peasantry of an island from whence Naples obtains her most beautiful and her most useful servants. Their costume is, in fact, a mark of servitude in Naples, but of nobility in their own island. Go and dress yourself as a Procitana," he added, turning to Graziella; "Antoniella will help you."

The shy and beautiful child went out with Antoniella, and returned in a few moments entirely transformed. It was like a scene in a play. On her feet she had little yellow slippers without heels, of which the leather was finely embroidered in red and silver; her blue stockings seemed not to be knitted, but wove in some kind of bright stuff. A woolen petticoat, with a multitude of fine plaited folds, and of a dark yet bright brown shade, fell to her feet; a boddice of green velvet cut square, and made into a point before and behind, revealed her neck and bosom, but both of which were modestly covered by a chemisette of fine lace and embroidery, closely buttoned down the front. The sleeves and waistband were trimmed with rich braiding and embroidery, and are alike for rich and poor. The head-dress, except on a journey, consisted of nothing but a profusion of raven black hair, rolled in a thick cable round the head, like a living turban. Her throat and ears were ornamented with a beautiful necklace and ear-rings of ancient Greek workmanship, and of very fine gold, the pendants of which clicked like the little bells of a horse in a circus. The blushing face of the child revealed a mixture of shame and bashfulness, partly with the consciousness of her own beauty, and partly with the sense of our appreciation of it. We looked at her with mute admiration; and had she been less of a child, I should not have dared to lift my eyes. In a few seconds she disappeared, and ran off to put on her every-day dress. But the effect had been produced and the blow struck. I could not forget it, and henceforth never saw her in her ordinary costume without recalling the Procitana, and looking upon her merely as a shadow of her real self. The dress she generally wore was only a common, coarse, brown stuff, fastened close round her throat, without any ornament whatever, and a simple blue handkerchief tied round her neck. Her beautiful little feet were disguised in untidy, heavy, black shoes, generally down at the heel. Such was the chrysalis — but what about the butterfly?

IX.

Virieu came to see me in the course of the day. His father, as I before said, had commanded the cavalry at the siege of Lyons. M. de la Chavanne had followed him in his last charge, and had been all but a witness of his death. They talked a long time of this fatal day. Virieu dined with us, and was as much struck as myself with the marvelous Grecian beauty of *la Procitana.* That evening Virieu and I went out together, and I accompanied him to his hotel. In passing the Via di Toledo we went in, from curiosity, to the Palazzo Fiorentino, opposite the theatre. This was the public gambling house, permitted but superintended by the police. Immense tables, surrounded with silent players, filled the rooms: great heaps of gold and silver were piled on the green table by the side of each player. We were soon drawn in to join the game, risked some *scudi* and lost. That evening, and the next, and the day after, we did the same. We could not understand why the luck was always against us. Whilst we were grumbling about it in the recess of one of the windows, an old Neapolitan came up to us, and told us, that as long as we played in that way, without sense or plan, we *must* lose; that this game was not one of chance, but of skill and science; that we were not to expect large gains but moderate profits; that he himself had once been a victim like ourselves; but that he now lived on what had formerly been his ruin. We listened to him with astonishment. He saw it, and lowering his voice, proposed to give us lessons at hazard, having been himself a *croupier* of a gambling table, and having masses of cards with which he could prove his theory to our satisfaction. With the ignorant and self-confident folly of youth, we accepted his invitation, and made an appointment with him the following evening in Virieu's rooms. The old man was punctual, and having thrown on the table a *mass* of cards, that is, ten or twelve packs, the game began.

"Play as you will, gentlemen," he said quietly, "and I will bet you anything you like that, by the end of the evening, I shall have gained and you will have lost." He threw down the cards, we played and lost, his gains were very small, but he always won.

We tried twenty times and always with the same result. We were confounded. "Why then are you not yourself rich?" I asked him at last. "Because riches are not the result of even successful gambling, but of honest labor," he replied. "I never promised that I should show you how to get millions, but small sums. Will you try again?" "Yes,' we answered. "Well, I am now going to show you my system, and explain on what it is based. Now listen to me. What is *trenta e quaranta?* A game in which the player, playing against the bank, gains every time that the color *black* or *red*, on which he has betted, approaches nearest to the number forty, without going beyond it, for, if it goes beyond, the player is dead. He must, therefore, calculate, as nearly as he can, which is the color, whether black or red, which offers the best chance of arriving at the winning number, and conform his play to that. Understand, once for all, there is in reality no *luck* in it, only skill and memory."

X.

The old croupier, without giving us more of his practice and experience, played for another hour, and following out the calculations he had suggested to us, went on winning, while we, trusting to luck, always lost.

He promised to return at the same hour on the following day. I was anxious to find out if it would always come to the same in the long run; and if he could *always* reckon on small but certain sums. The next day, and for twenty days running, we were confirmed in this belief; he steadily won so many *scudi* a night, and we lost as many Napoleons. It was becoming serious, and I asked myself: "But what is the cause? for, after all, chance is but an effect of which we do not see the reason; let us go on and try to find it out."

All the winter the croupier came, and we devoted our evenings to him, either at Virieu's hotel or at M. de la Chavanne's. One saw nothing but cards. One heard nothing but *trenta e quaranta.* M. de la Chavanne's French friends came and chatted round the braziers, in which the olive wood chips burnt without smoke or flame. Antoniella and Graziella worked on the sofa in the corner of the room. From time to time Graziella would look up at me and try to smile ; but then her face would suddenly become grave, as if she said, "What a pity that so sensible a young man should have a taste for gambling."

But the croupier cut his cards perseveringly, and we could discover nothing except the fact that he regularly pocketed our *carlini*.

XI.

In this way our Naples winter passed until the beautiful early spring lit up the waves and mountains of Castelamare. Vesuvius began to grumble and launch out angry puffs of smoke and flame, from time to time. Virieu was ill, and did not leave his room. I had met on the staircase of his hotel one day, M. Humboldt, the diplomatist, whom we had left at Rome. He received me like a son, and proposed to carry me off with him on a tour he was about to make in Calabria, after he had studied the volcano of which the threatened eruption had become more serious. I accepted his offer with joy; and yet I was sad at leaving Graziella when I thought of her. But as yet we had come to no explanation.

BOOK V.

I.

M. DE HUMBOLDT came to fetch me at M. de Chavanne's. At the moment of getting into his carriage he asked me: "Who was that beautiful child?" and I, looking up at Graziella, saw that her eyes were full of tears. Why did she cry; and why did she follow the carriage with her eyes till we were out of sight?

The horses rapidly took us on the road to Pompeii and Torre dell' Annunziata, a pretty village which you come to before arriving at Castelamare, and which is built at the foot of the mountain. We put up at a little inn still nearer to Vesuvius, and sent for guides and mules to conduct us to the hermit whose cell was built on the highest habitable cone. After two or three hours of fatiguing march, either upon cooling and slippery lava, or on hot ashes, of which the smoke nearly blinded one, we stopped on one of the lower spurs of the mountain. On turning round we felt as if we were floating in the sky: the sea, the islands, the capes, and Naples, all seemed to spring out of the earth at our feet. We could not resist an exclamation of pleasure. At last we reached the hermitage; the hermit had ceased to sleep there at night, fearing to be surprised in sleep by a sudden outburst of the volcano. We sat down on the bench at his door, gazing at the wonderful scene beneath us, which the ether seemed to have evoked from the void below. At last the hermit himself arrived on his donkey, which carried besides a quantity of flasks of Lacryma Christi; the hermit having catered for his guest as well as himself, and making us pay largely for the luxury. He was, however, a thoroughly good fellow, not belonging to any regular religious order, but one of those ambulatory friars who attach themselves to certain localities from whence they draw their means of subsistence. I should say that this monk was of the "Order of Vesuvius," and nothing else. He changed his cell according as the eruption changed its course. The rest of the time he entertained travellers; his cell was a picturesque and sacred house of refreshment.

M. de Humboldt and I sat down on each side of his little table, and talked to him about the mountain and the general prelude to the eruptions. I resolved next day to study it nearer by descending the crater. It was of no sort of use my doing so, for I was neither a *savant*, nor a naturalist. I did not even know the names of the scientific specimens which I proposed to bring back with me; but I was just at the age when one wishes to be thought rather foolhardy, let it cost what it might; somewhat of the race of Empedocles, who left his sandals on the borders of Etna. I induced two of our guides to return to Torre dell' Annunziata to fetch the cords necessary for the perilous descent of the crater. M. de Humboldt laughed at my preparations, and endeavored to dissuade me from so rash an act without any possible object. But I was only the more strengthened in my pride and folly, and woke the next morning as determined as ever to carry out my plan.

II.

Vesuvius had been silent through the night. The sunrise was magnificent; one saw nothing but a puff of yellow smoke belching forth at intervals from the pointed cone above our heads.

We started early, following our guides, who had brought the cords, which I had ordered during the night. It was no longer walking but scrambling. Several times we heard the stones and ashes falling round us, causing a sulphurous smoke which blinded us for a few moments until dispersed by the soft morning air. It would seem as if the spirits of this infernal region disputed every step with the human beings who ventured into their precincts. We often had to throw ourselves flat on the earth to avoid the rebound of the stones and pieces of rock as they fell; and only when the eruption ceased for a few moments, could we continue our route.

At last, we arrived at the mouth of the crater and sat down on the edge, measuring with our eyes, as far as we could, the frightful gulf, half in shade and half in lurid light, which yawned beneath our feet. It was the shape of an enormous funnel of which the base and the sides were colored, to windward, by the various streams of lava which recent eruptions had deposited on their course. On one side appeared a kind of crystallized salt, white as newly fallen snow; on another: fragments of sulphur as yellow as gold in the crucible. Farther on, the sides of the crater had taken the form of pointed, jagged, and still smoking rocks, with here and there bright stalactites which seemed to have frozen as they fell. One portion of this vast basin seemed filled with a brownish substance of which I did not know the name. But, towards the middle of the crater, masses of smoke belched forth, from the midst of which poured out at intervals rivers of flame lighting up the depths of this abyss of wonder and of terror, which might well have served for a picture of the infernal regions. My guides sat down with their cords and said, "What is the use of tempting Providence? How much more will you see if you do attempt the descent?" "I should actually have *touched* it," I replied. And rising from the hot sand on which I was sitting, I passed my arms through the knots of the cords, and prepared slowly to descend into the crater. Not one of the guides would consent to follow me; but they all hung on to the mouth of the basin, striving to direct my perilous course, and to induce me to return. I reached the flat brown surface I have before described in a few minutes; but the heat increasing in intensity as I neared the burning furnace in the centre, my shoes were at once almost burnt off, and scarcely any sole remained to preserve my feet. I strove to stand on such portions of the sulphur as had cooled a little, and springing across one of the rushing torrents of liquid fire, tried to rest for a moment on a less burning crust. I felt I was lost if the wind, changing for an instant, had driven back upon me the sulphurous flame and smoke, which fortunately it drove, at present, on the opposite side of the crater. My guides called louder to me than ever to retrace my steps while there was yet time. I hastily knotted together in my handkerchief some specimens of the burning metals around me, and at last gave the signal to be drawn up again from this very hell upon earth. My ascent was accomplished in perfect safety, only my clothes and shoes were burnt to rags. They hailed my return to terra firma with cries of joy, while M. Humboldt hastened to explain to me the names and characters of the specimens which I had brought up from the abyss. We went back to the hermit's cell, who could not recover his astonishment at my foolhardiness; and a good breakfast, with the help of the Lacryma Christi, made every one forget my folly.

That evening I would have given all the world to have had no part in this ridiculous adventure. If I had undertaken it as a man of science, to wrest some hitherto unknown secret from nature, it might have been sublime; but undertaken by an ignoramus like myself, the attempt was simply ridiculous. My vanity met with its due punishment; I had been egregiously vain — that was all; but I reaped what I deserved — that most bitter feeling of a thorough contempt of one's self.

III.

After our breakfast at the Hermit's we returned to Torre dell' Annunziata. The noise in the mountain seemed to increase in proportion as we went farther from it: the earth shook under our mules' feet. All the village had turned out. Every one, in mute despair, lifted their eyes and arms to heaven, and rushed from their houses to see which side of the cone of the crater would open out first and overwhelm with its burning stream of lava, the crops and the vineyards on which their whole existence depended. Every saint in the calendar was invoked in vain by these poor people. All of a sudden, at nightfall, a mighty cry burst forth — the problem had been solved. A great breach had been made in the cone to the south, and the streams of liquid fire were pouring down the sides of the mountain with resistless speed. What direction would the eruption take during the night? That was the anxious question. We got back to our little inn and supped, passing the greater part of the night at our windows watching the progress of this terrible devastation.

IV.

As soon as it was light, we ran, like every one else, out of the house to the base of the mountain. The heavy torrent of lava had made fearful progress during the night, and had already reached not only the vineyards, but the gardens and houses in the upper part of the village of L'Annunziata. Some of these cottages, perched on a little rising ground to the left, were already entirely encircled by the fire. The poor inhabitants were flying from their homes, with cries and tears, carrying with them whatever they could most easily save from the flames. It was a heart-breaking sight. Men were dragging great sacks of wheat, or bundles of Indian corn; women, their cradles full of children, on their shoulders. The animals followed, driven by the boys, and trembling with fear; the very cocks and hens, with half-burnt wings, were fluttering and striving to hide themselves amidst the vines. It was exactly such a scene as Pliny describes at the overthrow of Pompeii. As the lava slowly but surely encircled its prey, you saw the green vine leaves shrivel up, crackle and groan, almost like living human beings; and then the branches, despoiled of their now yellow leaves, in their turn becoming crisp, taking fire, and spreading the destructive element along the ground, which had become as a furnace. These agonies of nature were slowly repeated, till each vine had fallen a victim to the destroying element. For me the sight had a sort of fascination, and I forgot that I ran a like danger myself. We had certainly legs wherewith to fly; but if for a moment we were to forget, or that the wind had changed its quarter, the same burning breath would have devoured us like the shrubs, and our calcined bones would have crackled as rapidly as the vine branches. I did forget it several times, and drawing nearer to this bed of fire, the very stick I held in my hand was shriveled up in a moment. We suddenly saw, from the lay of the ground, that the flames had changed their course, and that we were in imminent danger of being encircled by them, unless we rapidly returned to the shelter of the town. At last, the lava torrent chose for its bed a narrow valley which led to the sea, crossing the high-road to Naples, along which both horses and foot passengers were flying at full speed. But anxious to study this phenomenon to the end, which had been the object of M. de Humboldt's visit, we remained on that part of the road which led to Castelamare and Salerno, till the eruption had ceased. The only sights and sounds which met our eyes the following day, however, were the tears and lamentations of the poor ruined inhabitants. After witnessing this terrible calamity, M. de Humboldt returned to Naples, and I started alone for Castelamare.

V.

After having driven through the picturesque forest of laurels which surround the beautiful villas in the neighborhood of Naples, I went to Sorrento, which gleamed on the horizon before me like a dream of Tasso's.

After some days spent in making expeditions from this lovely place, I hired, sometimes a *corricolo*, and sometimes a boat, to visit the Temple of Pæstum and La Cava, the most beautiful spot along the whole coast. After spending about a fortnight in these solitary excursions, I found that the high-road between Torre dell' Annunziata and Naples was again opened, a certain quantity of earth having been thrown upon the lava bed; so that I took a little carriage, and returned to Naples. My heart was still full of Graziella. I felt that all the emotions of which I could neither speak nor write would be shared in and sympathized with by that delicious child.

On going up-stairs at St. Pietro Martyro, I was startled at

not hearing her bright voice as usual at the end of the gallery Everything in the old convent seemed to be as still as death. M. de la Chavanne was in his counting-house. Antoniella was superintending the cigar-makers. My room was shut up. The only person I could find was the cook, who exclaimed, "Ah ! you will no longer find Mlle. Graziella. She is gone back to the islands to her parents. No one has had any tidings of her since. We suppose she was taken to her grandmother's house at Ischia, from whence she will not come back till after the summer. Oh ! by the bye, she left a little note for you, which she told me to give you on your return. Here it is."

I took the note, which was written, or rather scribbled, in Neapolitan *patois*, as follows : *Già che sei partito, non posser più restar. Non ti rivedrò mai. La damizella* ("From the moment you left, I felt I could no longer stay. I shall never see you again !" Two or three great tears had left their blots on the coarse yellow paper.

This note explained to me that which her eyes at parting had only partially revealed. I went into my room, threw myself on the bed, and burst out crying. Virieu came up a few minutes later, to know if I was returned. He found me in tears, and asked in utter amazement, what was the matter. Without speaking, I showed him the poor little note. "Oh," he exclaimed, "why, here 's the beginning of a beautiful romance ! You must go on with it. What a good thing ; for I was bored to death !" "Don't joke about such matters," I replied. "Tears at her age are serious."

I waited till Antoniella came in, and asked her directly where her little friend was gone. "I do not know," she replied. "I went to ask her father on the quay of Pausilippo. There was no one there. The neighbors told me that he had left off coming to Naples, and that they believed Graziella was gone back to her grandmother's house at Procida. Since you went off with that clever German, she never spoke or told me any of her little secrets ; only I remarked that she was often crying."

VI.

When M. de Chavanne came in from his counting-house, I asked him the same question. "Well," he answered, laughing; "it appears that *you* are at the bottom of the despair and the flight of poor little Graziella. We have tried in vain to find her out, and can only conjecture that to escape a sorrow which she could not conquer, she is gone back to her old grandmother at Procida. Her good common sense will soon make her see the folly of all this, and if you wish to meet her again, you may be sure to do so in the autumn."

I was destined to see her long before that. I knew where to find her, and I felt that she had left her comfortable position at M. de Chavanne's for no other earthly reason than disgust at my going off with M. de Humboldt. I knew that she loved me, and that her flight was nothing but a wild declaration of love. I was torn with grief. I felt I could not remain away from her any longer. I have described in my novel, how I rejoined her at Procida. The little details which I have now given to my readers, form the only difference between the fiction and the reality. It cost my pride too much to own that my first deep love had only a cigarette maker for its object, instead of a coral worker, as she became later. Where will not vanity find a peg on which to hang itself?

After this confession, I have nothing to add, but that the rest of the story is literally true. Graziella was as young, as naïve, as pure, as religious as I represented her in my novel. All the scenes therein described are drawn from life. The scene and the actors are simple daguerreotypes. The trade of the child was less vulgar in the novel, but that is all. Our voyage to Procida, and the purchase of the new boat as a present to the family, the joy of the grandmother at its reception, the exclamations of delight from the children, all this is not invented but simply related. So it is with our life in the island, and our mingled feelings of intense joy and sorrow, with our nights on the terrace where we had erected a tent, and our days under the shade of the vineyards where we lived the happy and simple life of the lazzaroni. [1]

VII.

Towards the end of the month of May, my family wrote to Virieu for an explanation of the suspicious life I was leading at La Margellina. M. de la Chavanne had evidently written to warn my mother. Virieu, in his warm friendship for me, returned post haste to Naples, and dragged me away almost by main force. I left Graziella drowned in tears, and as I got into the carriage she fainted away. I vowed to return and to live and die at Procida. At Milan I halted for a few days after Virieu had gone, being resolved to try the *rouge et noir* system which he and I had so conscientiously studied at Naples with the old croupier. I faithfully promised Virieu not to retrace my steps to Naples till I had seen my family, but to rejoin them in a fortnight at Milly.

Milan had a gambling table which opened daily at the theatre of La Scala. It was there that I determined to try my luck. I was extraordinarily successful. I resolved to reduce the old croupier's theories to practice. I thought, without always arriving at making the number forty, there was more chance with a good many low cards than with five or six higher ones. Experience had shown me that high and low numbers were dealt out, as it were, in sets and not alternately. I therefore concluded that, by watching carefully the dealing of the cards, I could make pretty sure of those which were left. I followed this method steadily, and won as steadily every night.

I remained a fortnight at Milan, and then started for Lyons with a Swiss merchant from Lausanne and his servant, who took immense care of me on the road, and insisted on my staying a few days at their house, when we reached their home.

After resting two or three days at Lausanne, I took a little

[1] See the *Romance of Graziella.* New edition, published by the company to whom M. Lamartine's works belong. Hachette & Co., 1870.

carriage and came back to Mâcon. My father was waiting for me, and received me with the greatest affection, without saying a word of my follies. I felt that I had come back pardoned, and that few sons had a father like mine. Still I was sad as death, though I did not say why. My poor mother cried for joy at my return, after so long an absence. If the rest of the family were displeased with me, they took care to conceal it. Everything seemed forgotten, except in my own heart and in the sick heart of my poor Graziella. Alas! I had not long to wait for news. A traveller passing through Mâcon brought me the tidings of her death, together with her letter of farewell. Her last thought had been for me.

BOOK VI.

I.

I HAVE now described my first loves, my happiness and my misery, and my first journey into Italy. Since that time, Italy became my own country, or, at least, the country of my affections. But my life was about to change entirely. We were in the year 1812–13. Bonaparte, like a man chased by the Furies, had returned from Moscow, where he never should have gone, while the other half of his forces were engaged in Spain, to which country he had no right to pretend. Of seven hundred and fifty thousand men whom he had had under arms, only a few thousand remained this side of the Vistula. But in the midst of his reverses he was grand. He never despaired. He gathered together the fragments of his glorious army, and with three hundred thousand men was fighting a brilliant campaign, though he could not recover the lost ground.

Austria offered him peace and neutrality. She proposed certain concessions not unacceptable to his ambition, or to his former glory. But he preferred fighting on for shadows, and threw the fate of the Empire and of France on one die. At Leipsic he lost all. He came back to Paris without an army. He brought but his genius, his pride, and his authority; in some eyes he became a hero once more, but a hero of adverse fortune. He was compelled to lay down his arms and the Empire at Fontainebleau, and went to the Isle of Elba to reflect upon his crime towards his country. It was the beginning of the end. St. Helena avenged Paris and France.

II.

On my return from Italy, I found France boiling over with indignation at, and opposition to, the Emperor. France never tolerates misfortune in her rulers; excepting the soldiers, there was not a soul who was not entirely alienated from him from one end of the country to the other. The Royalists conspired secretly with the Revolutionists in 1789, and even in 1792 against despotism. But in 1813 the conspiracy was open and unanimous. One proof of it was in the impossibility which the Emperor found to recruit his shattered battalions. The passion for glory had been satiated. Everything that has been written on this subject is pure conventionality, even the beautiful military histories of M. Thiers. His relations of the campaigns are admirable, but his views of public opinion at that time are erroneous.

III.

On the 31st of March, 1814, the patriotism which was the offspring of the Liberty of 1792 was expiring in the breasts of the French people. They felt that the Empire was coming to an end, in spite of the heroic exploits of its head. I was alone at Milly. The prefect of Mâcon, an old friend of my father's, had appointed me mayor of that little borough, without considering my youth and inexperience. My duties consisted in keeping order, and taking certain measures to levy contributions from the neighboring villages to feed the bodies of Austrian and Italian troops by which we were already invaded. Fortunately this was managed without much difficulty. Marshal Augereau commanded at Lyons, and feebly strove to repulse the Austrian forces, who were masters of Mâcon, with a handful of French soldiers who had just returned from Spain. Mâcon was taken and retaken several times, and finally submitted to the Austrians.

I was present at several of these skirmishes on the neighboring hills. Opinions were divided, between weariness of the Empire and pity for our brave fellow-countrymen, who were still shedding their blood like water for the Emperor and for France. Twice we advanced too far within the lines of the Spanish cavalry and the Hungarian grenadiers. I had my horse shot under me, and escaped with difficulty from the hands of the Austrians.

At last came the great battle, and the occupation of Paris by the allied armies, the abdication of Napoleon at Fontainebleau, and the proclamation of Louis XVIII. The Empire crumbled into dust amidst the confused cries of a whole people, cries of wounded self-love and patriotism; and yet of renewed liberty and peace. I went to Lyons and witnessed this curious conflict of opinions, and the coalition, in the name of the Bourbons, between the Royalists and the Revolutionary party. The Bonapartists had disappeared as completely as if they had never existed. I was Royalist by inclination as well as by family tradition, and at once declared myself for the King.

The next day I started on horseback with the Chevalier de Pierreclos, whose old father fastened the white scarf across our shoulders with trembling joy, and sent us as scouts to see how the land lay.

We arrived towards evening at the little town of Cluny, in the midst of a number of people assembled in the public square, who might, if they chose, have turned against us for our seditious colors, as Paris had not yet declared itself, and the Emperor was still at the head of his army at Fontainebleau. We rode boldly in amongst them, however, exclaiming, *Vive le Roi!* The crowd, which was composed of tradesmen and peasants, were at first mute from surprise and hesitation. Then they suddenly burst forth with cries of sympathy and joy at their deliverance from a yoke which had become insupportable. We got off our horses and mixed with the people, who welcomed us as liberators. Among such hundreds of men, not one lifted up his voice for the Emperor. Such was the popularity of the Empire at its decline. I do not pretend to praise their apparent fickleness; I only relate what happened. But I am writing the exact truth, and describing scenes in which I was both actor and witness.

IV.

In the evening we remounted our horses and went to sleep at the château of Cormatin, and home of Chevalier de Pierreclos, who had married the beautiful daughter of the famous Désotteux de Cormatin, a Vendéean general, noted for the treaty of peace he had concluded for the army of La Vendée, a treaty, be it said in passing, which he had taken upon himself to conclude without any extraneous authority.

General Désotteux had married a rich Mâconnaise widow, by whom he had had two beautiful girls. Madame la Comtesse de Pierreclos was the youngest and the handsomest. Her château was the rendezvous of the most agreeable persons in the county. I was invited there in common with all the other aristocratic and royalist families in the neighborhood, and found it very pleasant. There was every description of sport, plenty of horses for riding or driving, an excellent cook, and all the pleasures of a *maison bien montée.* Politics soon became a leading feature in our conversations.

I have already said that we arrived at the castle towards evening, where we found a numerous and friendly gathering. We sat down to dinner and drank to the King and Liberty. "Yes," I exclaimed, "our hopes spring from our very misfortunes. Let us drink to the Bourbons, who are going to bring us back peace and freedom! As to myself, I know not what fate may be reserved for me; but whatever it may be, no joy can equal that which to-day's news has given me." Every one cheered and declared that the upper classes were all of the same mind. During this political supper, the peasants in the villages lit bonfires of rejoicing on the hills, and in the magnificent grounds of the château.

V.

On my return to Mâcon I found my mother crying for joy, and the whole society of the place mad with excitement. Every one believed in the Bourbons as in the realization of their dreams. They looked upon them as the panacea for all the ills which this unhappy year had brought upon France. Every one, however, did justice to the personal heroism of the Emperor Napoleon during this last campaign. The Empire had fallen, but the Emperor had risen in public estimation on the very ruins of his throne.

A short time after, I started for Paris with all the youth of the country, whether noble or not, to enroll ourselves, though without any views of personal ambition, in the service of the King. To serve and defend the King, as the ruler spontaneously chosen by France, was our only object. What was curious in this movement was, that it infected at the same time every one capable of bearing arms, from Grenoble, Dauphiny, Lyons, Burgundy, and even as far as Dijon. Thus in a few days, led by the same feeling of enthusiasm, Virieu arrived; then D'Argout, who was afterwards finance minister; then M. de Mareste, who from his wit and ability is as great a favorite in Paris now at eighty years of age as he was at thirty; and a multitude of other young men, all distinguished in their different ways and all of the noblest blood in France. One and all burnt with the same sacred fire, and kindled the slumbering spark of royalty throughout the country. We took a species of little post-chaise drawn by one horse, and changed from one town to the other, with the cry of *Vive le Roi!* Such was the enthusiastic pilgrimage of young France to Paris at the dawn of the liberty which they dreamed secure under the new government.

My father, who had been wounded on the 10th of August, and who shared in our young illusions as we shared in his fidelity to his noble recollections, came to Paris himself a few days later. But not choosing to ask anything of the court, which was overwhelmed with applications and promises, he let the flood of emigrants and ambitious place-hunters rush by, and only came to express his devotedness to the cause, while he refused all pension or rank in the new army. Never did a father leave to a son a richer heritage of patriotism and noble disinterestedness.

As soon as he arrived, he presented me to the Prince de

Poix, who commanded the company of Noailles. As the sole recompense for his long and faithful services, he only asked to matriculate his son in the King's Guard. I see the whole scene before me even now.

VI.

It was in the hotel of the Quay Malaquais, which was afterwards taken by the Duke Decazes, minister of police. The Prince de Poix, who had been the great friend of Louis XVI., lived there at that time, and had turned the lower part of the house into a public office, for the formation of the new corps which he had at heart.

My father, who was a magnificent old man of sixty years of age, struck every one by his high-bred and martial appearance, which combined the simple dignity of his birth with the calm energy of one long used to command. To this was added the sort of plain frankness of a country gentleman, who had for many years laid down his sword, but whom patriotism had recalled to the service of his country. There was no anxious or ambitious expression on his face, mastering a feeling of joy at the crumbling of one dynasty, or the rise of another. My father was one of those who would never consent to emigrate. He considered that, as a loyal Frenchman, he was bound by a living vow to the national soil. The events of life never influenced his judgment. It was impossible to look at him and see in his face such a mixture of military firmness, frankness, and sweetness, without being irresistibly attracted and drawn, as it were, towards him. It was the beauty of goodness ; even to look at him seemed to make you a better man.

VII.

I followed him with some shyness through the great anterooms which led to the Prince's quarters. I wore, for the first time, a simple but elegant uniform, which yet rather drew attention to my youth and inexperience. My long sword, with its glittering scabbard, somewhat embarrassed my movements ; I passed it under my left arm as a badge, of which I was certainly proud enough, but to which I was unaccustomed. Every one stared at me as I passed, which added to my confusion. I cast my eyes down to hide my awkwardness, when we suddenly saw a little old man coming towards us muffled up in a white swan-skin dressing gown and draggled trousers rolling over his ankles; with his hair badly combed and only half-powdered, falling all over his face. I asked myself who this little man could be, who was so much at his ease in spite of his dress in the midst of a group of smart officers in full dress, covered with orders, when he suddenly came forward smiling towards us, with a face full of benevolent kindness.

Stopping all at once before my father, whose court dress, cross of St. Louis, jeweled sword, and noble bearing attracted every one's observation, he seized me by the arm, looked at me with a smile of satisfaction, and then turning towards my father exclaimed, "Sir, you are apparently the father of this young man, whom you are come to present to his general and companions, to form part of the new corps I am organizing of faithful defenders of the King."

My father replied with a kind of proud humility, "that I was in truth his only son, whom he had come to recommend to his care; that my name was Alphonse de Lamartine, and that I was not only his son but the one remaining scion of a family who had always been devoted to the cause of the Bourbons; that nought but royalist blood had coursed through his veins since that fatal 30th of August, 1792, when he had come, at the head of the gentlemen of his province, to offer to defend the King, Louis XVI.; and that he remembered the Prince perfectly from having seen him on that memorable occasion." But the Prince, after hearing my father's first few words, was no longer listening. Still looking at me, he took me by the hand, and leading me back to the apartments from which he had entered said, "Come with me, young man, and let me present you to my staff." I followed him from one office to another, till we came to a small room crammed full of officers. "I bring you a new recruit, gentlemen," he exclaimed pleasantly, presenting me to the one in command. "You will allow that I have chosen well this time, and that we are in luck." Then, to my confusion, he began enumerating my different military qualifications in a loud voice. "What a capital figure for a uniform! March, sir — very well; you have an excellent military step. Enter his name at once, gentlemen," he added. "You will soon teach him his trade." My father was much moved and almost ashamed of the laudatory exclamations of the old general. It was not exactly what he expected from an old soldier, and in fact the Prince had become somewhat of a carpet knight.

This reception was passed on from one room to another, and I was in consequence received everywhere with open arms. This was my first campaign. My friends, when I repeated it to them, laughed as much as I did; but I was foolish enough to be vain of it, while it roused in me feelings of real gratitude towards the house of Noailles.

VIII.

This sort of reception awaited me each time that my father introduced me to his old friends and companions at arms.

M. Henrion de Pansey, my mother's cousin, was then provisional minister of justice. We used to spend our evenings at his house. The lady who did the honors of it was a young widow, Madame de Pré, and my first cousin, who afterwards married a General Pernetty, of the artillery. She was a clever and accomplished woman and is still alive. My uniform was as popular there as at the old Prince de Poix's. M. Henrion de Pansey was the very soul of honor, and the pattern of a liberal royalist magistrate. There I found myself thrown with people of all kinds, and could glean the dominant opinions of the most eminent leaders of the day. General Carra St. Cyr, a relation as well as an old friend of my father's, who had been ill-used by the Emperor, showed us every species of kindness, and was not without some feeling of resentment against the injustice of Bonaparte. The beautiful and witty daughter of General Hoche, who had married my cousin the Count de Roys, was a link between us and the Republicans, who had become reconciled with the Bourbons. This friendship has lasted until now. Nothing is changed but the dates; and such changes only strengthen the feelings once engendered.

IX.

After leaving the Prince de Poix, my father took me to one of his old military friends, the Marquis de Busseuil, major-general of the body-guard.

He had lived for some time at Paray-le-Monial, the country of Marie Alacoque, whose name and holiness, ridiculed by Voltaire, had been the laughing-stock of the last century. The Marquis de Busseuil was not likely to vindicate her honor. He was a gentleman of the old school, leading a life the reverse of edifying, and who could only serve as a foil to his saintly neighbor. Under Louis XV. he would have found his place in the boudoir of Madame du Barry. But the return of the Bourbons made him keep within bounds, so as to obtain a restitution of his former rank and dignities. He received my father as an old friend and myself as his *protégé.* He was lodged under the roof of the palace, rather like a groom of the chambers in a great family, who is content with any accommodation provided he can serve his masters. The uniform he wore was sufficient to ennoble him in his own eyes. He proposed to my father to remind the King of the pension to which his long services and his zeal on the 10th of August entitled him. My father positively refused. He had simply done his duty, he said; and had followed his own honest convictions, without any thought of private interest. He did not choose to lower himself in his own esteem. He added: "Those who served the King for pay may perhaps desire that it should be continued; but a pension would tarnish the honors of those who served him for conscience sake. I have no wish to purchase my joy at the return of the King; it is enough for me to see him once more in his proper place."

These words sunk deep into my mind, and were a lesson to me for life. I knew better than anybody that my father was the reverse of rich; but he was a gentleman in the highest sense of the term; and he thus impressed upon me the feelings belonging to his rank.

X.

Either from the chance of service, or because the Prince de Poix had spoken of me to Louis XVIII. and wished to show the King a specimen of his newly-formed company, I received orders two days later to appear in uniform at a given hour to attend the King in person. Louis XVIII. had not yet seen the artistic spoils which the Louvre at that time contained, and which were exhibited to the French people as tokens of victory. He knew at what a price of blood and treasure, and likewise of injustice and violence, these *chefs d'œuvre* had become our property. But they were choice spoils which the peace had ratified, and which were still looked upon as trophies. The allies had not yet had the time to reclaim them. They were, perhaps, afraid of marring the effect of their great victory and humbling France too much. Only Domenichino's "St. Jerome" had been restored to the King of Sardinia. The year 1814 had passed over these galleries in silence. Louis XVIII. wished to flatter his people, and, above all, to make himself popular by appearing to take a pride in our least legitimate conquests. He thought thereby to conciliate the Bonapartists, in compensation for the large portion of Europe which the Congress of Vienna had compelled him to restore.

He wished, therefore, by a solemn and official walk through the Louvre, publicly to enjoy these wonderful works of art now brought for the first time in review before a King of France and a successor to Francis I. He had another object in view also, which he was too wise to despise; and that was, to conciliate the liberal and artistic party whom the Emperor had put at the head of these national museums. It was an innocent concession to the spirit of the times; an adoption of one of the national glories, and a sort of mute guaranty to the somewhat anxious possessors of the property of the French *émigrés*. M. Denon and M. de Forbin, one a classic courtier, the other a chamberlain of the Emperor, were the two presidents of the Fine Arts Committee. To pay them a compliment was to soothe the feelings of Imperial France. He was determined not to miss the opportunity. It did not compromise him in any way, and it pleased the so-called Liberal party. The ceremony was, therefore, arranged with the utmost care and pomp.

XI.

M. Denon, a man of taste and wit, had allied himself, no one exactly knew how, to the Imperial party. He was very old and very ugly, but with a classical kind of ugliness, and extremely clever. He was a man who could accommodate himself with skillful cleverness to all parties and all circumstances; a courtier by nature; a man of pleasure too and frivolity; an Athenian of the times of Alcibiades; the Anacreon of ugliness in France — such was M. Denon. I had some connection with him later on the subject of a celebrated beauty whom he won in spite of his advanced age, and whom Châteaubriand carried off in a like manner when his turn came. This lady is still alive. I never understood before how wit and cleverness could outweigh such ugliness and so many gray hairs!

XII.

M. le Comte de Forbin, father of the beautiful Countess de Marcellus, was, on the contrary, one of the most charming persons in France. He was equally happy with his pen and with his pencil. He wrote graceful novels, travels in which his genius rivaled that of Châteaubriand, and verses in which his gallantry verged upon passion. His talent for painting was equally remarkable; his pictures reminded one of Claude Lorraine. As to his exterior, nature had bestowed upon him all she had refused to M. Denon; a noble bearing, a beautiful figure, grace and ease of manner, fine features, luxuriant hair, the sweetest smile; nothing was wanting to this man save perhaps that quality which is of all others the rarest — being perfectly natural. I had a feeling sometimes that all this beauty and talent were put on ; but, in spite of that, it was very difficult not to be fascinated by him.

XIII.

My companion and I were placed on either side of the wheel-chair, pushed by two footmen, which was to be the moving throne of the King. I was to the left, my comrade to the right, with our swords drawn. The royal progress was to be too long and too slow for the gouty limbs of the King to bear on foot. We started through the long galleries which join the Tuileries to the Louvre. A crowd of courtiers and noblemen followed in silence. They all seemed to me to have that sort of look and set smile which people put on at court as they do their uniforms. M. de Blacas, the favorite minister of the King's household, walked nearest to the Prince, and explained to him as he went along the various treasures which the Emperor had accumulated. As for myself, at first I saw nothing, so dazzled was I at the royal pomp and the majestic figure of the King, with whom I for the first time found myself brought in such close contact. I heard nothing till we got to the Picture Gallery but the monotonous, respectful tread of those men who had served both dynasties, walking before and behind as courtiers of two centuries.

XIV.

But all of a sudden, a wonderful voice, soft and firm at the same time, like a voice which had coaxed men more than intimidated them, and which wished more than ever to please the ears of its hearers, roused me from my dreamy retrospect. It seemed to me as if I were listening to a voice of the past, formed by the habit of adversity of so many years' standing, coming forth from a breast which had been long silent, and speaking to men from the height of a throne.

"Let us stop here, gentlemen, and look around us, for I am not come here as to a rapid military review, but to see and admire what you have had the happiness of admiring before me. Now look here," he added in a lower voice to M. Denon and M. de Forbin; "you who are familiar with these art marvels, come and show them to me. I love Art in all its branches, and esteem all who make it their profession. Tell us to stop before all the best pictures, and don't leave out any, for I love glory, too, especially when it reflects upon France. Talent is a dynasty which has no usurpers."

A murmur of admiration ran through the court. M. Denon and M. de Forbin were beckoned on each side of the royal arm-chair, M. de Blacas yielding his place to them.

XV.

I then saw a little old man with a forehead in which art had in vain endeavored to efface the wrinkles, draw near to the King, and say a few indistinct words in his ear, all the whilst pressing his senator's hat to his breast. The King looked at him from head to foot with the superiority of eternal youth, and pointed out a remarkable sketch, which his experienced eye told him was that of a first-rate master, asking him at the same time the name of the painter. M. Denon being unable to satisfy him at once, he appealed to M. de Forbin. The difference was between a courtier of Cleopatra and of Alexander. The King appeared struck by it, and kept him for a long time by his side, listening to his observations. Whilst M. de Forbin was speaking and the King was listening, and giving little signs of approbation from time to time, I had then a good opportunity of looking at the monarch myself. I do not know whether I was more pleased or surprised. To be just towards him, one must forget Béranger and La Minerve, the two caricaturists of the Bourbons at that time. Disparagement is not truth. I am now going to give you an exact portrait of Louis XVIII.

People called him an old man; but he was not so. His vigorous and manly figure rose above the crowd of ministers, marshals, and artists, as if to impel them to admiration rather than obedience. His blue dress had nothing to distinguish it but the military epaulet. This was a compliment to the army, which had nothing ridiculous about it except to the eyes of the fanatics for the long gray great coat and straight collar. Any man of sense would at once perceive in this costume the modesty of a wise man who did not wish to usurp the glory of his predecessor, yet was bound to appear as the sovereign of a military people. A white waistcoat with a sky-blue ribbon across it, which was the order of chivalry of his family, marked his birth, and identified him with his nobles. His gouty knees were covered with the trappings of his horse, like a sign of peace to reassure Europe and his people.

As to his head, I have seen thousands of men in my life, and never saw any countenance which corresponded so well to the idea of one sent by Providence to fill the place of sovereign to a people whom a hero had compromised and lost by a series of hazardous battles, and who had been called to the throne to reëstablish peace and order. There was neither pride nor insolence in his face. One felt that he reigned because it was his proper place; he honored those who had served his rival, but he reigned because it was his divine right to be king over France. He was, in fact the exponent of Legitimacy, and ruled by the force of right alone. No one could reproach him for ambition. Europe and France had unanimously pointed to him with the words: "Thou art the man!" and he had answered, "Here I am." He had come without drawing the sword or shedding a drop of his people's blood. The words, "*I pity, I forget, I forgive,*" were his only war-cry.

XVI.

Those noble words were written without affectation in his clever mouth, his graceful manner, and his benevolent look. His eyes, which were the color of the blue sky after a storm, were the finest I ever saw. They had the gentle pride of a man born to the purple, and yet the calm tranquillity of a patience which was ready to wait, but which never doubted. It was the royalty of Nature. These eyes looked as if they were made of China and *lapis lazuli.* All the blood of his ancestry seemed to be revealed in them as in a mirror. They never kindled with anger, nor fell from timidity. They were the eyes of a king who sees everything, understands everything, and judges everything with serenity and calm.

But this apparent quiet had nothing of the impassable indifference of the Homeric "Juno with the ox eyes." It revealed, on the contrary, abundant intelligence and understanding of hidden motives and intentions. Royalty, revolution, misfortune, exile — he had passed through all. There was a something in his look which seemed to know or to guess everything; but he was careful not to reveal his thoughts. To be silent, and yet with an expressive silence which is at once understood — this was the eloquence of the king. It was especially through his eyes that he spoke, to the highest as to the lowest, for he neglected no one, and by his look apostrophized each one in turn. I felt myself, standing as I did for four hours by his side, that he knew all about me, that he had been told my history; and a smile of intelligence lit up his face as he looked from time to time at his young guards, whose appearance evidently pleased him. In spite of the respect which forbade my giving expression to the least sign of approbation or disapprobation of the royal speeches (when I was only permitted to assume the mechanical attitude of a living piece of furniture), yet nature was stronger in me than etiquette, and an almost imperceptible movement of the eyes or lips showed now and then an admiration which I could not conceal, and which pleased the King the more as it was involuntary. At intervals his ready smile responded; he felt himself understood; it was the flattering and mutual surprise of royalty on the one hand and obscurity on the other. His eyes sought my face several times as if to glean this mute homage. Years after I knew, through one of his ministers, that he had remembered this day, when, in 1820, my name came before him as that of a poet, and when he sent me a complete edition of the poets of Greece and Rome. He thought himself an Augustus discovering a Virgil. I was flattered, but not dazzled; it was not the fault of the King, but of the times.

This official promenade lasted four hours, which, however,

seemed to me only too short. Every one had had the right word and the right look. M. Denon and M. de Forbin were swelling with importance. I went back modestly to my place with my comrades, and slept, as those on guard always did, on one of the straw mattresses in the antechamber.

XVII.

This was the only time when I saw the King close except once, when I accompanied him on horseback as an equerry by the side of his carriage, in the neighborhood of Auteuil and St. Cloud. He liked going at a great pace to get that amount of movement and air which his gout precluded him from taking in any other way; so much the worse for those whose horses slipped up in the sharp turns on the Paris pavement; that was the only danger of this duty.

Sometimes, at the Tuileries, I saw the Duc d'Angoulême, a prince with too much reserve to conciliate public affection; or the Duc de Berri, who was too confiding; or the Comte d'Artois, a good man but too much impressed with the divine right of kings; or the Duc d'Orleans, too cringing a courtier within the walls of the palace, and too popular without; one or other of whom always accompanied the King to the chapel. Very often we met the Duchesse d'Angoulême, walking slowly, with red eyes, through the rooms of the palace, without thinking of popularity, but keeping back her tears, not to wound by her filial sorrow those who had witnessed the death of her father and mother. At other times I followed, with a corps of the body-guard, the covered and sealed baskets which contained the breakfast or dinner of the King, so that poison should not be thrown into the dishes; and it was my duty to see those baskets opened, and their contents placed on the table of the royal family and their guests. Louis XVIII. had the reputation of being a gourmand; in reality he was only a delicate eater. The conversation at those little dinners was easy, witty, and agreeable, especially when the King himself spoke: it was a direct contradiction to the orgies which calumny attributed to the court out of doors. Fancy an orgie of any sort at a table where the orphan of the Temple was seated, which was blessed by a bishop, and at which an infirm French king presided with open doors! There might have been license in the streets; but decency and religion, and the remembrance of a deep sorrow, reigned within the walls of the palace. This is the simple truth.

XVIII.

After my turn of waiting was over, which lasted several weeks, my father left me, and I went into garrison at Beauvais, which was the quarters of the Noailles Company.

I led a solitary and almost ascetic life, quite to myself, at a little grocer's in the Faubourg d'Amiens, who let her rooms to the officers of the garrison. Her husband was dead, and trade bad. This poor widow, who was already of a certain age, lived (with a young servant) on the letting of her humble lodgings. I established myself there; and, to avoid the noise and distraction of the *table d'hôte* I proposed to her to cook for me, and bring me up my simple meals in my own room. Thanks to this economical arrangement, my allowance of 50*l.* a year from my father, with my pay, amply sufficed for all my wants.

XIX.

I lived like this for three months, getting up at five o'clock every morning to go to the *manége.* My passion for horses and the habit of riding from a child at my father's, made this the pleasantest exercise of the day. After my second lesson in the riding-school, I was put at the head of the squadron. My companions liked me, and I was never thrown or unseated even by the most vicious animals. Once or twice I went into the *café* of my corps on leaving the *manége.* A pretty woman served behind the counter, and reproached me for my rare appearance in the coffee-room. I answered civilly but avoided her advances, and kept myself strictly out of the way of temptation, however agreeable. The remembrance of Graziella was my safeguard. By degrees I made acquaintance with several of the corps about my own age, whom my quiet and retiring habits had interested. Among these was M. de Vaugelas, a young gentleman from Dauphiny, whose tastes in always coincided with my own. He was one of the most accomplished men I ever knew. He was a strong royalist, as we all were, and loved solitude as much as I did. The duty of the day once over, he fled from the frivolity of the crowd around us. Thus he came to seek me out, and I to receive him with joy. Our intimacy soon attracted other men to us of the same stamp. After a little time we formed a distinguished society of our own in the garrison, which, however, excited no one's envy. My room was often the place of meeting, and we discussed literature, philosophy, and poetry; for many of us were poets as well as soldiers, and it was at Beauvais that I first began to compose the verses which afterwards brought me into notice. My hostess (both mistress and servant) had a kind of deference towards me, as my friends were noted as superior to all others of their age. But this agreeable society did not prevent my seeking daily the melancholy pleasure of a more complete solitude, which from my childhood until now has been a sort of necessity of my existence. Nothing is worth an hour's quiet communing with one's self. It was in the country that I sought and found it. There was not much beauty there certainly, but it was solitary; there were not many fine trees or beautiful flowers; but there was God and his works, and that was enough. . . . .

XX.

After three months of barrack life at Beauvais I got leave. I returned to Paris, and started for Mâcon. I own to having felt very proud of my martial apprenticeship, and still more vain of my uniform. I was longing to show myself to the young men and young women of my own neighborhood in my military dress. My hopes were not disappointed; every one said I was quite another man. I was the object of general attention, and even touched a few hearts. The only thing that troubled me was a murmur of opposition against the new dynasty which seemed to be grumbling around me, and which filled me with some bitterness. However, I did not at the time foresee that any serious events would trouble the future; so I gave myself up without reserve to the enjoyment of a brilliant winter without any sinister anticipations of evil.

A young gentleman and lady, M. and Madame Germain, kept open house at the Prefecture with all the luxury which a large fortune could give. M. Germain had been chamberlain to Napoleon, and had been overwhelmed with imperial favors. Madame Germain was the daughter of that Countess d'Houdetot, whom the passion of J. J. Rousseau had immortalized without tarnishing her good name.

Young, tall, well made, and thoroughly amiable in character, she was a great favorite with my mother, to whose house she came constantly with a loving and winning familiarity. She had everything which would have attracted me also, if she had not been already united to one of the most excellent of men. These two loved each other as such a husband and wife were sure to do. I could not help admiring her; but it was without envy or jealousy. If I had been J. J. Rousseau, I should have had a hopeless passion for her, but I was as careful and reserved as she was good and pure. She was to me like a holy picture. I believe she is still alive, but I have never tried to see her again. Her husband, who adored and was really worthy of her, died not very long after, in the prime of life. She went sadly mourning for the rest of her days.

XXI.

All of a sudden, in the midst of our *fêtes*, and without any previous warning, the great and astounding news arrived: "*The Emperor has escaped from Elba, and is marching with a handful of troops across the mountains to Grenoble.*"

There was great amazement but no panic. His abdication at Fontainebleau was too recent. The Congress of Vienna was still sitting; the allied armies were not yet disbanded; France had scarcely had time yet to be disgusted with peace and the Bourbons. Bonaparte had mistaken the hour. No one expected him, and few wished for him. His coming was out of place; there was no question of him. Even his army had ceased to think of him. This was the general feeling. I own that, as far as I was concerned, so far from believing in his success, I was rejoiced at his rashness. "He is about to accomplish what the treaty of Paris only did by halves," I said, — "the *dethronement* of his glory."

XXII.

We remained in this state for several days, always imagining that the Government would act on the defensive. At the end of six days, we heard that Labédoyère had rejoined the Emperor at some leagues from Grenoble; that the King's army had disbanded itself at the mere shadow of Napoleon's name; that Grenoble had opened its gates; that a large body of troops were gathering there round his standard; and that he was marching upon Lyons.

At Lyons, the Comte d'Artois, the Duke of Orleans, and Marshal Macdonald had been abandoned by the troops, and seditiously pursued on the road to Paris. At Lons-le-Saunier Marshal Ney had given it up. The Paris road was open. No orders came from the King; one felt one must go and seek them.

I started on horseback with the Chevalier de Pierreclos, and we determined to take a cross road which would lead us quicker to our destination. At a few miles from Mâcon we met Colonel Duluat, a great friend of ours and aide-de-camp to Marshal Suchet. He stopped us, exclaiming, "Well! where is he?" "At Lyons," we replied, "and marching upon Paris." "Upon Paris!" he retorted, with a wild joy which he did not attempt to repress. "Well done! *Vive l'Empereur!*" and digging his spurs into his horse he set off as hard as he could go towards Mâcon "See what the army is!" I exclaimed to my companion. "It begins with a little indecision, and then becomes as mad as Duluat!" We could not help making some rather bitter reflections. "It is no use fighting against popularity and glory," I continued. "The army has no right to rise against the country, against liberty, against our solemn oaths, against the very people from whom they spring! But you will see what has happened here will happen elsewhere. We who have our honor to think of, let us go forward!" And we galloped on towards Paris.

At the beginning of the line of mountains where the Charolais diligence conveyed its passengers from Moulins to Paris, we left our horses, and took our places in this primitive conveyance. My journey had nothing remarkable about it save a sword-thrust which I inflicted on a young Polish officer in the garden of the hotel, who had been sent to corrupt the troops, and whom I reproached for meddling with things which did not concern him, as he was not even a Frenchman. They carried him to his bed wounded in the chest, and we, delighted to have thus got rid of him, made the best of our way to Nemours. Here a good many of the officers of the King's household joined us, and we travelled together in a coach. My sword-thrust and royalist feelings won me golden opinions, and we arrived almost gayly at Paris.

XXIII.

The town was in a strange state of dumb consternation, like a place where there is but one feeling.

I went to lodge at a little inn which I knew, and which still exists, called the Hôtel du Hazard, Rue du Hazard. My landlady assured me that the court was determined to fight in the plains of Villejuif, with the King's household, the musketeers, the body-guards, and the whole population of Paris. On hearing these words, I felt as if I had found France again. The cries of *Vive le Roi!* which followed Louis XVIII. to the Chamber of Deputies the next day, seemed to me like the oath of the whole nation. Unfortunately, enthusiasm is not discipline, and Bonaparte was steadily advancing.

XXIV.

The day came when we were to meet him at Villejuif, and there were already neither soldiers nor leaders. The court was quickly prepared for a retreat ; we would not believe it. We passed the night armed, lying at our horses' feet, in our quarters, and expecting every moment the orders which never came. At twelve o'clock they led us to the Champ-de-Mars ; at six o'clock we were brought back to the Place de la Concorde. We remained there in battle array till ten o'clock at night. At midnight we were ordered to move quietly on to the boulevard by the Rue de Richelieu.

Nothing can paint the despair of the people when they saw, through the glimmering darkness, that the last defenders of the King were leaving the city. The inhabitants were crying at their doors ; their wives and children brought us wine and food ; our own tears fell, while consternation filled every breast ; curses on the Emperor echoed from house to house, and we ourselves knew not where we were going. At last we were ordered to halt before a barrack, in a great square full of troops, at St. Denis. We resumed our march at five o'clock in the morning. The King's carriage had passed us amidst the silence of the night, and had taken the route to Lille. We understood at once that he had determined to yield to the Emperor without striking a blow. The Maréchal Marmont, with about twenty general officers, on horseback, mingled with our ranks. The Comte d'Artois, the Duke d'Angoulême, and the Duke de Berri, marched sadly at a little distance under an incessant fine rain. No one spoke. The pride of France was humbled to the dust. This universal desertion of a great cause was best expressed by a solemn silence. I was very young at that time, but I really felt as if the weight of twenty revolutions lay on my heart.

XXV.

I followed my column sadly and silently through the Flanders mud, and under the freezing March rain ; while the Marshal who commanded us rode on doggedly, with an expression of disdain and indifference ; and the Duc de Berri, wrapped up in his waterproof cloak, went up and down our ranks, endeavoring to cheer us now and then with a few grateful and kind words. But the people in the provinces wept at the doors of their cottages as we passed by.

After marching a few leagues on the road to Lille, we suddenly received an unexpected counter-order. We retraced our steps to take a branch road leading to Béthune. It was the King himself who sent us this counter-order from Lille. He had found there the Duke of Orleans and the Maréchal Mortier, with 10,000 or 12,000 of the Emperor's army, who were still hesitating between fidelity and defection. They would not allow us to enter the gates of Lille. The Marshal said he could not answer for the conduct of the troops if the body-guard of the King followed him into the citadel. The Duke of Orleans, who did not wish to compromise himself with Bonaparte or his troops, was already negotiating a departure for London. The King resolved to quit Lille and to take refuge in Belgium. This was the secret of the counter-order which we had received, and which we could not understand. I fell ill in a poor little hut by the roadside. It was only a slight attack of fever. The care taken of me by the kind inhabitants of this cottage was what they would have shown to their own son; and the mother and daughter took it by turns to watch by my bedside. In a day or two I was quite cured, and my horse, who had benefited as much by the rest as myself, soon enabled me to rejoin my column. Towards evening we arrived at Béthune. To the right we saw bodies of cavalry commanded by Excelmans, an intrepid general as well as diplomatist, watching us from the woods, and following us at a certain distance. His orders were to keep us in sight without fighting. The Emperor did not choose to fire a shot first against the King of France. He wanted to be able to say to Europe, "I have restrained every species of violence. France calls me, and I come. Where then is my crime?"

XXVI.

Our entrance into Béthune, the gates of which were immediately closed upon us, was effected amidst some confusion. Excelmans's cavalry regiments had made a circuit round the town, and were waiting for us at the opposite gate. A shot was fired by accident. The horse which the Count d'Artois rode gave a sudden start, and nearly threw his rider, who was, however, a first-rate horseman. I saw this brother of Louis XVIII. spring suddenly upwards with the rearing of his horse, which looked as if he had been hit by the shot; but it was not so. The beast took the bit between his teeth, and galloped off outside the town, with the Duc de Berri and Marshal Marmont at his heels. A regiment of the Grenadier Guards followed; two regiments of the Imperial army, Lancers and Carabineers, were ranged in battle array at two hundred paces off, in a menacing but undecided attitude.

The Duc De Berri advanced alone and spoke to them. "Fire, if you dare, on the brother and nephew of your King; or go back, and have the decency, at least, to respect misfortune."

On hearing the Prince's words they retired accordingly, and left the road open for us to Armentières, by which we might enter Belgium. The Count d'Artois, the Duc de Berri and Marshal Marmont reëntered Béthune. We could hardly satisfy the hospitality of the people, who all pressed food, lodging, and stabling on our little troop of men and horses. I went to a blacksmith's who had a large shop full of workmen in the principal square of the town. They lavished upon us everything that was necessary for man and beast. We drank with our hosts to the health of the King, and felt that their hearts were entirely with us.

XXVII.

After resting and refreshing ourselves, we went out to stroll in the "Place" at Béthune, to talk over the events of the day. The Royal Princes desired our pay to be distributed amongst us with their last words of thanks and acknowledgments. "We are going beyond the frontiers of France," they said, "and do not ask you to accompany us farther. We know too well the consequences and cost of emigration to press upon you to adopt it. We have nothing to offer you but what awaits ourselves. Where the soil of our country ends, therefore, stop and leave us."

On hearing these words, opinions were divided amongst us. My mind was made up. It was the first time I had had the courage to speak in public. My adversary was the nephew of M. Royer Collard, a young man who felt and argued hotly on all subjects. He spoke well, and won all hearts to his views. But I fought against his proposal with all the energy of which I was capable. "To emigrate," I said, "is to declare ourselves defeated on the soil we are bound to defend. We are more useful to the King's cause in the country itself than in following his fortunes as soldiers in a strange land. It is by the force of public opinion that we shall win, and not by arms."

Five or six of our company insisted on following the King into Belgium; but the rest of us remained behind. A few moments later a proclamation was read, announcing that we were all to be disbanded, and that, in virtue of a convention entered into by the generals on both sides, we were to return unarmed to the bosom of our families. Until Béthune was evacuated, however, we were to guard her gates.

I and about twenty of my comrades were to have charge of the Paris gate, and prevent the enemy's force from entering the town before the day stipulated in the convention.

After two or three nights passed in this manner, we heard some one knocking at the gates under cover of the darkness. A voice cried out, "Is there an officer here named Lamartine?" "Yes," was the reply. "Well; tell him that an officer of Hussars, named Descrivieux, wishes to speak to him." I was summoned; Captain Descrivieux was admitted, and we embraced each other cordially. "I am come to fetch you," he said. Descrivieux was an amiable young man from Bourg en Bresse, a relation and friend of my family's whom I had left at Mâcon a few days before the 20th of March, and whom the defection of his regiment had compelled to follow the cause of the Emperor in spite of his own opinions. He belonged to Excelmans's corps of cavalry. "Follow me," he said, "your duty is accomplished. I will give you a tradesman's disguise, a horse, and money to get back to Paris. You must not wait till the regular disbanding of the King's troops has scattered them all over the country, for they would, of course, be looked upon with suspicion by the Emperor's forces, and your return would be both dangerous and difficult. Your mother put you specially under my charge; so come along directly."

I did not hesitate, and followed my guide through the faubourg of Béthune. He bought me a capital horse from the stables of the Prince de Condé, whose accoutrements and bridle were still marked with his cipher. I exchanged my own clothes for those of a horse-dealer in the neighborhood, which disguised me completely, and, after having wished Captain Descrivieux an affectionate farewell, I rode off, with a jockey's whip at my wrist and a pair of pistols in my portmanteau. "God protect you," exclaimed my friend; "and remember me to Madame de Larmartine." "We are sure to meet one another again in life." I did meet him often in after-life, and, at last, as a colonel of Hussars, beloved, and deservedly so, by his whole regiment. Waterloo had spared him. His had been one of the twelve regiments whom Grouchy, unjustly accused, had brought back to Liège. He had a prosperous and happy life, and died two years ago, always gay and good and bright, and always a devoted friend. Were all the world to forget him, I should ever deplore his loss, and remember his kindness to me at the little garrison of Béthune.

XXVIII.

Nothing happened to me on the road. My childish face was rather inappropriate to my pretended trade; but the troubles which filled every heart in the rear of the great army were my best protection. Moreover, the good people of the North of France would have died sooner than betray a friend of the King's.

I had a return of fever on arriving at Abbeville. I remember the great Hôtel de l'Europe, where I had lodged before, and, dismounting, I gave my horse to the ostler and asked for a bed. The mistress of the house and her three charming daughters, seeing that I was tired and sick, showed me into a most comfortable apartment; they directly saw through my horsedealer's disguise, and treated me as a young man of good family. The doctor came and said that all I wanted was rest. For several days I was nursed by these good people with a tender care of which I was really ashamed. The political state of the horizon seemed to have redoubled their natural kindness. My own mother and sisters could not have looked after me better. They always opposed my departure. At last, I had no excuse for remaining. I told them my name. They did not own to having recognized me till that avowal could only add to their kindness. They would not hear of any payment for their hospitality. "Allow us, sir," they exclaimed, "to consider ourselves your hostesses and not your servants; we can only beg of you to keep a place for us in your remembrance. Wherever the King is loved you will find friends."

I promised I would not forget them as long as I lived, and I have kept my word. May Abbeville always contain such good and loyal hearts! Gratitude is like friendship, and takes no note of time.

XXIX.

When I arrived near Paris, I began to reflect on the way I should manage to get into the town without exciting suspicion. I wrote to a good fellow named Michonnet, who let out horses and carriages in the Rue St. Marc, an old Vendean hero, whose body had been riddled with shot in the days when people fought for their opinions. I had known Michonnet during my first visit to Paris, and had made acquintance with his wife, who was as good and loyal as himself. He used to let me have horses and carriages on hire, and would even lend me money at a pinch. I wrote to him explaining my position, and telling him that I should arrive on such a day at St. Denis with a fine horse. I implored him to come and fetch me himself in his gig, with a groom to take my horse, and to let me lodge for a night or two at his house. I arrived towards evening at St. Denis, and found that he had arranged everything according to my suggestion. I took his groom's place in the gig by his side, the groom riding my horse, and so we entered Paris without the least difficulty or suspicion. He took me to my old quarters in the Hôtel du Hazard. My landlady gave me a graphic picture of the state of Paris. I wanted to remain here privately for some days. Every one who had belonged to the household of Louis XVIII. had been forbidden to stop in Paris; but I reckoned on getting out of the city as I had entered it, through the ready wit and good-nature of Michonnet.

After having, accordingly, stopped a week there, and been witness to the scandalous scenes in the theatre (when the Bourbons were given up to the coarse raillery of the dregs of the people to please the conqueror of Elba), I left it, as I had come, by the intervention of Michonnet, and mounted the same horse which had brought me to Paris. I had an uncle, whom I have before mentioned, a venerable ecclesiastic, who had given up his ministerial employments, and lived in a beautiful and solitary château in the forest in the neighborhood of Dijon. He was my father's favorite brother and most intimate friend, and I wrote to say I was coming, and that I felt it would be to a second father. I took the least frequented roads towards Burgundy; but I found the people far less Royalist than those of the North. The cries of *Vive l'Empéreur!* met me on all sides, with menacing looks and provocations to insult, even from the peasants who were working in the fields or mowing the meadows by the roadside. Sometimes the cry varied to *Vive la Mort!* But I went quickly on my way, only chewing the cud of bitter reflections.

At Châtillon-sur-Seine, however, on climbing the hill which led to the town, I felt I could not resist driving back those who were pursuing me with such gratuitous insults. I had a little sword-stick which hung on my wrist by a leathern strap, and I drew the sword, galloping after them for a few seconds with the naked blade. They all took to flight, and hid themselves in the vineyards. I put back my sword in the scabbard and walked on. But my impatient movement had broken the stick and the sword alone remained in my hand. Fortunately I found it out on crossing the little bridge which led into the town, and hastened to get rid of my sword by throwing it into the stream below the bridge. I went on my way quietly, not thinking I had been observed, and stopped at a little inn in the centre of the town to ask for some dinner. I saw that my horse was well cared for, and then sat down to dine. Hardly was I seated, however, than a captain of the National Guard came into the room and asked me what was the arm I had thrown away in the stream. I saw that I was discovered, and felt that it would be wiser to tell the truth, that my sword having slipped out of its sheath, I thought it was safer to throw it away rather than compromise myself by wearing it thus through the town. The captain saw directly with whom he had to deal, and that I was not a brigand. He asked me my name and my country. "But I know your father!" he exclaimed. "He was one of my great friends. You are one of the King's household, which has been disbanded, and you are going home: there is no harm in that. I will leave you for a moment to finish your dinner, and give you the time to be ready before me. Tell the ostler to take your horse half a league from here on the way to Vitteaux, and then leisurely go on foot in the same direction. I will take care you are not molested." I finished my dinner and started as I was bid, without being in any way hindered on my road, and rejoicing in the kindness of the captain who thus enabled me to escape an awkward interrogatory and several hours of prison, if not more.

The next day I started for Sombernon. I knew the country perfectly. At Pont-de-Pany I followed a narrow path through a gorge in the woods, which brought me at night-fall to my uncle's solitary château, where I found my father also, and we had a merry supper together. I stayed there several days to rest my horse. I saw that my Royalist feelings were far more keen and zealous than theirs. My father had become hardened to changes of government, and my uncle was not very sorry for the events of the 24th of March, whereby he was rid of a clergy whose pretensions gave him some umbrage. At Mâcon I found I had no alternative but to serve the Emperor. I had sworn not to bear arms but for the Bourbons or Liberty ; so I determined to leave France for a time and pass into Switzerland ; and my mother did not thwart or oppose my wishes.

BOOK VII.

I.

I HAD a great friend, who was an old *émigré* of Condé's army, living in the mountains of the Jura. I resolved to throw myself on his hospitality for a few weeks, and spend a little time with him in the heart of the Swiss mountains, from whence I could easily go farther if the state of things became worse.

This gentleman who was a good deal older than I, was one of those charming people who suit all ages. He was a Royalist, but not a very keen politician, and enjoyed life as he found it. He had that witty and keen sense of humor which rather laughed at enthusiasm or over-zeal, even in the cause of the King. He was a widower; his beautiful young wife was from Mâcon, and had died in her first confinement. Having left his little boy to the care of one of his sisters, he lived alone, half sadly, half joyously, in the midst of these wild mountains. All parties loved him, because he hated no one, and that he looked upon all opinions, if sincere, as deserving of respect and consideration. His name was M. de Maizod. His little château was only a house dignified with that feudal title, but which the peasants considered as belonging to the village. His nearest neighbors lived at the little town of Moirans. There was an old middle-class family in Moirans, which was not far from St. Claude, who were immensely looked up to and respected in the country. They were called, like the Scotch clans, the Chavériats. Léonard Chavériat, who belonged to every one of note in Moirans, was looked upon with affectionate admiration by the whole population. He was, in fact, all powerful; being lawyer, sportsman, fisherman, and one who could turn his hand to anything, while his greatest delight was to be of use to everybody. He was a Royalist; but his opinions were subordinate to his instincts. It would seem as if the heart of all the mountains beat in that honest breast. The moment he appeared, all, even the little children, would smile and cry out, "There 's Léonard!" This man, by analogy of character, was the friend and constant guest of M. de Maizod — that is to say, all Moirans was his.

Léonard Chavériat, who knew the history of every stone and ruin in the place, came directly to the château de Maizod to welcome in me the original owner and child of the soil.

II.

The château of M. de Maizod was a little square building perched on the extremity of a flat bit of table-land, which rose, isolated as it were, amidst the farms of the village. At some steps from the house, the terrace, formed by the gray rocks, slopes suddenly down in a precipice towards a retired and wooded valley. M. de Maizod opened his arms to receive me with a joyous cry; he was waiting for me at the front door.

"I come to you," I said to M. de Maizod, "like a bird who is poising himself on the last branch of the last tree in the forest, undecided whether to stay or to take his flight across the fields of Liberty at the first appearance of the sportsman. Do not let me disturb any of your usual habits, but let me only live here a little while in peace."

I spent a month, in fact, in this quiet solitude without being troubled by the convulsions which agitated the other provinces of France.

III.

Things were in this state when Léonard Chavériat came to inform me that war having been declared, and the Emperor being in need of men, the prefects had received orders to find out all the young men who had served in the King's household or body-guard, and to compel them to march against the enemy, and join the Imperial army. My decision was instantly taken. I exclaimed, "I would rather take flight or die than fight against the King!" I had told my father so, and I repeated it fifty times a day to myself. Neutrality may be accepted, but apostasy never! I had no time for deliberation. Léonard offered to guide me to the Swiss frontier through the forest of Fresnoy. I accepted the services of so true a friend. His known habits as a sportsman, and the way he was looked up to in the neighborhood, insured my safety on the road. I wished good-by to my host — that best of men, and followed Chavériat. My gun served as a pretext for my departure, and we started towards evening for St. Claude.

We stopped on our way at Combe, a little village at a stone's throw from the town. It has a pretty waterfall, which had been diverted a little from its course in order to work a saw-mill belonging to M. Reverchon an old tenant of my father's in this part of the Jura. He lived with his wife and sons on the borders of the forest, out of which the stream rushes in the most picturesque manner. We were treated less as guests than as masters of the house, and after supper we talked of family matters. I confided to them my plan of escape. Every one was ready to second me in it. I went to sleep lulled by the regular rush of the waterfall and the melancholy creaking of the wheels of the saw-mill. As soon as the day dawned, Léonard woke me, and after having warmly thanked our hosts, we started on our way. Our dogs trotted after us in couples. After following an oblique course across the fields on the lower edge of the mountains in sight of the custom-house officers who knew Léonard, we suddenly entered the magnificent forest which had shaded my cradle, as it was now sheltering my flight. We took the least frequented paths, under the grandest old firs, and walked on in this way for two or three hours. These trees resemble the giants in the Californian valleys, and rise like the great masts of a ship with their leafy sails. I exhausted myself in trying to measure by the eye their height and diameter. We appeared like dwarfs at their feet. What are revolutions which displace men, as the swaying of the branches displace the birds, compared to the kind of perpetuity of one of these primeval forests? We were never weary of talking of and admiring them. At last, a kind of twilight towards one end of the wood showed us a break in the dark cathedral-like shade we had been so long traversing. Here Léonard stopped. "Follow," he said, "that hollow and unfrequented path which leads up the hill until you come to a shelving bank, which is the boundary or frontier between the two countries. If I see the custom-house officers watching you, I will go and divert their attention till you have passed it. You will then find yourself close to a high-road, in which you are safe and free. It will lead you to St. Cergues, a Swiss hamlet on the summit of the Jura, from whence you will see at your feet the lakes Léman and Lausanne to your left, and Geneva to your right. God have you in his holy keeping! You are now in the country of William Tell." So saying, we embraced and parted. A quarter of an hour after I saw on an upright stone the arms of the Pays de Vaud. I cried out loud for joy at my deliverance, and walked gayly on to St. Cergues. I asked for the house of M. Reboul, which was immediately pointed out to me. It was the well-known home of a noble Swiss, who had been the guide of Madame de Staël and her friends during the first great Revolution. It was there that Mathieu de Montmorency, Benjamin Constant, MM. de Noailles, and countless other distinguished men, had shaken off the dust from their feet when flying from a land of tyranny to one of liberty. I thanked God who had allowed me to follow in their steps.

I was courteously requested to come in. M. Reboul was gone to see his cows, which were fattening on the rich pasture of *La Calme.* A young lady of remarkable beauty came forward and begged me gracefully to await his return. This young girl, or rather this angel from a higher sphere, had nothing either in her face or dress like any woman I had ever seen before. Her voice was not more strange and fascinating than her features. The calm of the mountainous region in which she lived seemed to have impregnated the tones in which she spoke to us, ordinary mortals.

But her face, with her blue eyes and her rose-leaf complexion, had a mingled expression of joy and sorrow, which struck me the moment I saw her. I did not then know that she had only lately lost her mother, and that time had not yet effaced the traces of her grief. She was plaiting a large straw hat with a wide border to defend her neck from the sun, and little bits of straw were scattered on the parquet floor at her feet.

She offered me a glass of wine whilst I was waiting for her father; and we began to enter into a quiet kind of conversation. She, with that calm soft voice, which thrilled me through and through, and I, with a totally new feeling which made my words tremble on my lips. I had a letter of recommendation from Léonard for her father, so that I had no alternative but to await his return. He came home very late, but by that time I had become accustomed to my hostess, and it was Reboul who appeared to me the only stranger.

I gave him Léonard's letter. He read it carefully, and then said we would speak of its contents on the morrow. He told his charming daughter to go and prepare my room for me. She left us at once, but my thoughts followed her. I do not know how it was that recollections of Graziella mingled with this new vision. I could not tell why this angelic apparition gave me at once such a feeling of security and such an inclination to cry.

I supped afterwards with Reboul; his daughter waited on us. Her soft and holy face seemed to me a good omen on the threshold of an unknown future.

IV.

During supper, M. Reboul spoke to me openly of his adventures as guide to the many hundred proscribed or voluntary exiles whom for the last fifteen years he had concealed and conveyed from one country to another. He began by Madame de Staël, whose château of Coppet was not far from St. Cergues. The wish he felt to save his friends had insensibly led him to make a habit of that which had at first been only the impulse of his kind heart. His reputation was spread throughout France and Switzerland, and he had always been fortunate in his ventures. He attributed his success to the protection of God, which the prayers of his saintly wife and child had obtained for him. At the mention of his wife his eyes filled with tears. His daughter turned her face away, and covered it with her apron to hide her tears. "Do not let us talk of this any more to-night," said her father. "It is time to go to bed. You will stay here till to-morrow," he added, turning to me, "and I will give you the best advice I can after I have heard your story, and have found out what I can do for you." His charming daughter helped the servant to make my bed, and I went to rest to dream of the future. But the face of the Graziella of the Alps prevented my sleeping for a long time.

The next day, at day-break, I was up and ready to accompany her father. She wished me good-by, recommending me tenderly to God's care. "You are very young," she said, "to be thus thrown by yourself into an unknown future. Your mother must have many anxieties on your account!" "Ah," I replied, "I have a mother and sisters also, who pray to God for me. They are younger, but not better or purer than you." She wrung my hand, and we parted.

After having walked for some time on the brow of the mountain which the dawn had hardly yet lighted, I suddenly burst into a cry of admiration. The whole horizon of Switzerland seemed to me to be emerging from the morning mist; it was like a second creation. At our feet the Lake Leman sparkled, half in light and half in shadow. The mountains of Meilleraie and the rocky Tooth de Jaman, so wonderfully described by J. J. Rousseau, formed the barrier on the Italian side. The Valais, a country of innocence and of shepherds, seemed nestled in a little hollow to the left. Then Vevay and the Château de Chillon shone like fallen stars in the lake. Never, not even at Naples, had I seen so wonderful and glorious a spectacle. At each rung of the marvelous ladder of terraces which we began to descend, new bays, new ports, new towns, new villas, new gardens opened out on our delighted gaze. It seemed as if we were really assisting at the creation of a new world. After we had walked for about two hours, always bearing towards the left, Reboul suddenly stopped and showed me a large and imposing modern castle, which rose like a fan with its succession of terraces above the village at the head of the lake.

"Look!" he said to me. "We will wish one another good by here. That is the Château of Vincy, to which I have led you. I will not go any farther, for you cannot lose your way. This castle, which is one of the most beautiful on the borders of the lake, belongs to the illustrious House of Vincy, Lords of Berne — once very rich, now ruined by the vile revolution of 1799. It is now inhabited by the youngest and last brother of those who commanded the Swiss troops in the service of France, and of whom one or two passed into Holland. Some of the other members of the family are married, and have become once more French proprietors. Others have seen long service in the household of the King, while this one spends his winters at Geneva, and his summers in this old family mansion. He is the best man I know to give you the information you seek, and to put you in the way of obtaining what you wish. He has, as it were, the kernel of a little French army, composed of men who wish to fight for the cause of the King of France without joining themselves to strangers. He is, in fact, the principal Royalist agent for the French in Switzerland. Go and introduce yourself to him in my name, and ask him to look at your papers. They will tell him all."

I thanked Reboul, sent many heartfelt good wishes to his daughter, and strolled on alone for the château of M. de Vincy. I was not without some uneasiness as to the manner in which I should be received, for I had only this note from Reboul, and my personal appearance was certainly not in my favor. I went down the hill, therefore, rather reluctantly, and arrived, almost with a feeling of regret, at the iron gates which led to the castle.

V.

I pushed open the gate for myself. One felt, by the solitude and the absence of any porter or servant, the ruin which had fallen on this noble and Royalist house. I walked on till I came to a magnificent flight of steps, and was admitted by a servant, who took in my card to M. de Vincy. He was a wizened, ill-dressed little man, and everything about him indicated a certain degree of poverty. He made me sit down in his own room, and asked me to what circumstance he was indebted for the honor of my visit? I presented M. Reboul's note in answer.

"I know nothing," he replied, "at this moment, of the state of affairs in France. The armies gathered against the Emperor are composed of English, Prussian, Russian, Austrian, and Italian troops. There are no Frenchmen, I fear, except a handful gathered together by the Prince de Polignac in a village near Neufchâtel called La Chaux-de-Fond. The Abbé Lafond, Malet's only accomplice, is at the head of this little troop. I will have your passport viséed for Neufchâtel."

I thanked him, and stood aside whilst a multitude of people and farmers came to transact different affairs with him, or to receive his orders. The same servant introduced them one after the other. I saw many of these men leave miserable little sums in copper on his desk, which was evidently their rent, and which he counted with the anxiety of an apparently rich man who did not know where to turn for the necessary expenditure of the house. Everything showed the pinching of penury in the midst of external opulence. I was filled with pity for him in spite of my admiration for his magnificent home.

When the farmers had finished their payments, M. de Vincy came back to me and gave me my passport viséed. I wished him good-by, feeling more and more for his unhappy position, and took my departure. Scarcely had I taken half a dozen steps towards the iron grille than a carriage drove up and stopped at the steps. Two ladies and a little child got out of it. They were a mother and daughter, and a pretty boy of ten or twelve years old. I glanced at them and raised my hat as they stopped for an instant on the lower step of the staircase, where M. de Vincy had joined them, and was speaking to them in a low voice. During this conversation I had turned away and had just reached the iron gates when a soft voice recalled me. It was Madame de Vincy. "Sir," she exclaimed, "be so kind as to come back."

I did so, shyly enough. When I drew near them she added, "Sir, forgive me for having called you back without having the honor of knowing you. But when M. de Vincy told me the object of your visit, I feared you might not have dined, and as we are just going to sit down to dinner, I venture to ask you to share our humble repast. There is no inn in this village, and it is three hours' march from here to Rolle. Do not refuse us the pleasure of being your hosts to-day."

I refused on the plea of my dress; but they insisted more amiably than ever, and I was compelled to yield. The dinner was served immediately; my hostess was most indulgent and kind. Madame de Vincy, the mother, was one of the most beautiful and imposing women I ever saw. She was born a princess of some sovereign house in the Palatinate, of which I have forgotten the name. The Vincys had noble birth on both sides, but Madame de Vincy did not belie her origin. Her height, which was five feet and seven inches, gave her the majesty of a goddess without taking away her grace as a mortal, and the blue eyes of a German princess impressed a certain amount of dignity even on her smile. Her face alone revealed the goodness of her heart; the sound of her voice spoke to the heart even before it charmed the ear. Her civility was indeed true Christian courtesy. Never had I seen so remarkable a face. One felt that she was a mother, and there was something filial in the emotion with which her beauty inspired me.

Her daughter, who was infinitely less beautiful but as good and sensible as her mother, was gentle and sympathizing in manner; I saw that her soul was a reflection of Madame de

Vincy's, and that she was a shoot of the same stem. She was about sixteen. The boy of twelve had a fine German countenance. Madame de Vincy had two other sons, one in the Dutch service and one in the household of Louis XVIII., who had followed the King to Ghent. They were fine well-grown lads; in fact, their mother was made to bring forth noble-looking sons.

VI.

Our conversation became more and more familiar. We had plenty of subjects in common in the political aspect of the times, and in the strangeness of my own position. They insisted on hearing my history, which I related simply and naturally. I saw that it made a great impression on my hostess, and that the father and son were of the same opinion. The dinner over, I took up my little bundle, and prepared to continue my journey. "But, sir," exclaimed Madame de Vincy, "an idea strikes me. My husband tells me that you are going, at all risks, to join the little gathering of French at La Chaux-de-Fond, in the neighborhood of Neufchâtel. I highly approve of your determination not to serve your country with strange troops, who any day may become our enemies. But if you find this French corps dispersed, what do you mean to do?"

"I really don't know," I replied.

"Well, then," she rejoined, "if you can put up with such accommodation as we can offer you here, why should you not stop a few days till we can obtain some information as to the state of things at Neufchâtel, and let us, for a time, replace to you your mother and sisters?"

I colored; but my face showed the pleasure I did not dare express. The ladies understood me at once, and Mademoiselle de Vincy, at a sign from her mother, taking my little bundle from my hands, laid it on the table.

"Well," added Madame de Vincy, smiling, "try and fancy that we are your mother and sister for the moment. You will not refuse to let us shelter you for some weeks till we can see our way a little more clearly; and will you not be as comfortable here as on the high-roads, or in some bad Swiss inn? Make up your mind to stop with us, for I already feel towards you as to a son."

"Ah! madame," I exclaimed with a broken voice, "how can I resist such kindness, and go against my own heart's leanings?"

"Well, well, then it's all settled," exclaimed husband and wife at once. "We will go and order your room, and I hope you will be as comfortable or more so than at the inn of Rolle."

They gave me a room with a most glorious view over the lake of Geneva, and I found myself treated in all respects as one of the family.

VII.

From that hour my life become most enjoyable. The mother and daughter took possession of me, whilst M. de Vincy, busy with his domestic troubles, was painfully collecting his rents from the tenants of Vincy. I had almost forgotten the object of my journey. But I soon found that the so-called French army, which had been organized in Switzerland by the Royalist agents of the Pays de Vaud, was reduced to nothing, or contented themselves with some insignificant movements without any result. In the mean time I reveled in the enjoyment of the confidence which my circumstances and age had inspired in the bosom of a hospitable and virtuous family.

One day during my stay with them I went to dine in the little town of Nyons, to try and glean some news to bring back to my hosts at the château of Vincy. There was at Nyons an inn dear to all old emigrants, kept by a maiden lady, who was well known in the country. Madame de Vincy gave me a line of introduction for her, and I went there for a night. She received me as an old friend. There were about thirty guests at the *table d'hôte*, at which she presided. Hardly was I seated, without any intention of being remarked by anybody, than an angry squabble arose at the other end of the table between some people who had been quietly occupied in eating their dinner in silence, and a Swiss officer belonging to the canton of Berne. I could not help listening to the quarrel, which seemed to get warmer every moment.

"No!" at last exclaimed the officer, "I am not one of those mean Frenchmen who renounce the great man who has been the origin of all their glory in Europe, and who are at this moment forming wishes for his second fall from the armies of the allies. And if you don't like my principles, you may, if you please, call me to account for them. I am ready to answer any one who chooses to contradict me."

Everybody was silent. Some of the company went away. I was the youngest, the most unknown, and the farthest from the speaker, who was at the extreme end of the long table. I therefore held my tongue, when a young man and two very pretty women who were with him, started up close to a side door which led into the dining-room. Their speaking faces, the deep frown on their foreheads, and the eager eye with which they looked up and down the room seeking for one who would answer and avenge their cause, made me instantly resolve to break the silence.

"Very well, sir," I exclaimed, rising and turning to the officer from Berne, "as no one seems disposed to answer your insolent speech, I shall take it upon myself to reply in my quality as a Frenchman. Yes, sir, I am one of those Frenchmen whom you call mean, because they believed in the reality of abdications, and in the sacred nature of treaties; and did not think that the caprice of a voluntary exile in the island of Elba could dispose at his will of France and of Europe. They still hold to these opinions; and if you wish to be answered otherwise than by words, I am ready, and will meet you where you please."

At these words a low murmur of applause ran through the whole length of the table, which went on increasing till the officer, looking thoroughly ashamed of himself, retired, and I remained confused at the praise I had unexpectedly received.

I sat down quickly, rather ashamed of my easy triumph, when the two pretty women, whose presence had inspired me to speak, rushed towards me, and drawing me towards the door I have before mentioned, carried me off through the corridor of the inn to their own room, and congratulated me in terms which I have since heard in the House of Deputies.

"We are proud, sir, to be French women," they said, "and to have by chance heard one of the youngest of our countrymen avenge our country by such words after the insults of that miserable wretch, whose only admiration is for tyranny. As to ourselves, believe that we have never made a pact with those who look upon glory as the one good, and that we hailed the restoration of the Bourbons as the return to right and liberty. Tell us who you are, and pray make use of our little apartment here while you are staying in this hotel."

They brought some punch, and I drank to the health of my enthusiastic friends; after which, thanking them warmly for their kindness, I went back to Vincy. A note from the landlady of the hotel had preceded me: my little adventure, colored by her good-nature, seemed heroic. They received me in consequence as a Royalist hero. Fortune had served me. I had defended at the same time the cause of the Bernese aristocracy, and that of the King of France.

These two ladies were Mesdames de Bellegarde, doubly famous from the part they had played during the French Revolution of 1792 and 1793, and by their enthusiasm for the restoration on the return of Louis XVIII. in 1814. Although very different in expression, they were still very beautiful, a beauty which had exposed them in former times to all the snares of human love and admiration. The eldest, the Countess de Bellegarde, had a face like that of Judith by Allori. She was tall, large, dark, with passionate black eyes, a living picture in fact of enthusiasm. The youngest, also tall and with a beautiful figure, was a great contrast to her sister; she was fair, delicate, and sensitive, with blue dreamy eyes, which often wore an expression of great sadness. They were natives of Sardinia, the daughters of a Count de Bellegarde, and had been left orphans very young. Their father had been in the service of the House of Austria, and their name had long been distinguished among the generals whom the Emperor was fond of selecting from the Italian states, such as the Montecuculli and others. Left in the country home of their ancestors during the beginning of the French Revolution, they lived in a magnificent château called Des Marches, in the midst of the beautiful valley of Grésivaudan. After having conquered Savoy and Geneva, the revolutionary general, De Montesquieu (then in the full height of his power, though soon after proscribed), had taken refuge in the mountains of Switzerland, to wait for better times, and the province of Savoy had been given up to the proconsul Hérault de Séchelles. Before the days of the Convention, Hérault had been a magistrate and a philosopher, and a model of honorable and high-principled conduct. His beautiful face and figure resembled that of Antinous ; he was the "Barbarossa" of the aristocracy. Elected unanimously by the legislative assembly, he had obtained a high position there, not only by his eloquence and the dignity of his bearing, but by his Jacobin enthusiasm. With his great zeal, his voice, and his expressive face, he became the idol of the neophytes of those days ; but, insensibly dragged on by the revolutionary torrent beyond his own convictions, he had, like Le Pelletier de St. Fargeau, yielded to the popular tumult, and sacrificed the King to the exigencies and barbaric violence of the republic. Popular favor, however, had rewarded him for this weak compliance as if it had been a virtue. Sent soon after to republican Savoy, he was at the same time a conqueror and conquered : he came to the château of Marches, and saw these two beautiful orphans without a guardian or protector ; the one in all the splendor of her grown-up beauty, the other with all the tender grace of budding girlhood. A passionate love for the Countess de Bellegarde took possession of his heart ; while his burning eloquence inspired these young girls with an enthusiasm for his own opinions. The two sisters had been introduced by him as models to the fanatical people of those provinces. A little later he became unpopular with his party from his moderation, and Hérault de Séchelles followed Danton to the scaffold, and died an honest republican, a victim to the crimes of the people.

The Countess of Bellegarde and her innocent sister wished to share his fate ; but even these brutal judges, dazzled by their youth and beauty, would not condemn them. They had lived ever since that time in the Château of Marches, sharing in the society around them, and in the reaction against the Terrorists, of whom they had so nearly been the victims The events of the 20th of March had revolted them ; they had quitted their château and come to Nyons to live with the Royalists. It was thus that I first became acquainted with them, and in their enthusiastic declarations I recognized the pupils of him in whose political school they had been brought up.

VIII.

Two days after, I resolved to profit by my near neighborhood to see, at least once before her death, Madame de Staël, who had long been the object of my antipathy on account of her father, and of my enthusiasm as regarded herself. Coppet, which was the abode of M. Necker, had been previously bought by my grandfather, who had kept it a long time without living in it ; but all of a sudden the canton of Berne passed a law refusing the rights of proprietorship to any Catholic ; so that he ceded it to I know not whom, and bought in its stead the beautiful castle of Ursy, in Burgundy. I felt that it would hardly be right for me, as a guest of the Vincys, to go and introduce myself at the château of Coppet as a pilgrim at the tomb of M. Necker, whom it was impossible for me to admire or to love. " I should be wanting to two persons," I said: "to Madame de Vincy and to myself. I will not go ! " Only, as the high-road is the property of everybody, I thought a cat might look at a king, and that a glimpse of her would satisfy without compromising me. I knew that Madame de Staël went twice a week to Geneva with certain friends of hers, among whom were two beautiful women, one Madame

Récamier, her great friend, exiled, like her, from all countries under the dominion of the Emperor; the other, Mlle. de Constant, a German, of still wider reputation; but, at this period of my life, the admiration of genius extinguished all other in my heart.

IX.

I got up, therefore, very early one Saturday, which was the day they told me Madame de Staël made her weekly expedition to Geneva, and putting a piece of bread in my pocket, I hid myself at a turn of the road from Coppet to Geneva, being partly concealed by a great ditch on the high-road, by the side of which her carriage must necessarily pass. I remained there from nine o'clock in the morning till two o'clock in the afternoon, hidden by the shrubs at the side of the road; during which time I amused myself by reading "Corinne" (that beautiful work of that modern Sappho), and listening with a quick ear to the least sound of a carriage coming from Coppet. In spite of the poetic interest of this beautiful book on Italy, the day appeared to me rather long, and I at last determined to quit my hiding-place, when to my great joy I heard the rolling of two carriages, which left me no doubt as to their occupants. They passed like the wind; the first contained only two gentlemen with Mlle. Constant; a beautiful person in the flower of her age. I could only, however, snatch one look at her, which was followed by an involuntary cry of admiration. The next carriage, which was an open one, contained two women, whom it was impossible not to recognize. One was Madame Récamier, whose angelic face could bear no other name, and of whom it was said that one look sufficed to bind your heart to her forever; but her beauty, although it dazzled, did not distract me. Her companion, who was speaking to her in a loud voice, was, however, the person of whom I was in search. I had time to take in her features thoroughly, for the horses slacked their speed at a little rise there was in the ground. Madame de Staël was, as usual, dressed in an Indian turban, of which the varied and well-assorted colors seemed to be magically reflected upon her forehead. The forehead was large, prominent, and high, as if to give space to a whole world of thought and new ideas ; it shaded two prominent eyes of magnificent shape and brilliancy ; all her expression, in fact, lay in these eyes ; they spoke more than her mouth. Her nose was short and finely shaped ; her lips thick and open, made for eloquence or for love ; her complexion was pale, but brightened by a look of inspiration. Her arms, which were always in movement, and exposed by short, open sleeves, were white and magnificent ; her whole person, though large, was not wanting in a grace which called forth admiration ; in fact, it commanded it. The little hill had been climbed. The horses started again at a trot, and nothing remained to me but the dust they left behind them. Genius had passed me with its escort of beauty ; but what remained on one's memory was the genius. I could not finish the volume of "Corinne" after having seen its author ! I came back very late and found my friends waiting for me for supper. I was obliged to own to Madame de Vincy what had been the cause of my long absence. "Why did you not tell me of your very natural admiration ?" replied this noble woman ; "in spite of some differences of opinion, we have for Madame de Staël as much enthusiasm as yourself. We would have taken and introduced you to her. It is impossible to see without admiring her, or to be her neighbor without loving her. Her faults are those of her training and her wit ; her good qualities belong to her own heart ; the foundation of all her glory is really her goodness." "No," I replied to my kind hostess. "I would rather have seen her quietly without knowing her ; I have had a glimpse of genius, and it was as rapid and fugitive as itself ;" and then we began to talk of other things.

X.

I had spent three weeks in this delightful house in a delicious intimacy with the Vincy family ; but I knew the extreme poverty of the house, and I was afraid of being indiscreet, and perhaps burdensome. I settled, therefore, to delay no longer my start for Neufchâtel and La Chaux-de-Fond, to seek the French royalist military gathering. They smiled at my enthusiasm, but they let me go. A gentleman from Lyons, who was a great agriculturist, came in the same way that I had done to present himself to Monsieur de Vincy, and gave me a pretext for departure. I took leave of my kind and generous hosts with a pang; it appeared to me as if I were again parting from my own family. Madame and Mlle de Vincy had tears in their eyes at wishing me good-by. I started with my Lyons companion, but promised to return if the gathering at La Chaux-de-Fond disappointed my expectations. At Rollo we chartered a kind of Swiss car to conduct us to Neufchâtel. Our vetturino brought us there in three days, the road winding round the base of the Jura mountains, amidst the most beautiful scenery possible, with the Lakes Leman, Yverdun, and of Neufchâtel to the right, and grand rocks and pine forests to the left. We were perfectly charmed with our expedition, and as our opinions were identical, there was nothing in our conversation to mar our enjoyment of this magnificent scenery. The first question we asked on arriving at the hotel at Neufchâtel was about the French military gathering at La Chaux-de-Fond. No one had an idea of what we meant! I began to fear our royalist visions would vanish in smoke. My companion was so discouraged that he decided to return to his Lyons property. I, however, was determined to persevere in the search, and next day started on foot for La Chaux-de-Fond. The path led through a beautiful forest of sombre pines and magnificent waterfalls, and I did not arrive there till the morning of the following day. La Chaux-de-Fond was then a poor little Swiss village, situated on the extreme frontiers of France, and inhabited by peasants who were all clock-makers. Its picturesque wooden houses were scattered here and there over the plain which led to the pine wood. My appearance and dress were rather those of a journeyman watch-maker, who was coming to seek employment from one of the clock-makers in the district. I went into the first public-house I came to, and asked for the address of the head of the staff of the French army. The people looked at one another with surprise, and after having said something in a *patois* unintelligible to me, concluded with a smile that I was wishing to find a French priest named L'Abbé Lafond, who had been living in the only decent hotel in the village for one or two months, and to whose lodging they proposed to conduct me. I began to doubt the existence of a staff corps, which thus disappeared like a mirage, and which seemed to be represented by an abbé in a wild village on the side of the Alps ; however, having come so far, I was determined to see, and I saw. What was called the great hotel of La Chaux-de-Fond was a little house at the end of a long solitary street, on the opposite side to that by which I had come into the village. A young girl, who had volunteered to be my guide, said smiling to the innkeeper, "Here is a gentleman who is looking for the French army ; they told him at our house that its head-quarters were with you, and that its general was L'Abbé Lafond!" "It's quite true," replied the innkeeper ; "we have got here a gentleman who calls himself the Abbé Lafond, but who says he is a major-general in the French army. If you, sir," he added, turning to me, "wish to speak to him, I will go and ask him to come down-stairs ; in the mean time, here is a little table, with some fresh bread and cheese, and beer, to refresh you after your hot walk." They brought me, accordingly, this primitive breakfast, and I sat down to eat it in the best parlor of the little inn.

XI.

I was hardly seated at the table, however, before I saw a little man with a beaming face, between thirty and forty years of age, come rapidly down a little wooden staircase. "Oh! there is Monsieur l'Abbé Lafond," exclaimed the servant, and she brought him to where I was sitting. He was dressed in a brown great-coat, which was half military, half ecclesiastical. His black stockings carefully drawn up over his well made calves, reminded one of a priest ; while the black cravat and military collar made me fancy that he was an officer.

He thus represented a double character, the ecclesiastic below and the soldier above ; he was, in fact, made to suit every taste. I got up and bowed, while he came forward smiling, and asked me, " What had brought me to see him in this out-of-the-way part of the world ? " I begged him to sit down. He said he would breakfast with me, and ordered some eggs, and we entered into conversation while filling our glasses with beer. " You have come from Monsieur de Vincy," he said to me at last. " Here is a letter from him," I replied. He read it, and then said quietly ; " This is just what I had supposed." I continued : " I am come to join the little army which is being organized, I am told, under your orders, at La Chaux-de-Fond. I will not serve with strangers against France, but I am dying to fight for the King against the Emperor ; where is the army ? " " The army ! " he exclaimed ; " why, it is I ! there is no other. Was not I alone, two years ago, the army of a general, who, with the help of a single man, put a whole ministry in prison, and an empire in his pocket ? Men after all are nothing ; it is the idea which is all in all ; the idea is mine, and if I can persuade every one from here to Besançon (as I have done) that a formidable army has been formed on this frontier, ready to act when the time comes, is it not as useful, and as much dreaded by the enemy as if indeed numberless battalions were prepared to enter France by this route, to bear succor to the Royalists ? Without money, without pay, without soldiers, without arms, I keep a whole province in check, and paralyze both Besançon and Belfort. You see that you come yourself to join us, and you find only a head instead of arms ; believe me, it is enough ; stay with me, we shall be two instead of one ; and when the Emperor has been defeated in the open fields by the armies of Europe, we shall have been believed to have led a general insurrection, and the East of France will think that their deliverance is owing to us." I fairly burst out laughing. " From this statement, Monsieur l'Abbé, am I to imagine that shadows are as powerful as bodies, and that imagination surpasses reality ? " He replied : " Have I not already clearly proved in 1813, that if General Hulin had consented to allow himself to be convinced by a ball in his jaw that the Emperor was dead, the empire would have died in reality?" "You are right, Monsieur l'Abbé," I answered; "but a surprise is not a revolution. Some man comes, more curious, or perhaps, you will say, more obstinate than others. Instead of a well-appointed army he finds nothing but an ecclesiastic; and if he does not want to pass for an adventurer, he blows upon the shadow, and its nothingness is made apparent. Let us have our breakfast together in peace, and I will take leave of you afterwards. I shall not believe again so lightly in representations from a distance, and shall content myself with waiting; while you must be satisfied with my good wishes." He saw that his army would never arrive at more than one man; but he comforted himself by giving me all the details of Malet's conspiracy, in which he had played the principal part. Fifteen or twenty innocent Bonapartists had been shot to convince the Emperor of the reality of the conspiracy; the Abbé Lafond, who was the only guilty one, escaped. He evidently hoped to play the same game a second time; but I refused to act as his second. I must do him the justice to say, that he was a man of wonderful genius and resources. When he was chaplain of a madhouse close to one where General Malet was expiating a previous sentence, he felt that he wanted a soldier to pull the strings of a military conspiracy, and persuaded him to undertake it. He had but one man, it is true, but he very nearly succeeded. He was confident of succeeding again, but miracles do not happen twice in a man's life. It was impossible to hear any one relate a story which one might think little to the credit of an ecclesiastic, with more confidence in the purity of his motives. He was really a master in political intrigue; but he had not the art of varying his subject; he always played the same tune. After having studied him for one whole evening, although immensely struck by his genius, I left him the next day without regret, and went back to Neufchâtel, my illusory search after military glory being dispelled. I came back by Berne to the Château de Vincy, where I gave them a full account of the puerilities of the Abbé Lafond. I always wonder what has become of him since, but I never could find out. He lives, and probably conspires still. I have always been astonished not to hear of him as having been shot in some great conspiracy strangled at the birth ; but I believe that there is a special Providence which watches over men of this sort, and that L'Abbé Lafond will probably go to his grave in peace.

XII.

At Paris, the Emperor could not live long on the conspiracy of Elba, and the Royalists and Liberals gave him little time to decide on any line of conduct. He was continually promising reforms ; but his only real hope was in the army. Before he was really ready, he made up his mind to take the field. Waterloo was to cut the knot ; that day, so fatal to military France, was drawing near ! In the mean while I resolved to pass into Savoy on the other side of the lake.

There was a boatman in the Savoyard village of Narnier who spent his time in ferrying over the inhabitants of the two countries, from the Swiss to the Savoyard side of the lake. He was known to Mademoiselle ——, the mistress of the hotel where the Mesdames Bellegarde lived. I took leave a second time, therefore, of my kind hostesses at the Château de Vincy, and went to Nyons. I begged the mistress of the inn to recommend me to the boatman of Narnier as a good Royalist flying from Imperial France, and only wishing to live in peace until the political horizon brightened. The boatman, himself a devoted Royalist, consented on these terms to ferry me over. I embarked in his little open felucca, which was loaded with cattle, towards the end of June ; but it was one of those stormy days which made the Lake Leman as tempestuous as the Archipelago. We had, in consequence, a very dangerous crossing, and the waves increasing in violence as we approached the shores of Savoy, prolonged our voyage till far into the night. Luckily, one billow, larger than the rest, threw us safely on the sand. At Narnier I went to lodge in the house of the boatman himself, who consented to shelter me for some hours. During supper I asked him if there were any lodgings in this place which would receïve me at a very low price, for my journey to Neufchâtel and Berne had made a great hole in my fifty pounds; and if my exile were to be prolonged some time longer, I began to think I must pass over to England or to Russia, and earn my bread by teaching French. The boatman spoke to his daughter (a young woman about twenty years of age) about a little empty house on the borders of the lake, which had been used as a guard-house by the custom-house officers of the King of Sardinia until the breaking out of the war; but which he would be very willing to let to me if I could content myself with such humble accommodation, and if the hay of his poor neighbors, which he yearly deposited there, was no inconvenience to me. "The house," he said, turning to me, "is about a quarter of an hour's walk from Narnier: if this arrangement should be agreeable to you, I would let you the apartment for twopence-halfpenny a day, and would feed you for sevenpence-halfpenny a meal; without meat certainly, but with excellent bread, lake trout, and cheese." That would come to tenpence a day, and his proposal suited not only my purse, but fully satisfied my love of solitude; so that the bargain was struck, and the very next day his daughter took me to my new quarters.

XIII.

On leaving the village of Narnier, an unfrequented little path leads across some beautiful meadows by the side of the lake. After walking for some minutes in silence with my guide, I heard the regular noise of the waves of the lake grating on the rocky promontories, and dying away softly on the yellow sand of the shore, while the fresh breeze from the lake refreshed my whole frame. At a litttle distance I perceived a square and solitary building very much like the hull of a shipwrecked vessel; the walls on the shore-side had only a low door, which was partly hidden by a group of osiers; on the water-side was a little window, low and narrow, like a loophole, from whence you could watch the lake without being yourself observed. Window and door, all was shut; there was no sign of life about the place, nor a sound in the house or out of it; it reminded one of the dwelling of a leper in the Middle Ages, such as Xavier de Maistre described in his "Solitude" some months before; only there was no leper. "Here is the house, sir," said the young boat-woman to me, not, however, without a look of some anxiety, as if she were afraid that the mournful appearance of everything would disgust me with the place.

Whilst speaking she put a great wooden key into the lock, and the heavy door rolled on its hinges. A bat, the only inhabitant of the place, flew in my face, blindly knocking its wings against the wall; but I was not thereby dismayed, and we went up-stairs to the only room in the house, which had served as the head-quarters of the custom-house officer. The room was not more than eight or ten feet in diameter, with the exception of a window, which remained open to give some air to the forage. Everything was full of hay. "This is the room," said hesitatingly and modestly the girl; then, as if ashamed to offer so extraordinary a lodging to a stranger, she hastily added, "But, of course, it will be emptied and cleaned; and we shall put a nice bed and table in the place of the hay." As she spoke she gave unintentionally a little kick with her sabot to the dried grass before us, and out rushed a whole army of mice, which began racing about the room. "Oh! what pleasant bed-fellows," I said, laughingly, to the girl: "Bats and rats!" Well," I added, after a few minutes, putting my head out of the window and contemplating the beautiful waves which dashed gently against the walls of the cottage, the glorious scenery of the mountains of the Pays de Vaud in front of me, and the two promontories which formed the bay of Narnier, "well, I find the house charming, and I will take it." Her face expanded with pride and satisfaction, while I sat quietly down on the hay. "I don't want any other bed," I continued; "a pair of sheets and a counterpane are all I need; I shall do very well here. I am used to campaigning, and the smell of the hay is rather pleasant to me than otherwise. Are you married, mademoiselle?" "No, sir," she replied; "my father is a widower and old. He would remain quite alone here if I were to leave him; there would be nobody in the house to make his soup; no one in the boat to mend his sails; no one at the helm to guide the rudder. I could not make up my mind to leave my father." "You are a good and noble girl," I answered, "and God will bless you for it." I looked at her with an expression which seemed to say, "Any man would have been happy to have won so fair a face." She rowed me quietly back, without speaking, to her father's house. "I will bring you some fresh bread and milk and cheese every morning for your breakfast," she said, as we landed; "and I will fry your fish and make you some coffee at home for your dinner; that is all I can do, I am afraid, as I am not a great 'artiste;' you will forgive, monsieur, such plain country fare; it is not like the inn at Nyons, you see!"

XIV.

The boatman was very much pleased to find that his strange little house on the lake would answer my purpose. Everything was arranged that evening to my satisfaction. I dined at Narnier with my host, and in the evening I went and installed myself in my new abode. All my baggage went in a pocket-handkerchief, and consisted of some books brought from Nyons and a pair of pocket-pistols, which I placed in front of my window. I slept on the hay as one sleeps at eighteen. The troubled mice ran about all night, trying to find their accustomed holes, and the bats cried out at dawn of day; but that only showed me that I was not alone. The swallows knocked their wings against my window early in the morning, and were very much astonished to find the panes of glass which had been put in the night before by the young boat-woman. I got up and opened the window, and they flew fearlessly about my room; then I took my pencil, and looking beyond the lake to the little white speck which marked the Château of Vincy, I wrote the following verses: —

Pourquoi me fuir, passagère hirondelle?
Viens reposer ton aile auprès de moi.

Pourquoi me fuir quand un ami t'appelle?
Ne suis-je pas voyageur comme toi ? etc.

The daughter of the boatman came to knock at my door at the very moment I was finishing these verses, which I mentally addressed to Vincy. I gave them to nobody, and I was very much astonished some years after to hear them sung at Paris and attributed to Monsieur de Châteaubriand. They were not worth his while to disown, nor mine to claim. We all remember his touching romance,

Ma sœur, te souviens-tu encore
Du château que baignait la Dore,
Et de cette tant vielle Tour
Du More,
Ou l'airain sonnait le retour
Dù jour ?

Châteaubriand was a great poet in prose, and I was nothing but the nightingale stammering by chance a plaintive air in my solitude. . . . .

I continued to live alone in my empty dwelling with my dumb companions. Oh ! how happy I should have been if Providence had granted me a dog ! One, at last, came to me from a castle near Narnier, who attached himself to me because I petted him, and he found me alone. Whenever a person is unhappy, God sends him a dog ; I have proved it twenty times, although man does not always perceive it. The moment the dog adopted me, my solitude ceased ; for he never left me. We loved one another, and so we walked, eat, and slept together ; and he understood me as thoroughly as I did him. I had now two friends, the dog and the boatman's daughter, and my days were calm, peaceful, and delicious.

XV.

The news of the battle of Waterloo came to me one morning in a little boat rowed by a messenger from Madame de Vincy. I watched it at sunrise out of my window like a seagull whose wing are colored by the rays of the morning, never dreaming that this little skiff bore for me a new fate — the fate of the whole world. The boat grounded on the sand; I put my head out of the window and the messenger asked me if I knew a young Frenchman who had taken refuge at Narnier? I replied that I was the person of whom he was in search. He gave me directly a long letter from Madame de Vincy, and a quantity of newspapers from Geneva. The letter ran thus: "I do not know whether you will be able to rejoice at the misfortunes of your countrymen; but as far as we are concerned we cannot help being delighted at the victory of Europe over tyranny. Bonaparte has been bitterly punished for his rash enterprise; he has been entirely defeated and put to flight at Quatre Bras. He is already at Paris, and has no longer any army. Oceans of blood have flowed on all sides, — the French are completely beaten; our own son is badly wounded; but the world is saved. I send you all the details in the inclosed packet of newspapers; send them back to us." The boat was moored to the shore; the morning breeze carried off the letter. I fell eagerly on the papers which were at my feet, but I could scarcely sit still and read of our disasters. It was impossible to rejoice at the destruction of the whole French army; but, if Bonaparte had won, the cause of the King would have been lost. I was silent and undecided from conflicting emotions. Finally I burst into tears. Was it from sorrow as a Frenchman, or from joy as a partisan? I could not explain this even to myself. Every one will understand this conflict of feeling; but no one can express it: my tears said what words could not. This is the misfortune of the bad actions into which the ambition of one man drags his country. . . . .

XVI.

I stayed eight or ten days longer at Narnier, waiting for further news before I returned to France. Fouché, the chief of the Provisional Government, held the strings; Carnot talked and let him act; Caulaincourt was furious at the slowness of the Emperor in deciding upon any distinct line of conduct. In the mean time Louis XVIII. reëntered Paris by selling his dignity to a regicide. My mother wrote to me by Monsieur de Maizod not to return till she could announce that the King was once more fairly established at the Tuileries. I could not leave my peaceful solitude at Narnier without the greatest regret. I continued there a fortnight longer, and employed my time in wishing good-by to the lake and to the sites where I had been so very happy. A secret instinct warned me that I should never find another spot so much after my own heart. The boatman's daughter rowed me in her father's little skiff to all my favorite bays in the lake. With my dog I retraced all my steps by the creeks and woods, where I had so often lost my way. All the trains of thought which I had followed during the past month returned to my recollection, and I garnered them up like the wild flowers which the traveller gathers and dries near his heart, so that their perfume might remind him of spots which he will never revisit. After these pious pilgrimages I watched the last rays of the sun lighting up the white walls of the Château de Vincy, walls which had been to me so hospitable and so friendly. The evening breeze carried with it from me all the blessings which could be showered on a spot which contained one who had been to me as a second mother. I was going to sleep my last sleep on my hay bed at Narnier.

XVII.

My night was sad and my awakening still more so. For the first time the heavens were dark with clouds. As I was to go to Chambéry by Geneva, the boatman and his daughter came to wish me good-by; the father remained to put back the displaced hay in my room, whilst his daughter, to shorten my land journey, proposed to row me on the lake to the Cape of Bellegarde, where I was to leave her. We embarked, therefore, at seven o'clock in the morning, and launched the little skiff into deep water; but we had hardly gone three hundred yards, when, looking back in the direction of my deserted house, I thought I saw something black swimming with effort in our wake. I recognized my dog, that faithful friend who, after our departure from the shore, thinking that we should speedily return, had discovered that we were about to double the cape to our left, and could not resist the impulse to follow his master to the opposite coast. The poor fellow had miscalculated his strength; his stertorous breathing came to us across the water in gasps and sobs. We instantly dropped our oars and turned our helm towards Narnier, striving to meet him; but it was too late, and when we stretched out the handle of the oar he could not seize hold of it, and was drowned, exhausted by his efforts. We got hold of him, however, and dragged him into the boat; but we only rescued a dead body, the loving eyes of which followed us still! We burst into tears at the death of this faithful friend, the victim of his tender fidelity. The boatman's daughter promised me to bury him on her return at the door of my little house. Then she resumed her oars, and cried quietly until we reached Bellegarde. I could not speak either, fearing that our farewell would end in a sob. Silence and tears, on both sides — such was our parting. The silence of emotion on my part; on hers tears and the dead body of the dog under her feet: what words could better have expressed our sorrow! The wind blew towards Narnier. Each time that a rise in the ground enabled me to see the lake I watched the poor girl motionless in the boat kneeling opposite the dog, wiping her eyes. She could not see mine, but they were equally full of tears. This event greatly saddened me. I arrived very late at Geneva, with my little bag on my shoulder, and went to lodge at the hotel called Les Balances. The next evening I slept at Frangy, and it was the end of the third day before I arrived at Chambéry.

XVIII.

I knew Chambéry since my first visit to Italy; my old college friend (of whom I long ago spoke) lived there, the nephew of the Count de Maistre, who was then Sardinian Ambassador in Russia, and whose family held a distinguished position in the town. This family, with whom hereafter I was to become so very intimate, was then composed of four brothers. The eldest was the Chevalier de Maistre, author of "Le Lépreux de la Cité d'Aoste" and the "Voyage autour de ma Chambre;" two inimitable books for agreeableness and depth of feeling. He was still in Russia, where he married a rich and distinguished wife. The next was the Bishop of Aosta, the author of several remarkable sermons, living at Chambéry, an accomplished man, still young, full of merit and originality, and one whom Sterne alone could paint. There was a sweetness in his goodness, and a natural fun even in his piety, which made him irresistibly attractive. You might imagine Yorick and Fénélon kneaded into the same mould and producing a thoroughly honest man. The third, who was the eldest in point of wit and cleverness, was the famous Count de Maistre, ambassador at St. Petersburg. He was certainly a writer of the first rank, and I should be the last to disparage his ability; but I, who knew them all so well later in life, infinitely preferred his two more modest brothers, the chevalier and the bishop, who were original without effort, and produced *chefs d'œuvre* without any pretension, as the marmot of the Alps produces its soft fur. I even preferred his youngest brother to him, who was only the colonel of a brigade in Savoy, and who had never written anything in his life, contenting himself with admiring his brothers; in a word, the whole family, — brothers and sisters, nephews and nieces — were all remarkable in their different ways: it was impossible not to esteem, admire, and love them all. These De Maistres were in fact an unique family, whose parallel could scarcely be found in Europe.

XIX.

The only member of the family with whom I was intimately acquainted at that time, although we had rarely met since the days we had spent together in the Jesuit College at Belley, was Louis de Vignet. His wit and his high character made him worthy of his uncles; but, although excellent at bottom, he was less simple and natural than they were. His genius was incontestable, but he was inclined to be willful. He knew his own worth, but he conceived, in consequence, as great an esteem for himself as he had an ill-disguised contempt of every one else. I must make an exception, however, for his own family, because his admiration of everything belonging to them reacted also on himself. It cost him nothing to allow the superiority of his own people as it completed his own. To praise his uncles was to praise himself. He was only a De Maistre on the mother's side, as she was their sister; but in that family genius had no sex, and she was as charming and remarkable a person as her brothers. To be a relation, however distant, of such a family was an honor; but Louis was very just towards all those of whom he had once appreciated the merit. In that way I had nothing to complain of. He had a higher opinion of me at college than I deserved. His friendship had blinded his judgment; in a word, he loved me passionately. No sooner had he heard that I had arrived at Chambéry than he rushed off to announce it to Colonel de Maistre, his uncle; to his aunt, the colonel's wife; to the Bishop of Aosta, and to some charming and very pretty cousins, the Mademoiselles Constantin, who lived in a country-house at Bissy with the colonel. He was just then madly in love with the prettiest and most interesting of these cousins; but this passion did not last. His fickle heart soon found other charms, while the object of his love lived sadly and died blind. She had lost her sight with crying at her cousin's inconstancy. The imagination of Vignet was far too vivid to be relied on. He was only faithful to his fancies for the moment; but these fancies had, while they lasted, all the seriousness and melancholy of a great passion.

XX.

Vignet hastened to seek me at the hotel and to carry me off to Bissy. He had predisposed all the family in my favor. We went first, he and I, to see the woods and the water of La Laisse, in that beautiful Cashmere valley which Chambéry hides in the folds of the Alps. Indian dreams accompanied us. From thence we went to Charmettes, the house of Madame de Warens, the lady who was so adored by Jean Jacques

Rousseau, and who was equally beloved by her. Here they lived together an ideal life of affection. Later, he was deceived by her, and abandoned her himself. He was ungrateful, and became an adventurer and a sophist, because he did not know how to be faithful to nature and to love. In those days we were not so severe in our judgments; youth and love made us believe that everything should be forgiven to genius. We spent a whole morning rambling over the deserted house of Charmettes, and especially the vine-trellised arbor at the bottom of the garden, where Jean Jacques Rosseau had given full vent to his tenderness.

XXI.

The next day Vignet carried me off to his tailor at Chambéry, where I changed my exile's clothes for a more decent traveller's dress. At dinner time he took me by a shady and picturesque path to Bissy. It is an isolated village, situated on the slope of the Cat Mountain, at the extremity of the lake of Bourget, which dwindles at this end into marshy meadows. Richly cultivated fields of Indian corn and a wood of old firs cover the slope of the *Mont du Chat* almost down to the court of the little square villa, where a fountain, of which the water falls into a circular basin, sends up continually its gentle murmur: here horses and cows quench their thirst, and white pigeons and dark swallows skim on its surface. The windows and door of the house open on the court opposite the mountain; on the other side is a terraced garden, and below, a meadow full of great walnut-trees, which I might call the tree of Savoy, and round which the vines twine and fall in festoons the whole height of the trunk, as if to accustom themselves to the olive and orange trees which they will embrace on the other side of the Alps.

XXII.

As soon as we arrived, Vignet called his uncle, the colonel, who opened the glass window of the dining-room which looked into the court, and came to embrace me as if I had been the eldest of his nephews. He was a little man with a cordial, gay, and sensible face, still wearing a blue coat without epaulets but of a military cut, which marked his profession. He introduced me to his wife, a charming person, whom the colonel had loved tenderly from his earliest years, even before the Revolution. She was his cousin, but he had been compelled to leave her at Chambéry in 1798 to fight for the King of Piedmont. On his return from his forced emigration he had joyfully married her, and they had been as happy as possible ever since. She was rather stout, with a face in which goodness and candor were happily mingled; and there was an expression in it of thorough content, as of the fruition of a love long waited for; while the sound of her voice seemed to say, "I am perfectly happy, and I now only ask of Heaven the happiness of others." Her two nieces Constantin were sitting at the table by her side. I at once recognized in the face of the eldest the girl of whom Vignet had given me such a glowing description. She had a languid grace which generally belonged to the young beauties of Savoy. All the family received me as if I had been their brother, and I felt as if I were at home. Louis had described me as a Royalist and a poet, but I only accepted their praises for the first quality. By the time we had arrived at the dessert, these acquaintances of an hour had already become to me like old friends. They gave me a room not far from that of my old college friend, from whence I had a charming view over the beautiful valley of Nivolet and the village of Servolex, where the eldest brother of Louis Vignet lived in a very pretty country-house. On the horizon to the left glittered the blue lake of Bourget, where, many years later, I was to know a love more pure and more faithful than that of Jean Jacques Rousseau. After dinner, Louis took me out and explained the country to me. We did not come in till sunset. Then we talked of Waterloo and of all the things that had happened in France. Savoy was undecided then, but we felt that when the peace came she would again become Piedmontese. Colonel de Maistre had already been pointed out as ambassador to arrange this in Paris. Joy and hope shone on every face, and I could not feel annoyed at the natural satisfaction of a country which was about to regain its independence. In the evening arrived the Bishop de Maistre, who, as I said before, was the colonel's brother; his simple benevolence and cordial gayety added to the pleasure of the evening. He told us all sorts of stories connected with his past life, and we laughed heartily at the amusing and innocent recollections of his friendship with Madame de Staël and other remarkable persons. His gayety, united to his piety and high character, made him the delight of the family circle. The colonel, his wife, and his pretty nieces were never tired of listening to him. He only stopped to go and say his office.

Thus passed our first day at Bissy. All the others were like it. Occasionally various relations and neighbors came to congratulate the colonel and the bishop on the restoration of the King of Sardinia and of their own fortunes. Piedmontese troops were marching upon Chambéry. The news from France left no doubt as to the reëstablishment of the Bourbons. I only waited for a line or a sign from my mother to rejoin her at Milly. The second invasion had been in all ways less serious than the first.

I have already said that all our days at Bissy were alike. Vignet treated me as a brother, Colonel de Maistre as a son, his nieces as a cousin. We passed our days in walking or driving in the fir woods, or in the meadows, or on the soft grass which sloped towards the lake of Bourget and the valley of Chambéry. At dusk Madame de Maistre and her pious nieces always went to a little chapel, where the old rector of La Motte said the Rosary as regularly as his daily Mass. We all shared in these services with regularity and devotion. The example of this perfect family, the happiness of thinking that I should soon be able to return to my own country, with my father and mother, and the knowledge that they were in safety in their country home, gave me feelings of gratitude which brought back to me the piety of my childhood. Except in the solitude of Narnier and at the Château of Vincy, I had never spent a more enjoyable time. At last the long-wished-for letter from my mother arrived, telling me that I had no longer anything to fear, and that I could return to Mâcon to rejoin the King's guard, which was about to be reorganized. I wished a joyous good-by to the colonel and to the charming family, whose home-life resembled so much our own ; and then took my place in the Savoy diligence to return to Lyons, and so on to Mâcon.

This is the whole history of my emigration. It consisted, in fact, of only three happy and innocent visits, where I was treated as the son of the house, without in any way having been wanting to the love of my country. I was happy not to have failed in my duty either towards France or to my King.

XXIII.

My father, mother, and sisters received me with a tenderness as warm as it was touching. They congratulated me on having been so well received everywhere, in spite of my being a perfect stranger; and my mother wrote a letter of heart-felt thanks to Madame de Vincy. When we came to discuss my future career, my father felt that my birth, however honorable, would not give me much chance of advancement in the King's guard, which was reserved for the sons of emigrant nobles. He told me, therefore, to go again and offer my services, but not to lose my youth in a fruitless waiting, and to resign after a little time with such of my companions as were in the same position.. I went to Paris, and then passed some days at Beauvais. Eight days after I was recalled to Paris, and ordered to resume my military service. I rejoined my corps accordingly; but, after having finished my turn of duty, I gave in my resignation as well as the greater part of my companions in the same corps, who had too much fortune to care for a pay of two hundred francs, and whose families were too distinguished for them to like to remain without a fortune in the King's guard. Soon afterwards I returned to Mâcon.

MEMOIRS OF MY MOTHER.

[THE second volume of "Twenty-five Years of my Life is devoted to "The Manuscript of my Mother." This "manuscript" is a diary, kept by the mother of Lamartine. It exhibits her as a devout Christian, a noble and worthy woman. From it there might be gleaned additional interesting details of the early years of her illustrious son; but as these would to a certain extent traverse the period covered by "Twenty-five Years of my Life," we are compelled to rest content with a few extracts.

In the introduction to the "diary" by Lamartine himself, we have the following sketch of his father and mother:]

I have found an old description of my mother at thirty-five, and I am going to give it literally to my readers.

"The evening is closing in, the doors of the little country-house are shut. The bark of the watch-dog outside gives notice from time to time of any strange step. A sharp autumn shower rattles against the window panes of two low windows, while the wind, blowing in gusts through the plane-trees, and sweeping their branches towards the outside shutters, produce that melancholy whistle which we sometimes hear in a great pine wood before a storm. The room I am describing is large but nearly bare of furniture. At the bottom is a deep alcove in which stands a bed. The curtains of this bed are of white serge edged with blue. This is my mother's. On four wooden chairs at the foot of the bed rest two cradles. They contain my two little sisters, who have been asleep for a long time. A cheerful fire of vine logs crackles on a stone hearth beyond, with a white marble chimney-piece, of which the revolutionary hammer has broken the arms in the centre, together with the *fleurs de lys* ornaments on each side. Even the iron plate at the back of the fire-place has been turned inside out, because it bore on its surface the arms of the King. The ceiling is of old wooden beams blackened with smoke. There is no carpet or inlaid parquet, only square unvarnished tiles, and these broken in a hundred places by the heavy hob-nailed shoes of the peasants, who had made this room a dancing hall during my father's imprisonment. No paper or hangings of any sort adorn the walls. You see that the plaster is broken away in many places, showing the stone of the outside wall, just as a torn frock would display a little beggar child's legs! In one corner is an open piano with different pieces of music (among the rest, Jean Jacques Rousseau's "Divin du Village") scattered over the instrument. Near the fire-place, in the middle of the room, is a little card-table, of which the green baize cover is all marked with ink stains and with little holes in the stuff. On the table flare two tallow candles in two silver-plated candlesticks, which throw a little light and a good many flickering shadows on the whitewashed walls of the room. In front of the chimney-piece, with his arms resting on the table, sits a man holding a book in his hand. He is above the middle height and is strongly built. He is still in all the vigor of youth. His forehead is broad and good, his eyes are blue, his smile is singularly winning, and displays the brightest white teeth. His dress, his hair, and a certain military stiffness in his carriage, betray the half-pay officer. Any doubts on the subject would be dispelled by a glance at the sword, cavalry pistols, helmet, and silver-gilt trappings of his horse, which hang on the walls of a little room opening out of the large one. This man was my father, and that was his dressing-room.

"On a straw sofa, in a little angle formed by the chimney and the wall of the alcove, sat a woman still young in appearance, though she had numbered thirty-five summers. Her figure had all the elegance and flexibility of a young girl. Her features are so delicate ; her black eyes have such a calm and penetrating look ; her transparent white skin with its blue veins still betray so vividly, by its ever varying color, the emotions of the moment ; her black, soft, thick hair still falls so silkily on her neck and shoulders, that a stranger looking at her would find it impossible to decide if she were eighteen or thirty-five. But no one who knew her would wish to sweep away a single one of those years which have only ripened her beauty by adding to its expression. This peculiar beauty of hers did not depend so much on the regularity of her features as on the harmony and grace of her whole person, and especially on the wonderful tenderness and love which beamed from her eyes, those true windows of the soul ; eyes which would have lit up the plainest face with that light coming only from above. This young woman, half leaning against the cushions of the sofa, held a little girl on her lap, whose soft curly head had fallen fast asleep on her shoulder. The child still held one of her mother's long black curls with which she had been playing before she had dropped into happy unconsciousness. Another little girl, somewhat older, was seated on a footstool at the side of the sofa, leaning her head of fair hair against her mother's knee. This young woman was my mother ; the two children were my elder sisters. The two little ones were in their cradle."

[Under date of Rieux, January 14, 1803, Madame de Lamartine writes :]

"I am going to write down now a strange anecdote of J. J. Rousseau and the Maréchale de Luxembourg, with whom my mother was very nearly connected. This lady, who was an old friend of J. J. Rousseau's also, ascertained that the lady with whom he lived was with child, and that she was in an agony lest Rousseau (as he had done three times before) should carry off this baby, and place it in the Foundling Hospital. She sought out another friend of Rousseau's, M. Tronchin of Geneva, and entreated him to bring the baby to her as soon as it was born, as she had decided to bring it up herself. M. Tronchin spoke of the matter to J. J. Rousseau, who appeared to consent, nay, to be even pleased at the proposed arrangement. He told the mother of it also, who was wild with joy. The moment she was brought to bed, the poor woman sent word to Tronchin. He came and saw the child, a beautiful little boy, full of health and life, and agreed with the mother and the nurse as to the hour the next day when he should come and fetch it. But at midnight, Rousseau, dressed in a dark-colored cloak, stole into the room of the poor mother, who had her baby in her arms, and, in spite of her cries and protestations, carried him off and left him at the hospital, without any mark or possibility of recognition! 'And this is the man of whose tenderness and fine feelings people are so fond of talking!' exclaimed my mother. I replied: 'It was the act of a madman, whose addled brain had made him forget his heart.'"

[Of some of M. de Lamartine's most serious escapades in the way of gambling, we in have the following record under date of January 31, 1813.]

"I have had a great deal of sorrow lately on Alphonse's account. From Lyons and from Italy, heavy bills have been sent in to his uncles and aunts for debts incurred by him during his travels. The family, who think I have spoiled him, consider me responsible for these extravagances. They have stormed at and scolded me, and I have shed many bitter tears; for, after all, the faults of one's children are in a great measure one's own. Why was I not more strict with him at first? He was afraid, above everything, of displeasing me. Perhaps, however, had I been more severe with him, he would have loved me less; and then I feared that later, should still graver circumstances arise, the dread of grieving me would have ceased to be a second conscience to him. Everything will be paid by the family. But they have made me pay too for the thoughtless follies of my child, a bitter price, in reproaches and tears.

"He is at Paris. M. de Larnaud, a very able and distinguished man, and a great friend of my brother-in-law's, lives in the same house. He has written confidentially to warn us that Alphonse's state of health gives him great anxiety; that he has lately developed a passion for gambling, into which he has been led by certain bad companions; that he spends his nights at M. de Livry's, where he might easily lose his whole fortune in a few hours; that he certainly studies and even works hard the greater part of the day; but that, what with work and sitting up half the night at play, his youth and strength are being rapidly undermined. He ended by imploring us to recall him from Paris as soon as possible. In consequence of this letter I started directly for Paris with my second girl, Eugénie, whom I let into my secret. I took out of my husband's desk all the money which he had left there when he went to his brother's in Burgundy. My old friend, Madame Paradis, my brother-in-law M. de Lamartine, and my sisters-in-law, helped me also; so that I could set off at once, writing to my husband at the same time to tell him all I was doing, so as to avoid, if possible, a scene of anger and reproaches, which must have ensued had he himself gone to fetch his son. When I got to Paris, I would not go straight to his hotel, for fear of giving him too sudden and too painful a surprise. I own too I was tremblingly afraid, after M. de Larnaud's letter, lest I should find him sadly altered in face, and that I might faint away if I saw him like that without any preparation. So I wrote to M. and Madame de Larnaud to tell them privately that I was arrived, and to ask them to arrange a plan for our meeting. I went to a little hotel not far from theirs in the Rue Richelieu and waited. It was still broad daylight. Oh! how I suffered at not being able to rush off to my boy and kiss him us usual, instead of having to wait till the next day for the visit or answer of M. de Larnaud! I was quite worn out with fatigue and anxiety, and at last threw myself crying on the sofa close to an open window. Eugénie went and sat on the window-sill to see the carriages going to the opera and to the French theatre. All of a sudden she cried out: 'Mamma, come quickly. I think I see Alphonse!' I ran to the window and recognized him directly. He was driving himself in a very smart cab with another young man alongside of him. He looked very gay and bright, which comforted me very much. It was certainly my own boy! All my foolish fears vanished at the sight of him. But I determined not to spoil his evening's amusement; so I went to bed quietly and had a very tolerable night.

"I got up the next morning dying to see him, but dreading what effect my unexpected arrival would have upon him. Also, I feared that he might not be inclined to come home with me, and that the state of his affairs might be much worse than I had anticipated. At last I made up my mind to write to him and tell him frankly the reason of my journey, He came running directly to our hotel, and seemed not only delighted to see me, but very much touched at the step I had taken. His health appeared to me far better than I had expected. He told me that on my account and for my sake, he would return to Mâcon; but that no one else would ever have induced him to do so. He only asked for a few days to arrange his affairs. I gave him a week, which I was not at all sorry for, as I wanted to show Paris to Eugénie."

[Then follows a description of Paris, the Louvre, museums, walks, etc.; also her wish to go to the play, which she resisted from religious scruples, and this entry concludes the history of the affair:]

"I have given all my money to Alphonse to clear his gambling debts, which were heavy, though he had begun by winning largely."

[The last entries in this journal bear the date of Milly, October 21, 1829. The following "Epilogue" relates so far as it can be done in words the unutterably distressing circumstances under which this illustrious woman met her death.]

It was the end of the autumn of 1829. Both in the Government itself and among the different parties in France, there was nothing but fever, trouble, and delirium. The Prince de Polignac, then Prime Minister, had so insisted in his letters (which were most kind and friendly) on my coming to Paris, and was so determined to keep for me the place of Under-

Secretary of Foreign Affairs, that I obeyed his summons: not to accept the office, but to explain, with proper gratitude and courtesy, the motives for my refusal. I loved the Prince, but I dreaded his policy. I wished, in speaking to him, to make a distinction between the man and the minister, both as to feeling and opinion. In my speech before the Academy I had spoken frankly but decidedly against the *coup d'état*, which destroyed the Charter, and against the opposition of the government to free thought and the independence of elections. This political programme (which was quite unexpected from me) was received with immense applause by one party; but was looked upon as an exposition of a retrograde or Royalist policy by the Republican and Bonapartist organs. M. Lainé and M. Royer Collard hailed me as their disciple. But on leaving the hall of the Institute, which was still fearfully crowded, the Duke de Rohan, my old friend, said in my ear: "Wish good-by to all promotion in your diplomatic career, You have thus disappointed all our hopes, and given pledges to the most factious members of the Opposition." I did not care whether or no I got my promotion. But I saw a gulf opening under the feet of Charles X., and I wished, as far as in me lay, to avert the danger.

The Prince de Polignac, full of hope in my future, had spoken to me, the year before, of his political views, in a way and with a freedom which had touched me very much. In those confidences, as in his occasional reserve, I felt that I had to do with a thoroughly honest and loyal heart; but with one whose mind had been warped by emigration, and who was alarmed by his own conscience.

The Duke de Rohan's prophecy was not fulfilled. I ought to remember it, to the honor of the King, Charles X., and the Prince de Polignac. The Prime Minister showed no resentment at my speech; but after having long and vainly argued with me, in private and in public, on the ill-founded reasons (as he called them) for my refusal, and the non-premeditation of the *coup d'état*, he resigned himself to my opposition, and offered me the place of Minister Plenipotentiary in Greece.

It was just at the moment when Europe, through a fleeting enthusiasm, had founded that artificial kingdom on the relics of past greatness. I shared in the general illusion of liberal and classical men about the Hellenic race, so brave in battle, but so undisciplined in government. The Prince of Coburg, widower of the Princess Charlotte (the heiress to the throne of England), had just been elected King of Greece by the united consent of the Western Powers of Europe. This Prince was then at Paris, and I had known him very well in Italy as an inconsolable mourner for the loss of his wife. The Prince de Polignac, therefore, introduced me to him as the most agreeable minister whom the French Government could offer him. I was rejoiced at the idea of going there under such auspices, and helping, however feebly, in the restoration of a kingdom on that sacred ground of classical memories in which I should thus share, like Lord Byron, the heroic poet of this resurrection. All of a sudden, however, the intended King took alarm at the insuperable difficulties of the task he was about to undertake, and renounced the responsibility of striving to regenerate the Greek people. He started suddenly one night from Paris, flying from a kingdom as one would fly from an abyss.

We learnt, on waking that morning, that there was no longer a head for that crown, which had been offered in vain to so many other distinguished personages. Diplomacy had to set to work again to find another. That took time; but I remained still Minister Plenipotentiary, at least in expectation, and continued to receive from the Prince de Polignac such testimonies of kindness and intimacy as were consistent with my obstinate refusal to form part of his cabinet.

My mother enchanted at my advancement in my political career, at the prospect of my future residence under the shadow of Athens, and, above all, at my election as a member of the French Academy, was at last at ease as to the future of the son who had been her one poignant anxiety, and who had now realized almost all the dreams of her life. I made arrangements to spend with her the few months that I thought

I should still have on the soil of France. I prolonged my stay in Paris only for a few days more, to collect such little presents of dress or furniture as it was my greatest pleasure to bring home to my mother and sisters on my return from my travels. Ah ! it was a poor return enough in love and gratitude for all the privations which they had borne on my account during my youth — to my mother especially, who had deprived herself of every luxury and jewel, down to the very rings off her fingers, to procure me an extra pleasure, a journey, or a treat of some sort ; or to hide one of my faults and extravagancies from the just severity and censure of my family.

The tables and even the bed of my rooms at Paris were covered with jewel-cases, ornaments, and pieces of stuff or silk for hangings, which I had collected with such delight, thinking of the exclamations of surprise and pleasure which they would call forth in my mother's simple home. I was rejoicing beforehand at her astonishment, and was quite absorbed in the thought of all the pleasure I was going to give not to her vanity but to her heart. That evening, at dinner-time (I will not insert the date for my own sake), I drove into the courtyard of my hotel, the cab loaded with pretty little bits of furniture and paper boxes, my face bright with joy at the thought of my start on the morrow, when, as I sprung out of the cab on the first step of the stairs, I saw standing by the porter's lodge, that dearest of my friends, the Comte Aymon de Virieu, whom Providence seems to have given me, from childhood to old age, as the sharer in all the joys and sorrows of my life. After having followed the same studies at the same school and college, the same pursuits in our respective homes, the same route in our travels, and the same society in the different capitals in which we had resided together, we were now embarked in the same diplomatic career. He was to start on the morrow for his post in Germany, and we had settled to dine together, and to pass the evening in my rooms to prolong the pleasure of a last talk together before wishing each other "good-by" for so long a time. On shaking hands with him, however, as I got out of the carriage, I was struck at his pallor, and at the distress which was visible on his expressive face. His eyes, which generally sparkled with fun, and sometimes with a kind of gentle sarcasm, seemed for the first time to be heavy with unshed tears. Instead of responding to my joyful exclamation of welcome, he seemed to avoid looking at me, while an inexplicable fear, mingled with pity, seemed to pervade his whole countenance. No smile met mine, while, on the contrary, he looked vexed at seeing me so confident and happy. He was troubled at my gayety, and seemed to reproach me for it involuntarily, without explaining why I should be otherwise. His whole appearance, in fact, struck me with a presentiment of coming evil. My face fell, and the smile died away from my lips. "Come upstairs," he said, with a broken voice; "I have to break sad tidings to you. Let us shut ourselves up in your room, and summon all your strength of mind to meet them bravely." I went up the staircase stunned by the threatened blow. He dragged me into my own room, shut the door, and made me sit down on the edge of the bed, where my poor dog, jumping for joy at my return, could not understand why his caresses, ordinarily responded to so warmly, should now be met by a rude rebuff. "Speak!" I exclaimed to Virieu, hiding my face in my two hands, and striving to brace myself up for some unknown misery, that worst of torments, which threatens all points of one's heart at once. Then, with all the tenderness and consideration possible, and the groping hesitation of one to whom has been committed the charge of delivering a message as terrible as it was unexpected, he ended by breaking to me, as he clasped me in his arms, the awful fact, "You have no longer a mother!" It seemed to me that the earth was sinking under my feet, and that I had no longer any existence in the past, the present, or the future. My soul flew upwards to meet hers who had been my life here below, and without whom I never seemed till now to have realized that I could live.

She was still so beautiful, and seemed so young, so full of life, activity, and energy, that the idea of a separation had never crossed my thoughts, save as a very distant prospect, softened by the gradations of age and by the shortness of time which I myself should have to pass in this world after a slowly protracted farewell. The separation had indeed come, and that without preparation and without an adieu. In the morning I felt as if I lived a double life, in her heart and mine, and in the evening only one was left in my breast, to cry and moan and live on alone for evermore. The best half of my life was gone. To make matters worse I was quite by myself at Paris. She who alone could have shared in my despair and mingled her tears with my sobs, was away. Neither mother, wife, nor child! Nothing but a blank in me and around me,— now and for evermore! — only a devoted friend, who strove by his tenderness to soothe the agony of my grief, and point out the only consolation. I remained sitting on my bed dressed as I was, and completely broken down, that whole evening and all that night. Every moment of that time is as vividly before me now as if it were yesterday. When I became a little calmer, I strove to gather from my friend the agonizing details of her death. The circumstances attending it were as heart-breaking as the event itself was sudden and unexpected. I dragged them one by one from the reluctant lips of M. de Virieu. He did not leave me till dawn, in order to prepare everything for my departure for Mâcon. Alas! it was already too late for me to be able to hold in one last embrace the mortal remains of her who had borne me for nine months in her womb, and all her life in her heart!

These are the details which my friend at last gave me, and to which my father and the servants added a few more circumstances when describing the agony of which they had been the witnesses. My poor mother was expecting me joyfully from day to day. The alternations of hope and disappointment, and the immense joy she had felt at my election to the Academy, and my appointment as Minister in Greece, had agitated her more than usual and brought on a slight attack of fever. On the 27th of November, after having, according to to her invariable custom, heard mass at dawn, she went from church to the public baths, kept by the Sisters of Charity in the town, adjoining the hospital which bears their name. The Sister Superior, who received her and talked to her whilst they were preparing her bath, said that she spoke as usual of pious things and works of charity with that grace and brightness which were her peculiar characteristics in her best days. The bath being prepared, she went in without being accompanied by the bathing-woman; in accordance with a vow she had made in her youth at the "chapter" where she was *chanoinesse* (and which she had preserved ever since her marriage), never to be seen undressed, or to employ a maid in personal services of that nature; always to dress and undress herself, and even to light her own fire, in continual remembrance of the humility and holy poverty which she had then embraced.

She had been only a few minutes in the bath, when the Superior, passing by the corridor into which all the doors of the bath-rooms opened, heard a cry, and then a groan, from her cell. She rushed in. The bath was overflowing with boiling water on to the floor; the swan's neck, by which the hot water flowed, was open, and streams of the boiling liquid were pouring over my mother's breast and arms, the effect of which had been that she had already fainted away. The strong arm of the Superior and of one of the bathing-women dragged her out instantly from this fiery cascade but she was more than half dead. It was evident that, finding the bath too cold, she had turned the hot-water cock; and that the sudden rush of boiling water, which was the result, dashing on her chest, had taken away her breath, so that she had neither the time nor the power to shut up the swan's neck again, which was rather stiff to turn. The fresh air restored her to consciousness; but she was terribly burnt. She embraced the Superior, who had scalded her arms and hands very much even during the moment of dragging her out of the bath, and thanked her warmly for her care. They laid her on one of the mattresses of the hospital, and four of the young incurable patients, to whom for twenty years she had continually brought linen, food, and medicine, bore her tenderly back from the hospital to her own home. The rumor of this terrible event had already spread like wildfire through the town. A crowd of servants, working people, and pious women, who were coming out of church, followed her with tears to her door, offering up prayers and vows to heaven for her recovery. Public lamentations burst forth in each street through which the stretcher was carried. It seemed as if the whole town were losing its mother as well as ourselves. The doctors hastened to her bedside. At first the accident did not seem to be so serious; but in the evening, when the dressing of her burns was examined, the gravity of the case became apparent to all. Fever ensued, followed by delirium. This delirium was, however, gentle and loving like herself. From time to time she recovered her senses sufficiently to thank those around her for their care, and to console my poor father, who remained motionless and despairing at the foot of her bed, overwhelmed by a blow which it was impossible even for his resignation to accept. She struggled against physical suffering and pain up to the last, so that her remaining hours might be given to those who loved her, and to God, whom she saw already through the light of faith. She wished to unite herself once more to Him in the Blessed Sacrament, in which she had so often anticipated the possession of the Divinity even on earth. The by-standers affirmed that her beautiful countenance, inflamed by the ardor of her convictions, and beatified by this mystical union with her Spouse, seemed to light up the whole bed, even more than the tapers which the kneeling choir boys of the hospital held in their raised hands behind her curtains. A great calm, a long silence, a sweet sleep, which revived the hopes of the watchers, followed this solemn rite of the dying. Alas! it was a false flicker of the expiring flame. She woke again but to expire, and that with perfect calmness and clearness of mind. She who assisted at that last agony towards nightfall, and who endeavored to supplement my absence by her own tenderness, has often repeated literally to me the words (broken by dreams) which she pronounced from time to time until dawn.

"My husband," "my children," "Alphonse, Marianne, Cécile, Eugénie, Sophie — may God bless them all!" "Why are they not all here that I may bless them myself?" "My Alphonse, my poor boy! Oh! how he will grieve at not having been with me at this last hour! Tell him, oh! tell him, that I do not suffer any more now — that I am already as if in a place of peace and joy, from whence I have a vision of heaven, and of all kinds of blessings for my dear children upon earth!" Then falling again into a dreamy kind of sleep, sweet and peaceful as that of a little child, and broken only by a word now and then, and a smile which hovered round her lips and finally lit up her whole face, she exclaimed, towards dawn, "Oh! how happy I am! Oh! how happy I am! Oh! how happy I am!" three times running; and then, "My God! thou hast not deceived me. I am so happy!" and, with those words, her pure spirit, with a gentle sigh, ascended to her God.

This is, word for word, the history of her death. All who were with her are still alive to bear witness to its truth, save my father and our poor Philibert, who, in losing her mistress, lost also her wish to live; and who only remained on earth long enough to continue to her master those faithful services which she had rendered from affectionate admiration to my mother. How beautiful is the tie between the servant who serves for love and the family who rewards that service by gratitude, tenderness, and equality in affection! It is the perfection of the different states of life on earth, diverse in fortune but equalized by love.

It was three days after my irreparable loss that I arrived at Mâcon, hoping to see at least her dear remains before they were hidden forever from human view. I was accompanied by an old friend, a true Samaritan, who had witnessed some of my anguish, Amèdée de Parseval, and whom a circumstance, already alluded to in this journal, had fondly attached to my mother, whose real son he had vainly wished to become. It was too late. The coffin was already buried under heaps of snow in the village cemetery. Owing to the absence of my poor father, who had been dragged away half dead from his home as soon as our mother had breathed her last sigh, and to the fact of all her children having been unavoidably far away in their respective homes when this terrible event occured, it had been entirely forgotten that my poor mother had particularly wished to be buried in the cemetery of St. Point, in the shade of the little village church where she had so often prayed during her summer residence in that peaceful valley. I could only press my burning lips on the bed on which she had died, and kiss every object she had last touched, down to the very floor of her room and the threshold of the door against which her coffin had brushed when she was carried (amidst the sobs of the poor) to her last resting-place. But my heart rebelled against the idea of any wish of hers being neglected, and also at the thought of being unable to go and pray by those dear remains except amongst a crowd of people who were unknown or indifferent to her. I resolved, therefore, while I had the opportunity, to repair this neglect of her secret wishes, and to exhume the coffin so as to transport it to the spot she herself had chosen. It almost seemed to me as if the eternal distance which separated her soul from mine would be lessened if her dear body rested between her own door and that of the church of St. Point, which almost adjoined the château. If I confess the whole truth, there was also in this exhumation a pretext for once more looking at the dear face which had been so ruthlessly closed from me, before time had disfigured or reduced it to the handful of ashes which would soon be all that was left of her human remains. The coffin, which bore no distinguishing mark to tell it from others, and the very site of which had been effaced by the snow before the gravedigger's spade had barely covered it, was to be reopened to prove the identity of her dear body, so that our pious intention might not be frustrated, or any danger exist of our bearing away an unknown corpse instead of our mother. I pass over these sad details. All was accomplished in the night, as I had wished. We swept away the snow which had fallen thickly over the uneven ground, and discovered, by groping, the right coffin among many others. Philibert, who had laid her dear mistress in it herself, recognized it at once. By the glare of the tapers it was opened that I might gaze once more on that sleeping face. She was there in all her beauty, save that the eyes were closed. The dear look, which ever thrilled through me, was gone ; but death had not yet marred her pure form with its corrupting touch. My lips were pressed with love and yet terror on that icy forehead, and bitter tears fell in that silent coffin. At last it had to be closed. I watched by its side with Philibert until the midnight hour, when the peasants of Milly were to come silently, one by one, and bear away noiselessly on their shoulders that dear burden to my home. At midnight we started on foot, through deep snow, past the suburbs of the town along the road which led to our château in the hills. Although I had limited the number of the followers in this sad procession to myself (of all the members of the family) and to the farmers and laborers of her dear old home at Milly, the wives and children of these poor fellows, all wearing some token of humble mourning, considered that they had a right of affection to follow the Head of the house and lengthen the black file of weepers, whose tears were her noblest panegyric. Not a voice nor a whisper broke the silence during the long march of this solemn crowd. Nothing was heard but the wooden shoes of the women as they marched on the crisp and frozen snow, holding their little children by the hand ; or, from time to time, the cavernous sound of a slight shaking of the oak coffin as it was shifted from the shoulders of one peasant to the other, each envious of his turn in bearing the holy burden.

At about two and a half hours from the town, we left the high-road and climbed up the steep hill leading to the hamlet of Milly. The path was slippery with icicles. Every household was awake and watching for our arrival ; and one saw, at the threshold of the doors, old men or children, each holding a little brass lamp, which lit up pale and tearful faces and hands, shivering with cold in that bitter December night. When we arrived at the courtyard of the house, the bearers, followed by all the inhabitants of the village, mounted slowly up the five steps which led to the hall door, and deposited the coffin in the centre of the vestibule — on the very spot where every morning she was accustomed to receive the old, the sick, or the needy; and to distribute amongst them the food, clothing, soup, or medicines which they required, while she dressed, on her knees, the wounds or burns of the sufferers. Those very walnut wood benches on which I have so often seen the legs of the peasants stretched out while she tenderly wound round them lint or bandages, now bore the coffin of her whose loving, skillful hand was forever still.

She was laid, as it were, among the very instruments of her charity. A long sob filled the hall into which the peasants had crowded. Every one drew near to dip a little box branch in the holy water placed near her head, and to sprinkle as many tears as holy water over those dear remains. During this halt under the roof which had sheltered her youth and early love, I retired to her own room and cried my heart out, my face buried in the coverings of her empty bed. I heard the dull tread of the sabots of the men and women, perpetually ascending and descending the steps of the front hall, to come and kneel and pray by turns round her coffin. We waited thus till the slow dawn broke of the winter's morning, before embarking in the defiles of the mountains, incumbered as they were with driving snow, which a cold north wind had blown over the paths, filling up the ravines and effacing all visible tracks. These roads would have been very dangerous for the little procession at night, and still more for those who were to bear their precious burden from Milly to the cemetery of St. Point. As soon as the dawn had reddened the distant peaks of that Alpine horizon, which at Milly was her great delight, we started again, escorted to the top of the first hills by the whole village in tears. On turning into the higher valley, we parted sorrowfully from the weeping crowd, who felt as if their only friend was being torn from them; and with a little knot of eight strong men, climbed up the steep defile which goes by the name of Croix-des-Signaux. Four of the men walked before the coffin to sound the path, whilst the four others carried her. I walked behind alone, following closely on their footsteps. The snow in some places was up to our knees; it deadened all sound except the sharp whistling of the blast through the crevices of the rocks. Two little half-frozen birds, not seeing any other solid ground for their feet, perched themselves on the black cloth of the coffin, which the bearers had laid down for a moment on the edge of a ravine, whilst with their knives they cut away the snow which was clogging the soles of their shoes. I do not know why, but these poor little birds, seeking help and shelter even from her coffin, made me burst into tears! It reminded me of all the miseries and sadness of which that loving heart had been the shelter whilst it still beat on this earth. The birds twittered for a moment and then gave a little mournful cry, after which they resumed their flight in the direction of St. Point. My thoughts flew towards the souls of Césarine and Susan, who seemed to come under the symbol of these wings to meet their mother and precede her to her place of rest. The heart is naturally superstitious when riven with emotion even beyond its strength. There are moments in the life of every one, whether man or woman, when all their powers of reasoning are dissolved in tears.

Our journey, which, in fine weather, ordinarily lasted but two hours, took seven in that ocean of snow, whose waves threatened every moment to swallow us up altogether. There were some turns in the deep ravines leading down to the valley of St. Point, where our only guides were the blackened stems of the chestnut-trees hanging over the abyss, and where we must have perished but for the skill and strength of those devoted Milly peasants. It seemed as if their very burden gave them power and confidence.

We did not arrive till towards the end of the day. We deposited the coffin in my mother's own room, and on her bed, which for the last few years I had taken for myself. I shut myself up in a little tower, which serves as a dressing-room to this apartment, and there watched alone, with the door of communication open between, during the whole of that last night which my dear mother was to pass under the roof of her old home. I do not know why, but I felt as if she were nearer to me while I thus prolonged my watch by her side. God alone can tell the prayers, the invocations, the tears, the remorse, the blessings, the revelations of that night! I fell asleep from very sorrow and exhaustion as the sun rose, and was woke by the sound of the funeral bell, which was already summoning all the inhabitants of the neighboring mountains to the mournful ceremony of her second interment. Strangely enough it was not the last; for, by a curious and unpremeditated combination of circumstances, it seemed as if the earth were to take, give up, and retake possession of the mortal remains of one whom the tenderness and veneration of those she had left behind, disputed even in her grave.

Looking out of the window on the two great pents covered with snow, which form the valley of St. Point, I saw crowds of black figures descending towards the church and the château, gathered from all the chalets and huts in the mountains. The whole country seemed to be in mourning, and the sighing of the wind brought even to the house the murmur of sobs.

Nothing had been prepared in the cemetery for the interment. Death had surprised us before we had time to think of her tomb. If our mother had been consulted (as my father was later) as to the place and mode of her sepulture, her humility and the dread she had of too much care being bestowed on her body, would have certainly induced her to leave a memorandum in her will begging only to share the last resting-place of the poor. But she had not the time to do this. She had only expressed a vague wish to be buried at St. Point. I could not make up my mind, however, both for my own sake and that of my sisters and their children, and that innumerable family of peasants who were united to her in heart as much as we were by blood, to lose in a few years all traces of her relics under a grassy knoll nibbled by sheep in the ordinary churchyard. I felt that such relics should be embalmed in a special manner to mark her holiness and our love. I, therefore, resolved to build a little family mausoleum, where some day we might be allowed to rejoin her should God give us the grace to die where we have lived and loved.

The site and laying out of the gardens at St. Point favored this thought. On a rising ground, in the middle of the valley, like the pedestal of an old temple, are built both the church and the chateau. The church is so inclosed in the terraces of the castle that it was evidently in old feudal times only the chapel of the manor house. Even now the gardens are only separated from the rustic cemetery which surrounds the church by a low box and filbert hedge, with here and there an old walnut-tree, of which the nuts fall (to the great satisfaction of the little shepherd boys) on the graves below. The walls and tower of the old Roman church, dark with age, add their shade in summer to that of the nut-trees, and give this part of the garden almost the look of a sanctuary. This was the favorite resort of our mother during the hottest hours of the day, when she came here for the months of harvest. I used to watch her with delight, from the windows of my little tower, sitting with her book in her hand, or else reciting the Rosary on a wooden seat, which had been placed under a large cherry-tree, of which the branches, heavy with fruit, used to hang over her head.

Even in the midst of my despair I felt a kind of sweetness at the thought, that she would rest exactly in this spot, under the same shade, and the same grass, covered with the fruit and flowers of the garden she had so loved during life. I resolved, therefore, to build the mausoleum in this very place, where I felt it would be the most cherished of all the family possessions. But as, in these days in France, no one can answer for any one family retaining their property long (not even a sepulchre !), and as misfortunes might necessitate the conveyance of this estate, mausoleum and all, to some creditor or indifferent person, I did not choose that my children or grandchildren should be robbed of this treasure, like an ordinary thing transferred for so much money from one hand to another. The idea of such a profanation in future filled me with horror. I thought over it a great deal, and finally decided on what I subsequently accomplished: namely, to make over to the village in perpetuity that portion of the garden on which the mausoleum would be placed, with a solemn charge to keep it from any sort of profanation. And lest that charge should become burdensome on the parish, I bound myself in return to give a piece of land on the hill adjoining the church for the building of a presbytery, which was much needed, and to build that presbytery at my own cost. The laws of the "Commune" could not refuse to ratify a contract which was so clearly to the advantage of the inhabitants of the valley, and, in fact, the deed was signed without any difficulties.

But, as I also wished that during my life-time, or during the life of those dear to me, this mausoleum should be reserved for our own private devotions, without being exposed to the criticisms or visits of strangers, I resolved to build a little low wall, covered with ivy, between the garden and the cemetery, which should enable us without observation, whenever we pleased, to pour out our prayers and our tears over her much-loved grave. All this passed through my mind during that long night's watch, by her coffin, which the morrow was going to carry away out of my sight, and which the instinct of tenderness, shrinking from the idea of an eternal separation, made me resolve to bring back, as it were, within my reach as soon as possible, in this mausoleum. I had dimly conceived the idea at Mâcon, and had obtained from the government permission, in the mean while, to place the coffin under the pavement of the church, in the vault of the old Lords of St. Point, of the illustrious house of Rochefort. What would I not have given that the miracle which was enacted a century ago in this very vault could be reproduced for us! A young Marquise de St. Point, whose prolonged fainting fit had been mistaken for death, had been interred in an open coffin under these very stones. The night of her funeral, the bell-ringer, coming in to ring the Angelus, heard a groaning under the pavement, where the tomb had been sealed down. Filled with fear, he rushed out of the church and up to the château to tell what had happened. The Marquis and his servants ran into the church. The stifled cry was again heard ; the stones were torn open by the half-distracted husband, who descended into the vault, and found the supposed corpse living and breathing in his arms. Wild with joy he carried her back to the château, where, still young and beautiful, she graced her husband's home for many years before returning (this time in good earnest) to her final resting-place. I had often in my childhood heard the bell-ringer and his old wife tell this story, as they had been witnesses of the miracle with several of the older people in the village. But, alas ! such prodigies do not recur in every sorrow of one's life.

At eight o'clock, the coffin was borne from the bed to the church, followed by the weeping inhabitants of twelve hamlets, and carried through the garden and by that same nut-walk, where I had so often met her coming back from the altar, her face bathed with tears of compunction, recollection, piety, and holy joy. With my own hands I placed her in her last resting place. Then I came back alone to my tower and locked myself in. Tears have their shamefacedness, like all feelings which are deep-seated in the soul of man. I stretched myself on the floor, my forehead buried in my hands, my eyes fixed on the church, my ears involuntarily listening to the sad toll of the funeral bell, that bell of which she so loved the sound, and which seemed to weep for her now as its mournful echo reverberated through the surrounding hills. My heart was full of unspoken thoughts. I only remember that, in consequence of all these days and nights of anguish and sleeplessness, my fevered brain seemed to be on fire with a pain which beat on my temples as with a sledge hammer, and vibrated through my whole being in unison with the funeral bell, so that my prayers were mingled with sobs, and physical suffering almost overpowered mental agony. Strange contradiction of our nature ! at the same time material and spiritual, when our senses are bewildered, and the ear takes in outward sounds, whilst the soul is riven with untold anguish !

Towards morning I fell into an uneasy slumber, after which I rose and retraced, with my guides, the snowy paths of the mountain, where we very narrowly escaped being buried in a fresh drift. The winter sun shone brilliantly, as if to mock both the season and my sorrow. I was anxious, however, to return as quickly as possible to my poor father, who needed every possible consolation. Our winter was as sad a one as this day; and all the remainder of his long life was henceforth as winter.

Thus we lost our mother, and the people one who had been their Providence, their example, and their guide in all grace and holiness. Ask any old man or widow whom you may meet by the wayside, — they will tell you the same tale! And for us, let us forever cherish her dear memory. It is for this reason that I have transcribed her manuscript. One by one we shall ourselves disappear from this mortal scene, carrying away with each one of us a portion of this tenderness and of these regrets. These pages will preserve for a little time longer, perhaps, the remembrance of her goodness, and the trace of her hand; then they will become ashes like all the rest. This is the end of all books and of all generations!

RECOLLECTIONS

BY

GEORGE SAND

RECOLLECTIONS BY GEORGE SAND.

I.

A DISCUSSION WITH EUGÈNE DELACROIX, CHOPIN, AND MICKIEWICZ.

ARIS, *January*, 1841. — I passed a portion of to-day with Eugène Delacroix. I wish I could remember exactly what he said. I cannot very well transcribe it, for he speaks better than I can write. When I first saw him I was in a state of distraction. I had just met that maniac, De ———, who had been revealing to me the strangest theories concerning outline and color, *separate* studies, according to his idea. I related to Delacroix our little dispute. "Do tell me, my friend," said I, "if this man is in his right mind."

Delacroix. — Well, yes! He is laboring under a mistake, but he will not believe it. He reasons upon his error, and clings to it, supposing it to be truth. How can it be helped? This heresy did not originate with him. It is of higher authority. It belongs to the school of M. Ingres, who has decreed that color is a superfluity, and that it is very dangerous to become captivated with a mere detail which is injurious to the purity of the outline. They have systematized the thing to such a point as to value only Raphael's first style, and to regard the primitive masters with perfect admiration.

Myself. — I know it. They hold in utter contempt the Venetian school, with Titian at its head.

Delacroix. — And the Dutch school, too! That dauber, Rembrandt, and that miserable Téniers! and all the Spaniards, Velasquez included! and the great Rubens, who excites their disgust! Does that make you indignant? I was indignant too when I believed them involved in serious error; but since I have assured myself that it is all a *humbug*, I am not angry, only amused.

Myself. — You are at liberty to become philosophical; but, at the same time, the public who are not artists and do not understand definitions, is satisfied with stupid sentences and ready-made phrases. "Rubens gives fine *coloring*, but he is no drawer. Rembrandt produces happy effects, but he bungles: he does not understand *outline*. Raphael alone knows how to draw. Michael Angelo is a fool who can produce only monsters. Pure art is the uniform tint, the silhouette." The Ingres school makes this assertion, and the *bourgeois* adds: "That appears to be the truth."

Delacroix. — Well! what is it to us if the *bourgeois* does talk nonsense?

Myself. — It is a good deal to me. The *bourgeois* is the fool that we should have been, if no trouble had been taken to perfect our taste and elevate our feelings. Why does not the critic, whose duty it is to enlighten —

Delacroix. — Oh, the critic generally comes from the *bourgeois*, or from literary bachelors who become *bourgeois* in order to secure readers. Look at the writers who possess taste, originality, and independence! They are not understood. They preach to the desert air.

Myself. — I am not such a pessimist as that. I am convinced that many literary men have no decided opinion, and that if art were explained to them —

Delacroix. — A mere fancy! Painting is something of which every one cannot be a judge. They must have a particular gift, or a special education. Young literary people who earn their living by writing articles for newspapers try to obtain an interview with some painter, and write from his dictation. If the painter reasons falsely, so much the worse. But do not make me talk any more. I have one of my sore throats.

Myself. — I will leave, especially as I smother my feelings when with you ; but I warn you that I shall go home only the more angry from your present indifference.

" Stop a moment ! You think me calmer than I am ; but I have seen Ingres' 'Stratonice' again, and, my faith ! I am as simple as the others ; I think it is charming."

" I am glad you like it ; but *I* think it childish and affected."

" I do not deny that ; but what pretty little touches ! what finish in the carving ! "

" *Carving* is the word. It is done after the manner of the Chinese fans with their little ivory figures fastened to one another. Well, good-by till we meet again."

" Yes, till we meet again ; but why won't you talk to me without making me talk ? I should like to know why you do not like M. Ingres."

" I never said that I did not. I like M. Ingres *although* and not *because* he is systematic. He is half a man of genius, has an immense talent, and is particularly high-minded. His failing is partly in coloring, partly in perspective, partly in a want of animation. We could forgive him these serious imperfections, however, if he did not convert his inability into a system."

" Stop ! When we view a book of art, it is not necessary to ask what the author says and thinks. We must judge of the work, and forget the man. I know very well that M. Ingres looks upon me as a booby and a mean rascal, and that he dismisses his pupils as soon as he perceives in them a tendency towards color. But I do not care to know anything of *him*, to judge of his picture."

" That will do very well for you ; but when this picture argues still more strongly a lamentable conviction, an overbearing blindness, a mental paralysis converted into a decree, I cannot help deploring the error of the master, and feeling indignant with the adulatory school that confirms him in his folly."

"Then you think that the 'Stratonice' indicates a decline" —

"Don't let us talk any longer. I must go. It is dinner-time."

"Is it? Where are you going to dine?"

"At home. Will you come?"

"To dine with you socially! That is a great temptation! You will not make me talk?"

"We will make you keep silent. Get ready, and I will wait for you."

He walked into his chamber, leaving the door open so that he could speak across, and requested me to explain to him what displeased me in the 'Stratonice.' But he did not give me the opportunity. The exercise of taking off his slippers and dressing-gown having restored his natural animation, instead of letting me criticise, he did it himself.

As we were on the way to my home, notwithstanding his resolution, he did not cease railing at the false coloring of the adherents of Ingres. He called them *pasticheurs* and illuminators of manuscripts. My anger was appeased through his. Chopin met us at the door, and the two walked up stairs discussing 'Stratonice.' Chopin does not like it, because the characters are affected and without any true emotion; but he is pleased with the finish of the picture. As to color, he said, out of politeness, that he understood nothing about it; not believing that he was telling the truth!

Chopin and Delacroix love each other, I may say, tenderly. They possess a great similarity of character, and the same grand qualities of heart and mind. In point of art, Delacroix understands and adores Chopin: Chopin does not understand Delacroix. He esteems, cherishes, and respects the man, but detests the painter. Delacroix, with his greater variety of faculties, understands and appreciates music. His taste is true and exquisite. He never wearies of listening to Chopin, who is touched by this adoration ; but when the latter beholds one of his friend's pictures he becomes distressed, and cannot utter a word. He is a musician, nothing more. His thoughts can be translated only into music. He possesses an infinite amount of wit, discernment, and sly humor, but has no knowledge of painting or statuary. He is afraid of Michael Angelo. Rubens makes his hair stand on end. He is scandalized by everything that appears to him eccentric, confining himself to the strictest conventionalism. Strange anomaly! His genius is the most original and most individual in existence ; but he would not like to have any one tell him so. In literature, also, Delacroix has a taste for what is most classical and most precise.

It was useless to attempt to enter into their discussion ; so I listened. Maurice began breaking the finger-bowls in his earnestness to have Delacroix explain to him the mystery of reflection, and Chopin listened with eager eyes. The master drew a comparison between tone in painting and sounds in music.

"Harmony in music," said he, "does not consist merely in the construction of concordant sounds, but in their mutual relations, their proper succession, in what I should call, for want of a better expression, their audible reflex. Well, it is just so with painting. Here, pass me that blue cushion and that red rug. If you place them side by side, you see that where the two colors touch, they blend. The red becomes tinted with blue ; the blue is enlivened by the red, and, from the two results violet. You can mingle in a picture the most gorgeous colors ; but give them the proper reflex, and you will never be gaudy. Is nature sober in her tones? Does she not abound in striking contrasts, which in no wise destroy her harmony? They are all blended by reflex. Some attempt to do away with this in painting. It may be done, but only at the expense of the picture."

Maurice remarked that the science of reflection is the most difficult of all.

"No," said the master ; "it is the simplest thing imaginable. I can demonstrate it to you as easily as that two and two make four. The reflection of one certain color upon another certain color invariably produces the same effect, which I have explained and proved to you twenty times."

"Very well," replied the pupil; "but the reflection of that reflection?"

"Mercy on us! How you run on! You are asking too much for one day."

Chopin moved uneasily upon his chair. "Let me take breath," said he, "before discussing *relief*. Reflection is quite enough for the present. It is something ingenious, new to me, but savors of alchemy."

"No," cried Delacroix, "it is pure chemistry. The tone is continually undergoing composition and decomposition, and reflection is as inseparable from relief as the outline from the model. They think they have invented; or at least discovered outline; that is, they believe that they can portray the outline. By no means! The contour laughs at them, and turns its back"

Chopin did not listen any longer. He sat down at the piano, but did not observe that we were listening to his music. He improvised a little, then stopped.

"Come, come," cried Delacroix, "that is n't finished!"

"It is n't commenced yet. I can think of nothing but reflections, shadows, and reliefs that will not stand still. I am looking for color, but I cannot even find the outline."

"You will not find one without the other," replied Delacroix, "and you will succeed in finding both."

"What if I find only moonshine?"

"You will have found the reflection of a reflection," remarked Maurice.

This idea pleased the divine artist. He resumed his playing, without, apparently, commencing anew, so vague and uncertain were his strains. Our eyes gradually filled with a soft moisture corresponding to the sweet modulations received by the ear. Now the blue note sounded, and we were in the azure of transparent night. Light clouds, assuming fanciful forms, covered the heavens, then pressed around the moon, which threw out great opal disks, and roused their dormant color. We dreamed of a summer's night, and listened for the nightingale.

Chopin talks little, and but rarely of his art. Yet, when he does speak of it, it is with an admirable perspicuity and soundness of judgment and purpose which would completely annihilate many heresies, if he wished to make an open profession. But, except in cases of intimacy, he is reserved, and lavish of nothing but his piano. He has promised, though, to write a method, in which he will treat, not only of the profession, but of the doctrine. Will he keep his word?

Delacroix has promised, too, in his moments of communicativeness, to write a treatise on outline and color. But he will never do it, although he is an elegant writer. These inspired artists are condemned to be always looking forward, and never to spare a day for retrospection.

Some one rang the bell. Chopin started, and left off playing. I called to the servant that I was not at home to any one.

"Oh, yes," said Chopin; "you are to *him*."

"Who is it, pray?"

"Mickiewicz."

"Oh, yes, of course. But how do you know that it is he?"

"I do not; yet I am impressed that it is. I was just thinking of him."

It was he, to be sure. He pressed my hand affectionately, then seated himself in a corner and begged Chopin to continue. Chopin went on. He was inspired, sublime. My little servant rushed in wildly, exclaiming: "The house is on fire! We hastened to the point of danger. The fire had originated in my sleeping-room; but we were in time, and quickly extinguished it. Nevertheless, it took us a full hour; at the end of which time we asked: "Where can Mickiewicz be?" and called, but he did not answer. We went back to the parlor: he was not there — yes! there he was, to be sure, in the very corner where we had left him. The lamp had gone out, but he did not observe it. We had made much noise and commotion, but he had heard nothing. He did not even inquire why we had left him alone, not having discovered that he *was* alone. He had been listening to Chopin, and the music still sounded in his ear.

This would have seemed like affectation in any one else; but the meek and humble great poet is as artless as a child, and, seeing me laugh, he asked what was the matter.

"Nothing is the matter now," I replied; "but the next time I am with you in a house that takes fire, my first step will be to put you in a place of safety; for you would burn up without knowing it, like a mere shaving."

"Indeed!" he exclaimed. "I did not know that there had been a fire."

And he left without another word. As Chopin accompanied Delacroix to the door, the latter, returning to the world of reality, began a conversation about his English tailor, in seeming oblivion of any other care in the universe than that of having his garments very warm without being heavy.

II.

AN ATTACK OF FEVER.

—TAMARIS, *near Toulon, February* 20, 1861. . . . . I still feel the effects of my late illness; but do not be uneasy, I shall get over it. I drive out every day, and in the evening I amuse myself by writing the "Romance of my Fever;" for, you must know, this illness has not interrupted my literary pursuits. I mentioned it to you at Nohant. Now I will give you an account of it, as an addition to our observations and researches concerning the phenomena of sleep, delirium, and hallucination. What passed through my brain is curious enough to be recorded.

The evening preceding my sudden and serious attack, I was feeling very well, and had sketched the commencement of a romance entitled, "La Famille de Germandre," one which I have just finished. I had decided on all my characters, and assigned to them their positions in the world, their tendencies, ideas, characters, and mutual relations. Their faces were familiar. All that was left for me now was to decide on what they were to do, and I did not trouble myself about that, feeling that there would be time enough for it the next day. Unconscious for several succeeding days, I thought no more on the subject, but I dreamed of it, probably at those times when I had been in the habit of writing, and the most unforeseen adventures entered into the story.

I seemed to be travelling with all my characters, without exactly knowing whence we came, or through what countries we were passing. This did not seem to trouble either of us, and we journeyed on, determined on reaching home, that is, *my* home, at whatever cost. I can only touch on the numerous events of the journeys. Sometimes we were in comfortable carriages which glided on with a rapid but easy motion, giving us an opportunity for conversation: of what nature, God only knows! Perhaps they were instructing me as to their respective parts. It seems to me now, at times, as though I had kept it in remembrance. Sometimes we were travelling in a cart over frightful roads. The cart would lose one wheel, then another; still we kept on, never overturning, and never thinking of making a stop, but endeavoring to ride upon the shafts in such a manner that our feet would escape the ground. The animal which was drawing us seemed to change every moment. At one time it was a donkey, at others a cow, a bull-dog, or a goat; sometimes it was nothing more than a blind beetle, which travelled as well as either of the others. Then the roads began to overflow with water, and, turning into brooks, became rivers, a pond, a lake, and, finally, the open sea. We kept on, however, our cart becoming first a ship, then a boat, a wreck, a plank, a floating stick. It still made its regular stops, however, and we put up at unendurable taverns, met with fantastic adventures, and saw strange cities; but this was all confusion, one idea being uppermost, to start again with my companions; and we renewed our adventures, extremely perilous and wearisome, without any of us being alarmed or fatigued. I cannot tell whether this dream, which from my remembrance was one of long duration, lasted throughout my illness; but I know that it commenced the first night, and that the last day, just as I returned to consciousness, I was so deeply absorbed in it that I was obliged to make an effort to distinguish the persons who were standing around me from those who belonged to my vision, who were exactly the same as when we started on our journey. A new incident had just occurred. From the extremity of Cochin China, perhaps, we had arrived at the castle of Motte-Feuilly, in the neighborhood of Nohant. The Germandre family, notary and major-domo included, took it into their heads to ascend to the tower, the circular wooden revetment of which I could distinctly see. The planks were broken and gaping, and I cried to my companions not to rely on these boards; but they paid no attention. Suddenly, amid a burst of laughter, they were precipitated from the height of the corbel to the pavements of the courtyard. They were uninjured, and the joke seemed to amuse them, for they hastened to repeat it. This thing seemed to me very funny, and yet I felt provoked at it; for they could not rise without my assistance, and as soon as I had picked them up and set them on their feet, like puppets, they made their escape. I reproached them, in vain, for their folly. "You will end by breaking your necks," said I; "and then what will become of my novel?"

I was just on the point of becoming angry in good earnest, and threatening to leave them, when the dream gradually faded away. I seemed to be alone in the castle, which had turned into a ruin, and I felt very cold. Some one spoke to me, and with delight I recognized my son, my friends, my room, my bed, and my real self.

All this may be included in the well-known phenomena of dreams; and I do not see that, in this case, it differed essentially, except in duration, from what would have taken place if I had been in a state of health. What strikes me in this act of obsession to which I submitted, is the important position held by fictions which have been voluntarily admitted into the brain. Every one who creates figures destined to live solely in the domain of art, has, probably, tried to picture them to himself in such a manner as to make them appear as natural as possible. Most likely, too, they have entered into his dreams, performing all kinds of impossibilities. My son, when very young, had a great desire for a manikin; but the first night it occupied his room, his sleep was much disturbed by dreams of it. This inert individual appeared to assume life, and performed all sorts of antics, driving nails into the inlaid floor, breaking the plastering, and tearing my son's clothes.

III.

PIERRE BONNIN.

June 25, 1866.—I made a visit recently to Pierre Bonnin and his old wife. It was on a delightful spring afternoon, neither too warm nor too cold. The sun shone brightly, and a slight breeze rustled along the corn-fields, relieving some of the overloaded ears of their surplus fruit. This exceedingly pretty place is called "The Elms." Five or six little houses are grouped together on a level plain, very wisely surrounded by trees and tall hawthorn bushes, and adorned with those pretty gardens in which our peasants were, formerly, so skill-ful.

They have plenty of shade and a good well; which is the cause of the grouping and intermarriage of families, as in the time of the patriarchs. The soil is good; and around the circuit of the gardens extends a belt of hemp-fields and lucern-fields, planted with walnut and cherry trees, and interspersed with charming little paths and a few fences easy to leap. Geese, goats, one or two cows, fifty sheep, a few pigs, and a quantity of hens, with the product of the surrounding lands, complete the wealth of this colony. To tell the truth, it is, at present, composed of only three families allied by marriage.

The principal representative, and a very peculiar one, is Pierre Bonnin. Whence did he derive that restless activity, that ironical and inexhaustible mirth, that sudden decision, that sort of mania for labor, and that disinterestedness so extraordinary for a peasant? I cannot tell, for I did not know his parents. The family have been peasants for generations past, and lived on this same tract of land, in old houses which were buried in ruins during my childhood; but they have left nothing to mark their existence. He himself had hardly known them. The history of the peasant is a blank; and yet, there must be here, as everywhere else, marked exceptions, intellects grown sterile for want of development, earnest minds extinguished for want of fuel. What account could be given of Pierre Bonnin, even in these times, when a peasant is a man? Nothing, indeed. He has done nothing remarkable; and, in a hundred years from now, no one will be aware that he ever existed; and yet, he is a man whom I shall never forget, if I survived him for centuries.

He is extremely old, but does not remember his age; like some old people with us, whose certificate of baptism has been destroyed and who have no record of their birth. He remembers *l'année de la grand'peur*, '89. A cry of distress arose, "There they are! There are the robbers!" and, without knowing what this meant, everybody hastened to conceal himself. Mother Bonnin hurried her little Pierre into the cornfields, and there they squatted all day. He might have been five or six years old then; now he is at least eighty-two He has no other recollection of the Revolution, nor of any domestic occurrence. When very young he learned the carpenter's trade, in the village of Father Lecante. To his great regret he had never been a soldier. He was fond of war and adventure; and all his life he had lamented that a military life had not fallen to his lot. When very young he married quite a pretty woman, with whom he quarreled on the eve of their wedding. She was proud and determined, as she is still. Did he find fault with her for drinking too much?—that was her failing. Or did she flirt with the groomsmen?—I know not. He remained three days at the public-house without coming home at night. At length he returned, and they have been a happy couple ever since; he very imperious, she very calm. Although there are only the two, they keep up the old custom in country households. He eats alone at a little table, and she waits upon him, eating her own meals near the fire, with a porringer upon her lap.

The earliest remembrance that I have of him is on his wedding day, when I was a child. He was very handsome, had eyes as black as ink, a straight nose with large nostrils, a fair complexion, a well-formed mouth, was tall, slender, and flexible. I was much struck with his wedding costume. It consisted of a complete suit of drugget dotted with blue, a waistcoat three fingers in length, the skirts of his jacket reaching to his knees, and a large black hat ornamented by a cockade at one side. He was much admired. His hair was cut short at the forehead, and curled at the ear, meeting the extremity of his black whiskers, which gave him, as his friends assured him, the appearance of a *real bourgeois!* He was the beau of the village, took liberties with the belles, was addicted to the use of light, home-made wines, took the greatest delight in making fun of others and teasing them, and overflowed with the spirit of wit. It must be confessed that he was not a very promising young man. When he was reproached for his levity, he used to reply: "I ought to have been sent to the army. I should have made my mark there."

But he had a good, honest nature, and as soon as the children came along he began to work like any four men. Father Lecante was dead. Bonnin did the jobs at our house, and upon the farm, which were considerable. The buildings were old, and always needing repairs. As soon as the Revolution was over, every one began to put in order his long neglected nest.

The steward was impetuous and exacting, and freely used his cane upon the lazy workmen. Pierre was quick to understand, quick to execute. The steward was struck with his intelligence, and employed him constantly; but one day, the work not being performed exactly to the liking of the steward, he became angry, unjustly, and threatened the workman. The latter replied: "Do not run any risks. I am hot blooded, and for every blow I return ten." A lasting peace was concluded.

He worked with renewed ardor. It seemed as though the combined vigor of this robust frame and enterprising spirit needed a violent effort for its expansion. He went at the wood furiously: it seemed like a sort of delirium; and when he superintended the work of the hewers, he scolded them with a decided contempt for their slowness and caution. "Wherever he comes, he raises a breeze," they would say; yet they liked him, for he was good-natured, and lavish in his expressions of tenderness when he was well served.

To zeal for strength he soon added zeal for invention, displaying great adroitness and intelligence; yet he knew how neither to read, write, nor draw; nor did he possess that knowledge of geometry necessary for his trade. He could not make a bargain nor rectify mistakes by calculation. If any one gave him a defective plan, he would not discover it until he had attempted to follow it, and then his anger was intense with *those who know, and yet do not know.* However, he never got discouraged, but commenced repairing the mistake, even if he had to go over his work ten times; but when he considered how he had been made to lose his time, his rage was so great that he became feverish and could not sleep.

My brother and I used to provoke him by playing with his tools, making wigs for ourselves of his shavings, stealing his pencil to write upon the walls, or teasing him to mend our wheelbarrows. He would scold us, make terrible threats, and then pat us on the back with his rule. We were not afraid of him, and so he loved us. "Those rogues," he used to say, "know very well that I shall not harm them."

He aspired to becoming a joiner; but Father Godard did all that kind of work, and did it very well too. So as soon as the old man joined his contemporaries in "The Garden of Nettles," as Pierre styled the cemetery, the latter set up for a joiner, without relinquishing his business as carpenter and wheelwright; for these callings are a little confused in the village. He had now more work than he could accomplish, and his zeal increased tenfold. He had children to bring up, but he did not complain of trouble. Universally beloved, he endeavored to give universal satisfaction. It must be acknowledged that he was jealous of any one who received the patronage of the public, and that, at one time, people used to go without necessary articles, in order not to incur his displeasure.

So it was at our house. Not keeping a steward, I engaged him myself. Where one lives in an old house all the year round, a great many things are needed; still I could not monopolize him; so we had to suffer. When I had made up my mind to find fault with him for leaving the work half done, he would return, and go to work so furiously that I was obliged to speak kindly to him to prevent him from hurting himself.

He accumulated money, although he was not at all greedy. He never asked for a cent more than his pay, nor ever disputed with the peasants whose *coche* was not as full as his own. The *coche* is a little square piece of wood upon which is recorded, by means of slight notches, the number of days' work. This account is kept by both parties, and sometimes the employer forgets to mark one or two days. Pierre Bonnin preferred to lay the blame on his memory rather than on his customers. He seldom kept an account of the days of the week, but he always remembered Sunday. On that day he carefully shaved his beard of a week's growth. This became gray very early; but he was still very fine-looking, with his scattering, silver locks brushed away from his forehead. From beneath his thick, bushy eyebrows he cast piercing glances. He conversed well, being neither a talker nor boaster, and preferring to make inquiries rather than give his own ideas. He was observing; but although he made fun of everybody, he injured no one. Very incredulous in regard to religion, he left others to think *their own way*. He never became intoxicated, but drank *too much*, as was apparent from the slight dimness of his eye and the hesitancy of his speech; yet he was neither quarrelsome nor tiresome, and Monday morning he was quite sober again. Though undemonstrative in his affections, he uttered words that went to the heart; and though he exhibited no apparent tenderness for his family, his infinite devotion was betrayed through his incessant toil.

His old house threatened to fall over his head. He built a new one, which, to-day, is in no respect superior to the other; but at that time it was esteemed a wonder. It was very convenient and comfortable, bountifully provided with closets, recesses, and shelves. A little corridor protected the principal room from the cold; and over the entrance was a glass light, which, I remember, was the astonishment and admiration of the neighborhood. No one had so fine a dwelling; but no one was quite so shrewd.

They were doing well, when, unfortunately, his wife, who was more practical than he, set her heart on the possession of a certain piece of land. It was at the time of their success, at that period of life when physical strength is greatest, and at a time when they were favored with a goodly amount of patronage; but after the house was finished and the children provided for, there was no money left. He yielded to his wife's entreaties, and borrowed; after which he was taken with sciatica, and since then has suffered from it every winter. Whether from some slight dissipation, or from the dullness of trade at that time, he failed, several quarters, to pay his rent, abused his creditors, and at last took sick to his bed. Soon after returning home from a journey, I learned that his house and garden had been attached, and that his creditors were about to take possession of them. I waited for him to come to me; but as he did not come, I went to see him, and questioned him. He was up, but was still feverish. He answered me in monosyllables, without appearing anxious concerning his situation, or supposing that his creditors would not allow him time for payment. Was he not an honest and hard-working man? In short, he was easy and careless.

But affairs had taken their course, and he was about to suffer the penalty of the law, when I hastened to send the sum for his relief. I met him a few days after. He spoke to me about some work that I had ordered, and, just as he left, he remarked: "While I think of it, you paid my debt. *That's right.*" He did not even add, "Thank you;' and some one who was present at the time exclaimed: "How ungrateful these peasants are! It is folly to do them a favor." "You are very much mistaken," I replied. "This man is so safe a debtor, that the service rendered by me amounts to almost nothing. He regards it as nothing more than an act of good-nature on my part, and he is right."

A few days after he offered to work for me gratis until he had acquitted his obligation. I begged him not to think of such a thing yet, and he answered, "You are very kind." He was right then, also. It was nothing more than an act of kindness. After he had gradually paid his debt, he said to me one day: —

"You are a person of whom I am very fond."

"Why?" I asked. "I have never done much for you: you never ask for anything."

"I have loved you ever since you were quite small. Your mamma used to go to mass on Sunday; and they used to lift you over the bad places in the road. You were a princess, and did not like to be carried in the arms of everybody; but you would come to me, and throw your arms about my neck; for my countenance pleased you. Afterwards, you were terrible. You used to provoke and annoy me continually; but when you said, "Please do, Bonnin," I yielded to your requests. Now it is your children who annoy and provoke me; but, for your sake, I do not pat too hard, and I love them too."

This momentary tenderness never prevented him from promptly dismissing me if I visited his work-shop for the purpose of engaging him to do a piece of work while he was busy with another job.

"Go away from here," he would say. "You are just the same as when you were four years old. You worry me."

His inclinations were as uncontrollable as his desire for independence. When he did not like any job, he would leave it, without giving any other reason than, "It bothers me." Why some kinds of work more than others? Why did he enjoy making inlaid floors, and yet had a horror of common floors? He did not know, or did not know how to express it.

He would leave, and, when requested to return, would reply, "I will not. You must get along as well as you can without it."

As he treated every one the same, people had to put up with his peculiarities ; for he worked so well and so fast when he chose !

But his attacks of sciatica becoming more frequent, and of longer duration, it became necessary to employ a younger and less capricious man. Bonnin consented, on condition that he should work *when he chose, and on what he chose ;* and, as his successor showed him great deference, he took it kindly, and worked by his side without any ill feelings.

He worked till last year. I was away from home when he gave up business, and did not hear of it until my return. On inquiry, I learned that his affairs were in an embarrassed condition, that he had lost his cattle, and that his wife was very much depressed. I went to see them, and found him in his garden, scraping the earth from the bottom of a spade which he had no longer the strength to use. He did not perceive me, and I walked up to him, without his being aware of my approach, and touched him on the shoulder. He turned around, and looked at me with a melancholy smile. I spoke to him, and he shook his head. "I cannot hear now," said he, "and I am not able to work any longer. I am used up ! "

His wife joined us. She was almost blind, but not deaf, and quite active still, though seventy-eight years old. She did not recognize me, and when he informed her that it was I, she began to weep, as she described in a dramatic manner the death of her last pig. She lamented that the old man was now worth nothing, saying that they would have to finish their days in misery, after having worked so hard. As the account of the death of her animals threatened to be prolonged indefinitely, I interrupted her with the news that I had brought the wherewithal to repair their loss. She was so excited that she continued her Iliad, without stopping to listen. Never was Trojan Hector the cause of so many tears as that last little pig that she could not save.

At last I succeeded in putting into her apron the money that I had brought in my pocket. She paused in amazement, and ran to her husband, who was sitting on an upturned wheelbarrow. Looking with indifference, first at the money, then at me, he said to his wife: "I told you she would come. It is foolish to cry about the animals."

Then, addressing me, he referred to having seen me as a child, and added: "*You* have always been kind to me. *That's right.*"

As, tired of the woman's repeated thanks, I started to leave, he called out: "You will never see me again at your house. It is all over! You must bid me good-by now."

He extended his hand, and, as he held mine, he seemed to have something in his thoughts that he could not make up his mind to utter. I made him understand that if he had any particular desire, I was always at his service. Then, coming to the point, he repeated that strange aspiration of his whole life-time: "I have no further needs. I am leaving this world without being able to declare that I have been unhappy. I enjoyed labor. I have nothing to regret but loss of health, and one other thing, which was fated not to be! I should have liked to be a soldier, and become a general — and emperor!"

"This same nonsense again!" cried the old woman. "He has always said, and persists in saying, the same thing. He would have liked to be emperor! Do you hear that!"

I remember having heard him make this remark several times, when he had taken too much liquor. Was there a vortex, then, in this peasant's solid brain? An inordinate ambition had he concealed under great wisdom of conduct. Was it the love of glory, restrained by a consciousness of his impotence? What was it? It was, assuredly, something — something besides an hallucination, perhaps. An inward revelation of some neglected power, for which he himself would not have been able to find a name. All that he could make manifest was an extraordinary vital energy, a great love of command, a horror of obedience, a natural dignity which yielded to no custom, and no compromise ; added to these, an exceeding goodness of heart, with no narrowness of mind. Who can tell what education might have made of Pierre Bonnin ? He has left, as the result of many hours' faithful employment, only carpenter's work, and furniture of Cyclopean solidity. He never finished anything without saying : " That will last longer than I do."

Sad and thoughtful I wended my way home through flowery paths. When I entered the great courtyard, where I was accustomed to see him at work, it seemed deserted, and larger than ever. No more will be heard here the heavy blows of his hammer, his angry exclamations, or merry shouts, which could be heard far and wide when old Bonnin was angry or joyous. Was he ill-natured ? He used to call out to the passers-by : "Walk fast. You make my blood boil at your ox's pace." If a dog laid his paw on a piece of his work that was finished, he would fasten a shaving to his tail, and people, hearing the animal's cries, would say to themselves : "Some creature has been disrespectful to Pierre Bonnin."

If he was in a jovial humor, he would address his jokes to those passing. He was the personification of noise, energy, and activity. All that is over now. His exuberant nature will be reproduced in other men, but in a different way. This particular type will soon join the great Mould that never repeats His models.

INDEX.

www.ingramcontent.com/pod-product-compliance
Lightning Source LLC
LaVergne TN
LVHW010159110826
845151LV00002B/560

* 9 7 8 1 4 2 5 5 3 6 3 7 4 *